"For people who love food and gossip, [*Alice Waters and Chez Panisse*] will be irresistible."   —*Pittsburgh Post-Gazette*

"Though much has been written about her, *Alice Waters and Chez Panisse* promises to be the definitive work on the life and career of this enigmatic and remarkable woman for years to come."
                                    —Tom Cooper, *St. Louis Post-Dispatch*

"The author's sensitivity to nature and his sympathy for his subject make this an engaging and tantalizing read."   —*Library Journal*

"A great pleasure for foodies."—*Kirkus Reviews* (starred review)

"Serious foodies will devour this memoir."   —*Publishers Weekly*

PENGUIN BOOKS

ALICE WATERS AND CHEZ PANISSE

Thomas McNamee was born in 1947 in Memphis, Tennessee, and grew up there and in New York City. He graduated from Yale University in 1969. His essays, poems, journalism, and natural history writing have been published in *Audubon*, *The New Yorker*, *Life*, *Natural History*, *High Country News*, *The New York Times*, *The Washington Post*, *Saveur*, and a number of literary journals. He wrote the documentary film *Alexander Calder*, which was broadcast on the PBS American Masters series in June 1998 and received both a George W. Peabody Award and an Emmy. He has written many book reviews for *The New York Times Book Review*.

PENGUIN BOOKS

ALICE WATERS

&

CHEZ PANISSE

THE ROMANTIC, IMPRACTICAL,

OFTEN ECCENTRIC, ULTIMATELY BRILLIANT

MAKING OF A FOOD REVOLUTION

THOMAS McNAMEE

Foreword by R. W. Apple, Jr.

PENGUIN BOOKS

Published by the Penguin Group

Penguin Group (USA) Inc., 375 Hudson Street, New York, New York 10014, U.S.A.
Penguin Group (Canada), 90 Eglinton Avenue East, Suite 700, Toronto,
Ontario, Canada M4P 2Y3 (a division of Pearson Penguin Canada Inc.)
Penguin Books Ltd, 80 Strand, London WCR2 0RL, England
Penguin Ireland, 25 St Stephen's Green, Dublin 2, Ireland (a division of Penguin Books Ltd)
Penguin Group (Australia), 250 Camberwell Road, Camberwell,
Victoria 3124, Australia (a division of Pearson Australia Group Pty Ltd)
Penguin Books India Pvt Ltd, 11 Community Centre, Panchsheel Park, New Delhi – 110 017, India
Penguin Group (NZ), 67 Apollo Drive, Rosedale, North Shore 0632,
New Zealand (a division of Pearson New Zealand Ltd)
Penguin Books (South Africa) (Pty) Ltd, 24 Sturdee Avenue,
Rosebank, Johannesburg 2196, South Africa

Penguin Books Ltd, Registered Offices: 80 Strand, London WC2R 0RL, England

First published in the United States of America by The Penguin Press,
a member of Penguin Group (USA) Inc. 2007
Published in Penguin Books 2008

10

A portion of this book first appeared in *Saveur.*

Grateful acknowledgment is made for permission to reprint the following copyrighted works:
"Food neither good to look at nor to eat" by Fritz Streiff. By permission of the author.
Chez Panisse song, music, and lyrics by Michael Tilson Thomas. © 2001 Kongcha Music.
By permission of Michael Tilson Thomas.
Selections from *California Dish* by Jeremiah Tower (Free Press, 2003). By permission of the author.
Selections from *Chez Panisse Menu Cookbook* by Alice Waters. Copyright © 1982 by Alice Waters.
Used by permission of Random House, Inc.

Photograph credits appear on page 381.

THE LIBRARY OF CONGRESS HAS CATALOGED THE HARDCOVER EDITION AS FOLLOWS:
McNamee, Thomas, 1947–
Alice Waters and Chez Panisse : the romantic, impractical, often eccentric, ultimately brilliant
making of a food revolution / Thomas McNamee.
p.   cm.
Includes bibliographical references and index.
ISBN 978-1-59420-115-8 (hc.)
ISBN 978-0-14-311308-9 (pbk.)
1. Waters, Alice.   2. Restaurateurs—United States—Biography.   3. Women cooks—
United States—Biography.   4. Chez Panisse.   I. Title.
TX910.5.W38M36 2007
641.5092—dc22
[B]
2006050334

Printed in the United States of America
Designed by Amanda Dewey

for

ELIZABETH

CONTENTS

FOREWORD
by R. W. Apple, Jr.

By now, everyone in this country who can tell the difference between an éclair and an entrecôte (and quite a few who cannot) knows who Alice Waters is.

She is, of course, the creator of Chez Panisse in Berkeley, California, one of the fountainheads of California cuisine, which some demanding judges consider the best restaurant in the United States. It is indisputably the most influential one. Before Chez Panisse, even the grandest American restaurants relied on imported, often canned or frozen products; today, the Waters credo—fresh, local seasonal, and where possible organic ingredients—is followed by hundreds of farmers' markets, thousands of restaurants, and millions of home cooks.

Her approach wins plaudits abroad as well as at home. I remember a conference at the opulent Manoir aux Quat'Saisons near Oxford, involving leading chefs from the United States, England, and France, where she dazzled her peers. They had arrived with trunks full of raw materials; she brought a few Meyer lemons and not much else, and relied for the rest on the Manoir's wonderful gardens and products on offer in the region, very simply prepared and served. All the chefs whom I asked said that her meal had been their favorite. It made the other meals seem somehow overwrought.

What is little understood, and what Thomas McNamee makes abundantly clear in this penetrating biography, is how unlikely a revolutionary Alice Waters is.

For one thing, she is no chef, at least in the generally understood meaning of the term. She has never attended cooking school and never served the same kind of rigorous apprenticeship, working in a succession of well-established kitchens, as have generations of European and more recently American culinary stars. She cooks, yes, and beautifully, but with some reluctance, and she has run Chez Panisse's kitchen only very episodically.

She isn't much of a businesswoman. Well into its period of ascendancy, Chez Panisse lost money, despite the best efforts of a series of business managers (including Ms. Waters's father) to impose fiscal discipline. Her habitual extravagance made their work hard and often all but impossible. In 1972, when the restaurant had been operating for less than a year, no less than thirty thousand dollars' worth of wine was unaccounted for.

Nor is she really a writer, despite the excellence and enormous success of her cookbooks. Like so much of her work, they are the products of her interaction with a group of friends, even when her name is the only one listed on the title page, as is sometimes the case.

Perhaps most surprising, the restaurant's mature style, marked above all by simplicity, evolved much more slowly than is generally appreciated. It is hard to believe, when one is faced with a trademark Chez Panisse dish like a salad with goat cheese, dependent for its impact on the quality of the greens and the care of the preparation, or a rustic soup of root vegetables, that Chez Panisse once served dishes of extraordinary complexity with no evident connection to northern California.

This was especially true during the tenure of Jeremiah Tower in the kitchen. He reveled in special dinners including surrealistic dishes inspired by Salvador Dalí or haute cuisine extravagances like duck stuffed with oysters, shallots, and its liver. A far cry, those, from the eventual house cuisine, influenced by Alice's experiences in the south of France, based on fresh herbs, newly picked vegetables, garlic, and olive oil.

So what assets did Ms. Waters bring to the project if not the usual skills of the successful restaurateur? Several.

Perhaps most important, what her old friend Eleanor Bertino calls "an iron will." A determination to press on when the staff or her private life was in turmoil, which has not always been visible to the casual observer, disarmed perhaps by her elfin appearance. Eleanor Bertino again: "There has always been this interesting contradiction between the delicate little way Alice looks and how she really is. . . . [She wore] these antique hats, delicate little hats that lay close to her head—she looked just like a Pre-Raphaelite angel."

"Of course it's possible," Ms. Waters would often say when someone told her that something could not possibly work. Another old friend, Greil Marcus, pictured Alice when challenged: "She'll simply smile and without any agitation at all, say, 'It can be done, it will be done, it's going to happen, you'll see.' She really does believe that she can change the world, she can change individual people one by one."

That determination has been hitched to a vision, one that has gripped Ms. Waters from the time of her first visit to France. As she told Mc-Namee: "I wanted civilized meals, and I wanted to wear French clothes. The cultural experience, that aesthetic, that paying attention to every little detail—I wanted to live my life like that."

So she made a restaurant about much more than food, taking infinite pains with flowers and lighting and color, menu design, the sequence of dishes, and the pace of service. An intensely social being, she has always been most at home in the dining room. To borrow a concept from Wagnerian opera, you might call Chez Panisse a *Gesamtkunstwerk,* a unitary work of art in which numerous elements play indispensable parts.

Not that food is slighted. By the testimony of her closest co-workers, Ms. Waters has an almost infallible palate and taste memory. If she tastes a dish and suggests that it needs just a squirt of lemon juice, that nearly always proves to be true. She knows that fava beans will combine well with rosemary, and she knows precisely how to make mulberry ice cream taste best.

And finally, she has that most valuable of leadership skills, the ability to build a feeling of camaraderie among staff members. No matter how turbulent things have become at certain moments in Chez Panisse's history—and they have often become turbulent indeed, fueled by gallons of Champagne, occasional dalliances with cocaine, and ample lashings of sex—Ms. Waters has managed to retain the loyalty of key figures like the chef Jean-Pierre Moullé for many decades, and even the humblest of workers is valued as a member of the Chez Panisse family.

The great triumph of her private life is her daughter, Fanny, named like the restaurant in homage to Marcel Pagnol's films. It was concern for Fanny's well-being, at least in part, that led her mother into her crusades for better food for children (the Edible Schoolyard project) and for college students (beginning with Fanny and her classmates at Yale). They may prove to be Ms. Waters's lasting monuments.

"How we eat," as this diminutive woman of grand dreams said confidently not long ago, "can change the world."

AUTHOR'S NOTE

Cristina Salas-Porras, at the time Alice Waters's assistant, first approached me about writing this book, presumably on her boss's authority, and in that sense it is "authorized," but I have had complete freedom throughout. Alice herself has been extremely generous with her time and resources. I have had unimpeded access to the Chez Panisse archives at the Bancroft Library of the University of California at Berkeley and to the archives stored at the restaurant. Alice has granted me many hours of interviews, and I have been free to interview her friends and colleagues as well.

Because Alice and my other interviewees have often been so well spoken and so candid, I have quoted them extensively. This approach has resulted in a frequent cohabitation of past and present tenses—for example, "'Amboise and Jean-Didier were their names,' says Alice."

Alice has been kind enough to talk her way through a number of recipes that illuminate certain significant times in her life. Lindsey Shere, the pastry chef of Chez Panisse for twenty-six years, has also provided two of these "narrative recipes."

On a few occasions I have interwoven individual interviews into a sort of dialogue that I believe more fully represents my interlocutors' recollections than presenting them separately would have done.

WHEN I WAS FIRST thinking about this book, I went to the home of Lindsey Shere and her husband, Charles, who has been a partner or director of Chez Panisse throughout its history. When I asked Charles what he thought my biggest difficulty would be, he answered quickly: "Too much information."

And how. Whenever I have mentioned this project to anybody who knows Alice Waters or Chez Panisse, I've been almost certain to hear something like, "Have you talked to Jean-Jacques Quelquechose?"

And I've answered, "Not only have I not talked to Jean-Jacques Quelquechose, I've never heard of Jean-Jacques Quelquechose."

To which the riposte came, "Well, I don't know how you expect to do this book without talking to Jean-Jacques. He was one of Alice's most . . ."

Too much information.

I'm sure I've made significant omissions that I will come to regret, and I'm sure I've made some outright mistakes. All I can say is that I've done the best I could, and I beg the reader's forgiveness for my errors.

1.

OPENING
NIGHT

1971, 2006

Late-summer sun streamed into the dining room, turning every westward surface gold—French gilt mirrors on ivory plaster walls, redwood trim, oak floors and flea-market oak chairs, mismatched flea-market china and flatware on red-and-white-checkered tablecloths, one great vase of flowers with a white-linened table all to itself. On the stairway to the second floor, a woman, on her knees, was nailing down an Oriental runner.

"Alice?" called a waiter from below. "It's six o'clock."

Alice Waters rose and turned and descended the stairs. She was twenty-seven years old but looked much younger, with the skin and guileless mien of a child. She was wearing a tan lace dress, of an earlier day, delicate, fine, exactingly chosen. She was tiny, barely five feet two, with wide-open, wide-set gray eyes and a soft, pensive mouth.

This little restaurant in an old house on Shattuck Avenue in Berkeley, California, was the dream of Alice's life, and tonight, August 28, 1971, was its opening night. She had named the restaurant in honor of Honoré Panisse, the most generous and life-loving character in Marcel Pagnol's film trilogy *Marius, Fanny,* and *César.* Alice wanted Chez Panisse to be an easygoing, unaffected gathering place, like César's Bar de la Marine on the Old Port of Marseille, where friends could laugh, argue, flirt, and drink wine for hours on end. At Chez Panisse, they could also have something simple and delicious to eat.

She threw her shoulders back, lifted her chin, and prepared to smile. She opened the door, and in poured a multitude. "We'd invited friends that first night," she recalls today, "but there was a line out the door and down the block. We just didn't know what to do."

Alice led them to their tables with a confident smile and a flourish of the hand as though she had been running a restaurant all her life. "In fact," she says, "my entire professional experience amounted to one summer making crab salad sandwiches at the tearoom in Bullock's department store, plus a little waitressing here and there."

The menu was chalked on a blackboard:

Pâté en croûte

Canard aux olives

Plum tart

Café

$3.95

And that was it. There was no choice except of wine—Mondavi Fumé Blanc, Mondavi Gamay, and, by the glass, a fine Sauternes, Château Suduiraut.

The dining-room staff had no uniforms and so were hard to distinguish from the customers, but there were a lot of them, in both the kitchen and the dining room. Chez Panisse on its opening night had fifty seats and fifty-five employees.

The pâté arrived promptly. It had been made in advance, and required only to be sliced and plated at the last minute. It was simple, an archetype of French bistro cooking: tightly packed chopped pork and pork fat flavored with Cognac and wrapped in an egg-glazed pastry crust. It was accompanied by the little sour pickles known as *cornichons* and crocks of

Dijon mustard. The customers dug in, and came up smiling. And then the wait began.

Behind the kitchen door was, in Alice's recollection, "sheer chaos." Victoria Kroyer, also twenty-seven, had been laboring at the sauce for the duck for three days, not shortcutting any of the many steps of the classical sequence set down by the imperious nineteenth-century master Auguste Escoffier. She had begun by making a *fond brun,* the classic long-cooked stock of vegetables, beef, and veal. She then thickened her stock with a roux of flour browned in clarified butter and set it to simmer through repeated skimmings of the scum that floated to the top. After six hours of that, she added tomatoes and *mirepoix* (minced carrots, onions, celery, and raw ham, with thyme and bay leaf), and skimmed it some more, reduced it some more, and strained it again, yielding *sauce espagnole,* the base on which many more elaborate sauces are built in French haute cuisine. To the *espagnole* she added more *fond brun* and reduced that combination by half; and then she spiked it with a bit of sherry and again strained the result, a demi-glace, which was still only a base. From the duck bones and trimmings and white wine Victoria then created a second stock, which she cooked for four hours, skimmed, strained, defatted, reduced, and finally combined with the demi-glace. That amalgam, in turn, she cooked with the olives for two hours. The sauce was magnificent, if a bit salty, but the braising of the ducks was now falling desperately behind.

Until Alice hired her as chef a few weeks prior to the opening of Chez Panisse, Victoria Kroyer had been a graduate student in philosophy, at the University of California at Berkeley, who liked to cook at home. She had never made *sauce espagnole* or demi-glace or, indeed, *canard aux olives* before this night. She had never worked in a restaurant kitchen. "Victoria had a certain confidence," remembers Alice, "which I lacked completely."

The ducks were fresh, not frozen, from Chinatown in San Francisco. Most of the produce had come from either the Japanese produce concession at the Usave on Grove Street or the Berkeley Co-op grocery across the street from the restaurant. For the salad, served after the main course though unlisted on the menu, the best they could get was romaine lettuce, and Alice ended up throwing away three-quarters of it. Alice and

Victoria had worried for days about which olives to use in the sauce, and as it turned out, says Alice, "neither of us was satisfied with the ones we ended up buying. Green Sicilian olives. They were much too salty." Alice and Victoria didn't even know that there were such things as restaurant purveyors. Not that it mattered, for the big suppliers didn't have fresh ducks, or beautiful salad greens, or the appropriate French olives either.

In the kitchen, casseroles of duck simmered on every burner and were crowded into the ovens, and still the meat refused to soften to the melting tenderness that Alice remembered from her seven months in Paris during her junior year in college. The dining room grew quieter as the diners' patience waned. Alice was in and out of the kitchen every few minutes, first cheering her crew on, then begging, then, finally, in a serious temper. Luckily, she did not know about the ash that had fallen from Victoria's cigarette into the sauce.

Between the pâté and the first plate of duck to appear in the dining room, a full hour went by. "I was going out of my mind," Alice remembers. "All these people waiting at the tables. More people waiting at the door to be seated. People waiting out on the sidewalk. And we just couldn't get their food out to them. And I was the one who had to talk to them."

At last, at intervals, waiters burst out of the kitchen to rush to a table with a few plates of unctuous, glistening, and delicious duck with olive sauce. At some unlucky other tables, as the kitchen bogged down further, the wait stretched to two hours. It was a good thing that so many of the diners were friends or family. "We had fifteen or more people in the kitchen," says Alice, "way more than we needed. Way more than there was room for. Not one of them professionally trained. Making it up as they went along. Same in the front of the house. Waiters and waitresses who were actually painters or poets or dancers. I hired them all, because I liked them. I didn't want professionals. We were just going to figure it out. That's what we were all doing, making it up as we went along. It was totally insane."

The plum tart—straightforward, almost austere, the plums at their peak of ripeness spread across a light custard and baked in a buttery crust—was the work of Lindsey Shere, a longtime friend of Alice's, who worked in calm isolation in a shack in the backyard and was, therefore, protected from the infectious nervous breakdown that had taken hold of Chez Panisse that night. The tart was perfect: warm, delicate, intensely fragrant, and ready to be served on time.

At the end of the evening, as the last late diners trickled out, Alice stood beaming in the doorway, her heart still pounding. One hundred twenty meals had finally been served. How many of those were actually paid for, no one would ever remember precisely. How much it cost to serve them was certainly much more than what they brought in.

There were still at least fifty people waiting in the street. "I'm sorry," Alice called to them. "We just don't have any more food. Come back tomorrow!"

Past midnight, Alice and the staff and the friends who stayed on opened some wine in the half-finished café upstairs and sat quietly together, exhausted, elated. "We were so happy. We were so young," she reminisces. "We were in love with what we were doing. And we were in the right place at the right time. It was sheer luck, really."

THIRTY-FIVE YEARS LATER, Alice Waters is arguably the most famous restaurateur in the United States, Chez Panisse the best-known restaurant. In 2001, *Gourmet* magazine deemed it the best restaurant in the nation; in the magazine's next assessment, in its October 2006 issue, Chez Panisse fell to number two (behind a Chicago newcomer called Alinea).

How the slapdash, make-it-up-as-we-go-along little hangout and its harried mistress became such icons is a story of adventure, misadventure, unintended consequences, steel will, pure chance, and utterly unrealistic visions. The characters who thread through its history range from hedonists to Machiavellian careerists, from the crazy to the coolly rationalist; nearly all have been driven by passion, passion sometimes so fierce as to be blind. The road Chez Panisse has traveled from there to here is neither straight nor smooth. It is potholed, booby-trapped, cliff-hanging, devil-daring, sometimes not quite a road at all.

In some ways, Chez Panisse today goes no further than Alice's first, modest desires for it. It still occupies the same old house in Berkeley. It is still an easygoing, unaffected gathering place where friends laugh, argue, flirt, and drink wine for hours on end—and have something simple and delicious to eat. Some of the same stoned hippies who were fumbling plates of duck on opening night are now polished professionals and still there—though their practiced manners mask the same antic, cerebral inner lives that attracted Alice to them years ago. There is not a Chez Panisse outpost in Las Vegas, or anywhere else; there is no Chez Panisse frozen pizza; and it is only in the last few years that Chez Panisse has become a genuinely profitable enterprise. Alice is a hero and a celebrity, hounded for endorsements and autographs, but she can still seem the same childlike, slightly out-of-focus dreamer who opened a restaurant without knowing anything about restaurants. Chez Panisse is a place of pilgrimage for gourmets and chefs from all over the world, but it offers no culinary fireworks, no vertiginous architectural assemblages on the plate, no wild combinations of exotic ingredients. It's still just a place to have fun and eat very good food.

But for many people, including many who will never eat there, Chez Panisse is a much larger enterprise than a restaurant. It is a standard-bearer for a system of moral values. It is the leader of a style of cooking, of a social movement, and of a comprehensive philosophy of doing good and living well. It is also a work of art—the work of many, the masterpiece of one.

With eight books, hundreds of talks, dozens of honors and awards, ceaseless media attention, and one not very big restaurant, Alice Waters has transformed the way many Americans eat and the way they think about food. Her insistence on the freshest ingredients, used only at the peak of their season, nearly always grown locally and organically, is now a ruling principle in the best American restaurants and for many home cooks. Her conception of a moral community based on good food and goodwill has helped to spawn a new generation of artisans and farmers. Like her, they are committed to stewardship of the land and waters. They settle for nothing less than the highest quality in what they produce. They see themselves as an increasingly potent force in American culture and politics. Under the leadership that Alice has reluctantly and somewhat awkwardly assumed, this new community has seen its ideals and methods spread across the country. You can now walk into a co-op or a farmers' market, or even a supermarket, in Montana or Mississippi, Ohio or New Mexico, and find fresh, delicious, organic foodstuffs, grown by people who share the values and vision of Alice Waters.

By the time Alice turned sixty years old, in 2004, she had far-reaching ambitions. Already she was seeing students, from grade school to college, being taught to grow and cook their own food. On a larger scale yet, she envisioned the soul-deadening machinery of corporate agriculture supplanted by a profusion of small organic farms, sustainable fisheries, and humane and ecologically benign animal husbandry. She dreamed of the fractured American family coming back together, and back to health, around the dining table. She saw that people worldwide could be drawn by pleasure to a new way of thinking about the earth and a better way of living on it.

Alice today is much changed from the girlish twenty-seven-year-old of 1971; Chez Panisse is in many ways much changed as well. But together— and their identities have become inseparable—they are still making it up as they go along, and every dinner is still a passionate experiment, often changing up to the moment it is served.

2.

SOUP

1944–1965

A lice Louise Waters was born on April 28, 1944, the second of four daughters of Margaret Hickman Waters and Charles Patrick Waters, of Chatham, New Jersey. Hers was an ordinary American suburban childhood, but Alice's experience of it was extraordinarily intense, because her senses were so acute. "Through the senses, always through the senses" is still how Alice Waters describes her lifelong way of knowing the world.

Her earliest memory is of the garden. Bad eyesight had prevented Alice's father, known as Pat, from serving in World War II. His part in the war effort had been to plant a victory garden. One Fourth of July, for a costume contest at the playground, Alice's mother, Marge, dressed Alice as the Queen of the Garden, with a skirt of lettuce leaves, bracelets made from radishes, anklets of red and green peppers, a necklace woven of long-stemmed strawberries, and a crown of asparagus.

Half a century later, Alice vividly recalls her mother's applesauce and apple pies, the strawberry patch, bacon sandwiches slathered with butter, running to the white Good Humor truck for a cherry-lime Popsicle, red on one side, with real pieces of cherry in it, green on the other, each half with its own wooden stick to be licked clean.

"The meal I loved best," she says, "was when my father was grilling a steak outside. The smell of the smoke, the sizzling of the meat and the fat. For my birthday, I always wanted a grilled steak, and we'd have green beans. That was my favorite meal, steak and green beans. Still is one of my favorites."

Alice remembers the aromas of the outdoors—the freshly cut grass on the hill she rolled down in Hacklebarney State Park, the musty smell of her snowsuit when she sledded the same hill in winter, the forsythia hedge in spring, the lilacs and the lilies of the valley beneath them, the newly turned black soil of the garden.

She remembers a good many things she didn't like, among them some elements of her mother's efforts toward good nutrition—brown, dry "health bread," oatmeal, vitamin pills that Alice sneaked into the bathroom to spit out. What becomes clear as she recalls her girlhood is that her senses were almost painfully acute. In the bedroom that she and her older sister, Ellen, shared, Alice was always too hot or too cold. When she complained of the cold, her mother would take her to the basement, stand her shivering in front of the furnace, and stuff her into her snowsuit. Hot summer nights, Alice would lie sleepless on top of the sheets. Then, in the mornings, through the open windows came the murmur of the creek beyond the raspberry brambles, squirrel chatter in the big oaks and maples, birdsong, and all the sounds of a summer morning.

As Pat rose through the ranks of the Prudential Life Insurance Company, the family moved to Indiana and then to southern California, and Alice grew from Mary Janes and cap-sleeved little dresses made by her aunt to pink Capezio pumps with a soft pink sweater and a straight pink skirt, through spin the bottle to serious smooching in the dark. In high school she discovered drinking, and boys—"lots of boyfriends, lots of driving up and down the main street in town, going out with older boys and ones from the other side of the tracks. Guys who had big Bonneville convertibles."

At Van Nuys High, she fell in with the intellectual crowd, and for college her parents urged her to go to the famously intellectual University of

California at Berkeley. But Alice chose U.C. Santa Barbara, which in her recollection is a whirl of skirts and hairstyles, parties, frat boys, and a great deal of drinking. "That was a dark period of my life," she says. "I was just moving from one party to another. There were various people I was involved with, but I don't remember a single person's name. I never got into pot smoking, but alcohol affects your memory too. Especially when you drink enough to pass out."

She was very smart, but she was in danger of becoming an irredeemable party girl. Rescue of a sort came from a fellow Van Nuys graduate, one she hadn't known there, a slim, cerebral beauty named Eleanor Bertino, one of her sisters at Alpha Phi. Eleanor was elegant, soft-spoken, and serious. She wanted to leave Santa Barbara, and she thought Alice would do well to join her. In the fall of their sophomore year, 1963, Eleanor, Alice, and another Alpha Phi, Sara Flanders, all applied for transfer to the University of California at Berkeley.

That moment was an early instance of what came to be a pattern in Alice's life: people stepping in to rescue her at just the right moment, and in doing so drastically altering her world. Although she has always seemed to lead a well-ordered life, Alice still sometimes characterizes herself as more acted upon than purposeful.

When they arrived in January 1964, the campus was nothing like the serene intellectual refuge they had imagined. The quiet, scholarly air of the 1950s had been shattered by the assassination of President John F. Kennedy, by violence against the civil rights movement in the South, by the arms race (indeed, nuclear weapons were being designed right there, at the Lawrence Berkeley Laboratory). That summer of 1964, the Freedom Riders James Chaney, Andrew Goodman, and Michael Schwerner were murdered by Ku Klux Klansmen in Mississippi, and President Lyndon B. Johnson pushed the fraudulent Gulf of Tonkin Resolution through Congress, setting in motion a war that would kill fifty-eight thousand Americans and three million Vietnamese. That year, the Republican Party, at its convention in San Francisco, named Barry Goldwater its presidential candidate. Goldwater wanted a much bigger Vietnam War (including the possible use of nuclear weapons) and much smaller federal defense of civil rights.

Years later, Eleanor Bertino looked back to the signal moment that drew them personally into the Berkeley whirlwind: "The Free Speech Movement erupted at our feet."

"And that changed everything," says Alice. "Changed my life forever."

BERKELEY WAS IN TURMOIL throughout the fall of 1964. Thousands of students were protesting university rules that effectively forbade political activity of any kind on campus. The administration met the protests with repression that grew more extreme by the week. The students' resistance took organized form that October as the Free Speech Movement. The FSM marked the beginning of the wave of political and cultural upheaval that would sweep around the world for the next ten years. Like many another venture in Berkeley, it was a first, and its leaders—some students; some older, long-dedicated activists; some mysterious characters who seemed to have materialized out of nowhere—tended to rely on intuition, improvisation, and a style of expression designed to shock their elders. They were remarkably successful nevertheless, and profoundly disturbing to the University of California system, its Board of Regents, the state legislature, and the governor. The movement made for sensational press, and that fall, emotions on all sides were mounting toward frenzy.

On December 2, 1964, the galvanic orator Mario Savio led some one thousand Free Speech Movement adherents in an occupation of Sproul Hall, the university's main administration building. Nothing like that had ever happened at an American university. That night, hundreds of policemen gathered at the edge of campus. All but a few of the students refused to leave. At three o'clock in the morning, 367 police officers stormed the building, and 773 of the occupiers were arrested. It was the biggest mass arrest of students in American history.

Real violence, southern style—with dogs, tear gas, and beatings—seemed imminent, and many of the students, inflamed with their sense of injury and injustice, were ready to welcome it. Many others were frightened and confused.

Alice had taken part in a few of the demonstrations earlier that fall, and her heart was with the protesters, but when her friend Sara Flanders showed her a brochure describing study at the Sorbonne, it did seem like a fine time to go to France.

ICELANDIC, the favored airline of young Americans traveling to Europe in the mid-1960s, flew crowded, scruffy turboprops from New York to Luxembourg, with a leisurely stop in Iceland to refuel, and a continuous party aloft. On those long and festive flights there was not much sleep to be had.

It was dark when Sara Flanders and Alice Waters arrived in Luxembourg, and they were already exhausted. Paris was another five hours by bus. It was February 1965, and freezing.

Alice had never been abroad. She had not come to France for the food, for she knew little about food, French or otherwise. She liked the idea of learning to speak French. She liked the idea of meeting French boys. She liked the idea of France.

"My rich aunt had told us about a place where we should stay, on the Rue Cambon, in the First Arrondissement, right behind the Place Vendôme," Alice recalls. "It cost ten times what we should have spent. We closed the curtains—the heavy, heavy blue curtains—and we went to bed, and we didn't wake up for a whole day. We missed the whole next day.

"Finally, we woke up. Our second day there, which we really couldn't afford. We went down to the dining room for lunch, and we didn't know what to order, so we just had the soup because it was the cheapest thing. It was a *soupe des légumes*. It wasn't puréed, it was just very finely chopped up, and it was so delicious. It felt like I had never eaten before. And everything that went with it—those big, old, thick curtains and a bed that was made with those sheets that had rolled-up cushions at the head of the bed—it was a sensibility that was not part of my life, had never been."

· WINTER VEGETABLE SOUP ·

You start with real winter vegetables, mostly roots, like carrots and turnips, parsnips, parsley root sometimes. And maybe winter squash and some greens. Maybe a little potato to give it body. You cut the vegetables into equal-size cubes and sauté them with onions and garlic and herbs till they're just starting to soften. Since it's winter, I would probably use a couple of thyme branches and a bay leaf. A little lovage leaf might be nice in there.

Then you add your liquid, just enough to stew the vegetables till they're nice and soft but haven't lost their shape—an hour and a half, or two hours at the most. If you cook them too long, the taste is too strong.

You can use just water, for the pure taste of the vegetables, or a little light chicken stock, but really light, made from uncooked chicken parts and nothing else. It's got to be more about vegetables than it is about the taste of the stock. Don't forget to take out the thyme and the bay leaf.

You don't want to use a blender or a food processor because that would make it too smooth. I use a food mill with the widest holes, so you still have a sense of the liquid in the soup. It's not emulsified. You still have all those different colors—the oranges, the yellows, the whites, the greens.

It might just need a little oil or a little butter right at the end. You want to serve it as soon as it's done. You don't want to keep it overnight in the refrigerator.

There are other sorts of vegetable soups, very long-cooked, with many vegetables, a soup that likes to be reheated. Minestrone, for example. But this one keeps the bright, live taste of the vegetables. I'll never forget that first time I tasted it.

"Well, we had to leave, and so we set out to find a hotel," Alice recalls, "which we found on the Rue des Écoles. It was a seventh-floor walk-up."

In their first days there, Alice and Sara were afraid to go to a restaurant because they thought their French was so poor. The Self Service Latin-Cluny, where you didn't have to speak French to anyone, was their haven. "They had pretty decent pâté, with *cornichons,* and *oeufs mayonnaise,* two hard-boiled eggs coated with mayonnaise. We'd have a glass of wine and a glass of mineral water and yogurt. I can still taste that yogurt."

For their permanent lodgings, the Sorbonne helped Alice and Sara find a studio apartment on the Place des Gobelins, with a bathroom down the hall. "I remember trying to make the true café au lait, with steamed milk," says Alice. Sara, now a psychoanalyst in London, adds, "And we would go out to this wonderful *pâtisserie,* for hot croissants and *pain au chocolat,* and bring them back to the flat."

"We would just sit there in that room," remembers Alice, "and eat this little treat, pastries and café au lait. Then we missed our first class, and it kind of went on like that."

It didn't take Alice and Sara long to overcome their fear of restaurants, and once they'd started going to them, they couldn't stop. Back in Berkeley, Sara had been the one excited about all the French food they were going to eat, while Alice's opinion, as Sara recalls it, was that they should be thinking about gaining some experience with French men. But it was food that Alice fell in love with. "And the culture," she adds now. "And the politics."

The dreary classrooms of the Sorbonne versus a joyous immersion in French cuisine in the sparkling, spotless dining rooms of Paris's restaurants—for Alice it was an easy choice. She reveled in the aromas of onion soup and Gauloise smoke in the bistros, the flowers on the tables, the meticulous geometry of the place settings. Down every Paris street, it seemed, food beckoned to her: roasting chestnuts, glistening oysters at the stands of long-aproned shuckers, the little outdoor markets that bloomed at dawn and were gone before lunch, with their exquisitely arranged fruits, vegetables, eels, chickens, and sausages, and their garrulous, mock-aggressive merchants.

Alice's meals card for the Sorbonne, 1965

She was enchanted by the rhythms, the old and inflexible customs, the sheer charm of Parisian dining. She loved the squiggly handwritten menus on the bistro chalkboards and the fact that the bill of fare changed every day. She loved the unvarying *"Bon appétit!"* and being called *mademoiselle*. Even in the most modest places, the napery was crisp and spotless, the flatware polished bright, the food better than anything she had ever tasted. Nevertheless, she recalls, "that was the time when no matter what we said in French, in a restaurant or to anyone, they said, *'Comment?'* They just refused to understand us. It was so demoralizing, and so painful. *'Comment?'* These good-looking French waiters. And of course I was dressed like a Russian émigré, with thick old boots and a giant huge coat and a huge hat, and it was snowing. These little French girls had on heels and spring coats, and they looked like they weighed about ninety-nine pounds, carrying their purses and eating a hard-boiled egg for lunch. I wanted to dress like them, but I was too cold. I was freezing. I did long for those beautiful French tight-fitting sweaters."

Alice and Sara's enchantment with French food grew into obsession. "We'd get up and have breakfast and figure out where we were going to go for lunch. That took some time, and nearly as soon as we finished lunch, we had to figure out where we were going to go for dinner. It was a wonderful time to be in France. It was real and genuine and honest. And really affordable. We were able to go to restaurants twice a day for five francs."

Sara adds, "I think I cared about the prices far more than Alice, who was—and is—extremely extravagant."

"I was still very intimidated everywhere we went," says Alice. "I didn't want to be gauche and order the red wine with the wrong course or the white with the wrong course, so I just ordered rosé. And I always ordered too much food. The waiters must have all been laughing hysterically in the back room. That's always how we felt, like no matter what we did, we were doing the wrong thing. But sometimes you learn well when you're on your knees, you know?"

Alice did show up for class from time to time, and began to acquire passable French. She remained afraid to use it, however, unless her interlocutor spoke absolutely no English. "Her French was better than mine," Sara Flanders recalls, "but she was paralyzed about talking, and I would be the one who would speak. Not because my French was that good, but because Alice used to start, 'Uh, uh, uh'—she just couldn't get it out."

"But I got the whole French aesthetic, from beginning to end," Alice says. "What those thick curtains looked like, what the fruit bowl looked like, how the cheese was presented, how it was put on the shelves, how the baguettes twisted. The shapes, the colors, the styles.

"Everything in Paris was magical to me. You'd walk past a church and you'd hear music, and you'd walk in and sit down and they'd be playing Bach at lunch. Concerts—we went to so many concerts. And those magnificent museums."

For spring vacation in 1965, Sara and Alice went first to Barcelona, and then to the south of France for three weeks. There Alice discovered the sort of elemental, boldly flavored food that would, years later, be the foundation of the Chez Panisse style: fresh herbs, just-picked vegetables, garlic, olive oil. Olive oil, especially the sharp, aromatic, green, first-pressing oil that was the single most basic ingredient in southern French cooking, was all but unknown in the United States. "I'd hardly even heard of olive oil at all, much less 'extra virgin.'"

After their return to Paris, Alice and Sara met two young Frenchmen. "Amboise and Jean-Didier were their names," says Alice. "They took us out in the country, and that was our real introduction to the food."

"Amboise, who was from Brittany, made an itinerary for our first trip there," Sara recalls. "This little chart, all the places Alice and I should go."

"I'll never forget those mussels in Honfleur," Alice says.

The fishermen brought them in from the boat, rinsed them off for a minute, threw them into this big cauldron, and then scooped them out. And I developed a whole crêpe obsession. I loved the *crêpes Grand Marnier* in Brittany. Buckwheat crêpes. I'd have a couple dozen oysters for lunch and a couple of crêpes, savory and sweet, and a bottle of apple cider. Oh, that cider. The first time we had it, we didn't know it was hard cider, and after lunch we were walking along the road getting sleepier and sleepier, and finally we just lay down in the grass and drifted off to sleep. I don't know how long we must have slept in that grass.

And the *fraises des bois*! I didn't know what they were. Strawberries of the woods. Couldn't imagine somebody out there picking them. We had them with crème fraîche and a sugar shaker. The waiter comes to the table with this big bowl, and you help yourself. Unbelievable.

In Paris, I loved the steak Bercy. All those shallots. *Entrecôte Bercy.* That was very expensive. And the salads and the skinny little green beans. And those big crudité platters. I loved standing at the bar at Au Pied de Cochon. I loved the idea of that restaurant, because it had those oysters out front, and then you'd go into the downstairs part and for four francs fifty you could eat at the bar and have a *blanquette de veau* and a glass of red wine and a basket of great bread.

I remember going to Caen, just to have those famous *tripes à la mode de Caen*. It was a sort of pilgrimage, really. But we set one foot inside that restaurant, took one whiff—augh!—and out we ran.

Late that spring of 1965, at a restaurant in a little stone house in Brittany, Alice had a meal that crystallized her conception of what good food ought to be. "Elsewhere, even when I found the food to be wonderful," she would write years later, the French "would say only that it was 'all right'; but after the meal in this tiny restaurant, they applauded the chef and cried, '*C'est fantastique!*' I've remembered this dinner a thousand times: the old stone house, the stairs leading up to the small dining room, which seated no more than twelve at the pink cloth–covered tables and from which one could look through the open windows to the stream running beside the house and the garden in back. The chef, a woman, announced the menu: cured ham and melon, trout with almonds, and raspberry tart. The trout had just come from the stream and the raspberries from the garden."[1]

After classes ended in June, Alice and Sara got rail passes that for a single price allowed them for the next two months to take the train anywhere in Western Europe on the spur of the moment. They went to England, and then to Italy, and from there on to the Salzburg music festival. Alice was not impressed with the food anywhere they went: "I was a confirmed francophile by then."

In September 1965, Alice and Sara returned to America by sea, sailing from Rotterdam on an old ship crammed with hundreds of students. One of them was a freshly minted Amherst graduate on his way to law school at Berkeley's Boalt Hall, Tim Savinar, who remains a friend of Alice's today.

"Almost immediately it was very rough, and just about everybody was sick as a dog," he says. "I don't get seasick—I'm an old salmon fisherman. And the other person who seemed not to be seasick was Alice. There we were, with this whole ship to ourselves, going to dinner, going to the bar, dancing. Alice said that she was going back to Berkeley, but what she really wanted to do was to operate some kind of a café, or some sort of meeting place that had the food that she had been awakened to, and combine it with people sitting around talking about film or something like that. She was quite romantic."

"When I got back from France," Alice remembers, "I wanted hot baguettes in the morning, and apricot jam, and café au lait in bowls, and I wanted a café to hang out in, in the afternoon, and I wanted civilized meals, and I wanted to wear French clothes. The cultural experience, that aesthetic, that paying attention to every little detail—I wanted to live my life like that."

3.

VERY SIXTIES

1965–1966

Alice's experience of Berkeley in the fall of 1965 could hardly have been less like the sweet and decorous life she had known in France. At this midpoint of the 1960s, Berkeley was undergoing all at once the cultural conflicts that would come to the rest of the United States through the later years of the decade. Social protest tended toward the vitriolic in Berkeley. Communal living often took radical forms, driven by ideology and lots of sex, some of it rather defiantly flaunted.

In Paris, Alice and Sara had read the *Herald Tribune* to keep up with the mounting discord in America, and they had heard French antiwar protesters chanting, *"U! S! Assassins!"* but there was a certain abstractness to it all. In Berkeley, the anger and the sense of danger were real. In Alice's absence, the Free Speech Movement sitters-in who had been arrested on December 2, 1964, had gone to trial and had been found guilty en masse. The black neighborhood of Watts in Los Angeles had rioted and burned; thirty-four people had been killed there, a thousand wounded. The first United States troops—thirty-four hundred Marines—had entered the Vietnam War in the spring of 1965, and by the end of the year, there would be nearly two hundred thousand Americans there. Berkeley was seething.

"I'll never forget the time Alice took us to one antiwar session," her sister Ellen Waters Pisor recalls. "We went to hear a speech by William F. Buckley, and afterward we could ask questions from the floor, so Alice immediately stood up. She was outraged by everything Buckley had said, and she said, 'What are you planning to do about the genocide in Vietnam?' Well, *genocide,* that was a pretty heady word for 1966."

"God, it was a wild time," says Alice. "A terrible time in many ways. But it all felt so important. History was being made in Berkeley, and we all felt that we were part of it. I didn't lose my French aesthetics, not at all, but what was going on at Cal seemed bigger, more important."

It was a very exciting time to be young and in Berkeley. The word *revolution* was heard constantly, and it meant not only the political uprising against war and racism but also a social and sexual revolution. While dour radicals debated all night in the dorms about correct and incorrect forms of violence, there was also the Sexual Freedom League holding weekly orgies and demonstrating naked on the campus.

Berkeley has a history of sexual freedom nearly as long as its activist tradition. In 1960, a professor (and Cal alumnus) at the University of Illinois, Leo Koch, advocated "free love" in the student newspaper and was summarily fired, but Berkeley welcomed him home the next spring with an outpouring of jubilation. Long before cohabitation was common anywhere else in the country, unmarried couples were openly living together in Berkeley. They didn't call themselves girlfriend and boyfriend, or companions or partners. They used the word *lovers.*

For Alice Waters, the radicals' romanticizing of violence was something to steer clear of. She and Sara Flanders and their friends were enacting their own sort of revolution, quietly devising a new way of living, grounded less in outrage than in pleasure, while also imbued with ideals of social justice. "I kept drinking my café au lait from a bowl," Alice says, "but I was also seeing the world beyond that now a little more clearly."

In 1966, Alice, Sara, Eleanor Bertino, and another former Alpha Phi sister from Santa Barbara teamed up to take an apartment with a well-equipped kitchen, where Sara and Alice tried to reproduce the French dishes they loved. There was a Frenchman living downstairs who was a good cook and a good teacher. Julia Child's television series on French cooking was in its third year and was a rich source of information. "My specialty," Alice says, "was crêpes with orange zest, just like I'd had in Brittany."

· CRÊPES WITH ORANGE ZEST ·

These were buckwheat crêpes—mostly buckwheat flour, but some white flour, and milk, and some beer, butter, eggs, a tiny bit of sugar. You let it sit in the refrigerator for at least a couple of hours. Overnight is better.

I have my own crêpe pans now. It's possible to use an omelet pan. It's hard to do it just free-form, because it's hard to get the batter very, very thin like you want to have it, and it's hard to pick it up if you have a high-sided pan. You need to have a very low-sided pan. In France, they sort of rake it out on a flat griddle with a little instrument, a little wooden snowplow-like thing, but I've never made them that way. I suppose you could try it, but you just absolutely have to have the right amount of liquid or you can't get it right. The batter's got to be as thin as possible.

You can use butter or oil, not too much, just about medium hot. I put the batter in, and then I pick up the pan and tip it all around so the batter goes out to the edges and forms a very, very thin layer. Then as soon as it bubbles and gets settled a little bit, I lift it up by one edge with my fingers—I don't flip it in the air—and turn it over and cook it another minute, and then stack them in a pile.

You make a kind of butter with orange zest and sugar in it. After you make the crêpes, you spread them quickly with that butter, *et voilà*. Maybe put in a touch of Grand Marnier or Cognac. I think the buckwheat is incredibly delicious, that flavor. Yes, I do.

With girls this pretty and food this good, the apartment was a popular destination for young men. "The door was always open," says Eleanor, "and we always had men who were just friends, which was something a little bit new. Things were open in Berkeley. The sixties started in Berkeley before anywhere else, you know. You could be a nice girl and still sleep with your boyfriend. Everything was kind of expansive. It was like the whole world was brighter and opening up. And of course we were the defining generation."

And for many in their generation, in mid-sixties Berkeley, the defining experience was LSD. Lysergic acid diethylamide was still legal. Its most famous manufacturer, Augustus Owsley Stanley III, universally known as Owsley, plied his trade nearby, in north Berkeley. Sara Flanders announced that it was time for them to give it a try, and Alice was intrigued by what promised to be an entirely new sensory experience. "Owsley was a friend of one of our downstairs neighbors," says Alice, "so we managed to get the good stuff. I had never even smoked dope before that. Well, it blew my mind, as they say. I was up there on the ceiling looking down at Eleanor, who was on the chair. I don't think I came down for three days. The whole world looked different to me after that. I just understood something about another way of thinking. It was an important experience, but it scared me terribly. There was that feeling that I was going to lose my mind. And that I would never ever come down. Never, ever, ever."

This was classic Alice: portraying herself as timid while also daring the high dive; having her adventure never alone, but always in the company of trusted friends; and describing a moment of intense sensory experience as somehow, inexpressibly, life-changing.

Alice's aesthetics and her political commitment came together in her study of the Romantic period in Europe. She was gaining confidence. She created her own major, in French cultural history, focusing on the period between 1750 and 1850—"in other words, the French Revolution. In part, I suppose, because it felt like the moment we were living in."

"She was never a shy person, exactly," says Eleanor, who has made something of a life study of Alice, "but she wasn't very articulate. Then, in 1965, when she was back from France, all this intellectual stuff and the arts gave her a means of expressing herself. She was super-energetic. Not a moment of self-doubt. I mean, if she didn't like your boyfriend, she was not nice to him. She knew who she wanted me to go out with, and I wasn't doing that. She made life very difficult for this poor guy I was going out with.

"She wanted to run things, and she had the strength and energy to do it. When it took two of us to take a mattress and struggle up this flight of stairs, Alice would just throw it over her shoulder and run up the stairs. That's how I always think of Alice, still—lifting things, carrying them, moving things, always moving so quickly.

"There's always been this interesting contradiction between the delicate little way Alice looks and how she really is. There was something very turn-of-the-century-to-1930 about Alice's appearance, and there still is. When you look at the furniture in her house, I think, some of it is from the thirties still. And she started wearing these antique hats, delicate little hats that lay close to her head—she looked just like a Pre-Raphaelite angel. She had this long, wavy hair, and was very, very skinny. Barely five-two. But an iron will. Always."

Eleanor understands Alice deeply enough to make Alice sometimes quite uncomfortable, but her cool take on Alice's foibles is in its way an expression of Eleanor's great affection. To the curious would-be analyst of Alice's complexities, Eleanor responds with unsentimental simplicity: "She has never wanted to stop. She is not a contemplative person. She's not somebody who likes to stop and really think about things. She's not one of those people who need to go off and read a book and be alone."

Alice and Eleanor and most of their fellow students foresaw a changed world in their near future, one they had forged themselves. Sometimes they saw it as generated by political action, and sometimes from within, close to home, in the way people lived.

"In the spring of '66," Eleanor says, "I remember sitting around together and saying, 'You know, we don't have to get married.' All our sorority sisters in Santa Barbara were getting married. And Sara said, 'It's kind of exciting—we can do whatever we want; there are no rules, there's no structure. We have to make them up ourselves, and that's sort of frightening.' And we decided that we wanted to have a restaurant... more than a restaurant. I wanted to call it The Four Muses. We'd get this great big old house, and Sara would make clothes there, and Betsy Danch, our other roommate, would have an art gallery, and I would have the bookstore, and Alice would do the restaurant. Alice had wanted to have a restaurant where a different person would cook each night, but where we would all go to eat. We were starting to think about a more community-oriented, communal way of life—creating a family in that way instead of the traditional mommy, daddy, baby."

Also in the spring of 1966, the editor of the radical magazine *Ramparts*, Robert Scheer, decided to run in the Democratic congressional primary, on an antiwar platform, and Alice volunteered for his campaign. "I didn't really think I could win," recalls Scheer, now a syndicated political columnist. "I just wanted to force the incumbent guy to come out against the Vietnam War. I wasn't a politician. Alice was only twenty-one, but I put her in charge of our press liaison, and she was so good, so unflappable, so passionate, so focused. And then damned if our campaign didn't take off. I lost, but I did come close to winning."

Alice would bring campaign materials to the printers at the Berkeley Free Press, where one of the leaders of the Free Speech Movement, David Lance Goines, was learning the printing trade. David was studious and reserved, with an elegant, rather formal way of speaking. He had been a classics scholar, studying Greek and Latin, until he was expelled for distributing a course catalog "supplement" in which students dared to evaluate their professors. "And now, thirty years later," he says with a laugh, "they're required to do it."

Alice soon learned that David also bore the radical's badge of highest honor: He had gone to jail. He had served a month in the summer of 1965 for his part in the Sproul Hall takeover of December 2, 1964, and would serve another thirty days in the summer of 1967.

David also appealed to her aesthetic sense. He was a very good graphic designer and calligrapher, and Alice found herself fascinated by calligraphy. "She had such a strong, bold hand," he recalls. In the summer of 1966, Alice moved in with David Goines.

Alice and David Goines, 1967

Alice and David loved to cook together. "Alice would try anything," David says.

Sara Flanders, with something of a shudder in her voice, remembers their serving her "these big mushrooms with a snail coiled in them."

"We knew that you were supposed to make soufflés using copper," David says. "You were supposed to whip the egg whites in copper. But we didn't know the copper had to be absolutely clean, so we made this wonderful soufflé that came out grass-green. We figured it would kill us dead if we ate it, which it would in fact have done. So we threw it away and had popcorn for dinner. We had a fair amount of failure. We were willing to fail, which is absolutely essential to any kind of learning. Truly momentous disasters occurred on a regular basis, both in my artwork, which I destroyed, and in her cooking, which she destroyed. All those failures are, needless to say, not around to accuse us at this point."

David and Alice lived on the same block as Charles and Lindsey Shere. Charles was a music critic, a composer, and the music director of the notoriously provocative radio station KPFA, whose printing David did. Charles was a towering presence, intimidating until you realized how soft a heart his bearlike demeanor concealed; David's manner was mild and formal. They made a good pair of friends. Lindsey and Alice both loved to cook. In the fall of 1966, the four of them began to dine together often.

Lindsey shared with Alice a commitment to using only the best ingredients and doing her best at whatever she undertook; like Alice, she had little use for shortcuts; like Alice she was slim and delicately featured. Their voices were both soft, and softest when they were together. They were instant soul mates. Usually Alice would cook the main course at home, and then the two couples would stroll down the street for Lindsey's dessert.

"There was a wonderful Wallace Stevens poem that hung on the wall in Alice and David's kitchen," Charles Shere recalls, "right by the kitchen table where we ate our crêpes ['Cy Est Pourtraicte, Madame Ste Ursule, et les Unze Mille Vierges']. In the text of the poem, Saint Ursula is distracted from the cruelty of the slaughter of the eleven thousand virgins by the beauty of the radishes growing in a field. Alice must have looked at that poem ten times a day.

"Those meals of ours were truly composed, like music," Charles says. "I spent years at KPFA making record concerts, and I was always really interested in how you design a program—how this piece of music goes with that piece of music. That was one of the things that really impressed me about Alice. Every item on each menu had a relation to all the other items on the menu. When you spend a lot of your time composing things, then I think you develop a mind that always looks to see what the interconnections are, what the running threads are. I think that Alice's awareness of interconnection ultimately flowered in her thinking about the whole concept of sustainability"—the idea that any human undertaking should be part of a larger ecology, in which the use of resources can be sustained indefinitely as they are replenished by natural processes.[1]

Alice decided to cook her way straight through Elizabeth David's *French Provincial Cooking*. The book was about more than just good recipes. It portrayed a way of life—honest, elemental, caring—from which a tactile, sense-engaging way of making food emerged as naturally as a plant from the earth. Alice was becoming a very good cook, although she could still curdle a béarnaise sauce. "She didn't even try to save it," David remembers. "Just threw it right in the garbage. I was shocked. She was very demanding, very exacting. Everything had to be, within reasonable limits, perfect, or she wouldn't serve it." They developed a crowd of regular guests, from university intellectuals to a topless dancer, and, though Alice was raised loosely Presbyterian and none of them was Jewish, they also always "set a place for Elijah"—a Passover tradition of welcome to an uninvited guest. In fact, as often as not, somebody would turn up just in time to occupy Elijah's chair.

4.

MONTESSORI AND
A DREAM

1967–1971

Because her semester abroad did not count toward her degree, Alice continued at Cal through 1966 and graduated in January 1967. That spring, she took a job at what David Goines describes as a "trying-to-be-French" restaurant in Berkeley named the Quest.

"I was a good waitress, I think," Alice says, "but in that kitchen I wasn't learning anything." She was already a much better cook than anyone there.

"It was an awful place," recalls Charles Shere.

That winter, Eleanor Bertino and Sara Flanders left for an extended sojourn in Paris, to be followed by Sara's psychoanalytic training in London. Alice herself didn't know what she was going to do. She did still daydream of having her own restaurant, but "the restaurant fantasy was still just that," says David. "A fantasy. Lots of people have dreams, and how many of those dreams are ever realized?"

Meanwhile, for the *San Francisco Express Times,* an "alternative" weekly newspaper, David and Alice began collaborating on a food column titled "Alice's Restaurant," after Arlo Guthrie's antiwar story-song. Each column consisted of one of Alice's favorite recipes calligraphed and illustrated by

LA SAUCE MAYONNAISE

it is essential to begin with all the ingredients at room temperature · beat together two egg yolks in a wide bottom bowl
using a fork stuck into half a potatoe with the flat side
exposed · beat in ½ teaspoon dijon mustard · ½ teaspoon of
salt · & ½ teaspoon wine vinegar · & ½ teaspoon of confection-
er's sugar · when the mixture is smooth · begin pouring a
constant thread of olive oil · the better the quality of the oil ·
the better the taste · stir vigourously as the oil is added · when
about ⅓ cup of oil has been poured · the mixture should begin to emulsify · continue · adding a sprinkling of vinegar every so often · after several additions of vinegar · switch to lemon
juice · it is possible to use as much as 2½ cups of oil · adding
lemon when necessary to insure the consistency & taste ·

David. In 1970, David would print them as a limited edition of litho-
graphs titled *Thirty Recipes Suitable for Framing*.

With Alice working nights and David at the print shop all day, their
time together was scarce. Late into the nights, they would cook together.
Alice fed David his first raw oyster. "Everything for us was about taste,"
he recalls. "I'd forgotten what real food tasted like. And I grew up on a
farm, just like Charles and Lindsey. When I was a baby, my mom squirted
milk straight from the cow into my mouth. We were discovering and re-
discovering, always exploring."

But the food Alice was cooking didn't live up to what she had eaten in

France. Was it a trick of memory, a magnification by nostalgia? That was unlikely, because Alice had learned by now that she was possessed of a preternaturally fine palate and a nearly flawless taste memory.

Much of the food that Alice had loved most was *la cuisine du marché*—market cooking. She had seen it in action many times. A French house-wife would stroll through a village market, sniffing, appraising, thinking. If some farmer's basket of bristling, just-harvested cardoons struck her fancy, and a particularly nice rabbit was hanging from the butcher's hook, the Frenchwoman would devise in her mind a rabbit-with-cardoons dish and then shop for harmonious accompaniments. The little blue-and-white boats would come into port with nets bulging with dozens of species of wriggling sea creatures, and the fishermen's wives or mothers would spread them, still flopping, on tables at the water's edge: The smells of the sea and the fish and the cries of the circling seabirds merged in an indivisible whole of sensory felicity; and the housewife would compose her *bourride* as she paced along the quay.

In the big French cities, and in the luxurious Michelin-starred estab-lishments of the provinces, such improvisation was either considered un-professional or not considered at all. A serious restaurant had to be able to turn out a consistent menu day after day. It was true that the grand restaurants' menus changed somewhat with the seasons, bringing game and truffles in fall, tomatoes and eggplant in summer, but their rigid sys-tem could not respond to the arrhythmic, unpredictable supply of prov-ender direct from the farm and the sea.

The chefs of more modest restaurants, however, the ones Alice had loved best, were in the markets every day, touching the food, smelling it, talking to the farmers and fishermen. A farmer might have only a half dozen ducks, but if they were really exceptional ducks, the chef would compose his *plat du jour* around them.

If Alice wanted to buy a duck in Berkeley, the only one she could get was a frozen-stiff Long Island duckling exactly like every other frozen-stiff Long Island duckling in the United States. But she soon discovered in the Chinatowns of Oakland and San Francisco ducks that had been raised on nearby farms being sold either still alive or freshly killed, with their heads and feet still attached, just as they had been in France. The Chinese markets were crowded and chaotic, but they had chickens that tasted like chicken, Dungeness crabs still waving their legs and smelling of the cold, clear Alaskan current just offshore, salmon spawned in the Sacramento River delta just a few miles north of Berkeley. There were live rock cod and catfish and sturgeon and prawns in tanks. The fish on ice hadn't been dead long enough to have lost the mucous sheen on their scales, the lively pinkness of their gills, the clarity of their bulging eyes.

"Ingredients!" Alice cries, remembering those first illuminations in the farmers' markets of France. "Sure, you had to know technique. But if you didn't start with great ingredients, you could never make great food."

THE QUEST was a nightly exercise in humiliation—impossible demands from customers and bosses, contempt from the kitchen, lousy tips, lousy food. At the restaurant Alice was dreaming of, the staff would be treated with respect, the food cooked with love. But she had no money, didn't know how to raise it, and had no idea how to run a business. Until she could figure all that out, she was going to have to find something else to do.

Barbara Carlitz had been the college roommate of Alice's sister Ellen, and had become a virtual member of the Waters family. She was also a Montessori teacher, and "I just had a feeling that Alice would love teaching," she says.

"And I did," Alice agrees. "Right from the start."

In the fall of 1967, she began assistant teaching at the Berkeley Montessori School and was enraptured. "Montessori went straight to my heart, because it's all about encountering the world through the senses. That's how kids learn best. The hands are the instrument of the mind—that was how Maria Montessori put it." The excitement of learning new things, growing rapidly into a new world, and doing so through sensory engagement—the Montessori narrative was a recapitulation of Alice's own life story. "Maria Montessori's great idea," says Alice, was to design a curriculum that accommodated the way kids were naturally, and the stage of physical growth they were in, and the emotional stage as well. She designed materials to appeal to kids through all their senses—for instance, these special color tablets or color squares. You begin with the most simple of matching—it's a little game where you're matching the blues, the yellows, and the reds. You have them all scattered out, and the idea is to put the two blues together, the two reds, and the two yellows, each one with a beautiful enameled center and a polished wood frame.

The idea is not to touch the color but to hold it by its side. You're not only teaching them this game, you're teaching them to pick something up carefully. All the games are designed so that the kids will be successful. If you say to a little kid, "Go pick up that glass," and then it's big and heavy and he drops it, and the mother comes over and says, "Why did you spill that on the ground?" the poor kid learns nothing. Maria Montessori would have a little tray of glasses in the classroom, and the child would touch the glass, and then he'd close his hand and feel how weighty it is, how big or little it is. You ask him, "See whether you can lift it up," and you say, "You put your hands like this, all the way around this side and all the way around that side, and you lift it up. And you bring it over, and you put it right here. And you let go." It's an observation that's not just with your eyes. You take a little broom and try to get up every crumb on the floor. You take your little tray and you put that back on the shelf. There's a place for it. You learn about everything in your environment. You become familiar with it. And you begin to really see what its value is.

The International Montessori Centre in London was supposed to be the best place in the world to train in the Montessori method, and Barbara Carlitz and her husband, Michael, had recently moved to London. Barb was teaching in a London Montessori school, and when Alice announced her intention to pursue certification there, they were delighted to put her up. But this meant leaving David behind. He was in the midst of several work and study projects, and he encouraged Alice to go ahead. He might come over and join her later in the fall.

Alice flew to London in August 1968. "I remember the time precisely," Barbara Carlitz recalls, "because it was just at the time of the fall of Dubček, when the Russian tanks rolled into Prague.

"She was working a couple of different jobs while she was going to school," Barb remembers. "She used to give me her money. She's always been quite bad about money. And she would say, 'Now, Barb, don't give it back to me no matter what I say.' Then she'd come and say, 'I've found the most gorgeous coat. Now, this is really important. This is a necessity. I have to have this coat. This is exceptional.'"

When the Carlitzes came home from a brief vacation in October 1968, they were astonished to find David Goines ensconced in their flat with Alice. "Hello," David greeted them, "I'm your certified commie creep."

Alice and David stayed at Barb and Michael's through Christmas, and then Alice went out looking for a place of her own. In Hampstead, her eye was drawn to a tall Victorian house with a turret. "I've always loved turrets," she enthuses. There was a sign out front advertising a room to let, and the room was at the top of the turret! The landlady was suspicious, informing Alice coldly that the room was for one woman only, no visitors allowed. The turret bedroom was barely big enough for the single bed in it. "There was no central heating. You fed a space heater with shillings. The kitchen was in a closet across the hall—a two-burner hot plate with a tiny broiler underneath. I didn't care. I was living in a turret."

In the London of 1968, no matter how "swinging" its international reputation, unmarried couples did not live together. David was going to have to find digs of his own. The flat he found was at least near Alice's. And thanks to the Carlitzes' broad-minded hospitality, Alice and David did manage to spend the occasional night together—and to cook together again.

"I nearly froze to death that winter," Alice recalls, "but I cooked up a storm. I was cooking for anybody who would come over. I'd go down to Harrods and just look at all the beautiful things. I would eat in this Indian restaurant down the street, having the prawn-and-spinach curry for lunch while I was supposedly doing my homework, and reading Keats and thinking about cooking. I loved London.

"And I loved the Montessori work. The thing about Montessori is that every kid has something that he's good at, and you just have to find out what that is, help him open that door to find what he has a passion about. Kids can find that out very early on, and it's what gives them a sense of confidence and gives them a passion about their life. That's what I was getting, too."

Alice and David decided to get married. The wedding would be in February 1969, in London. It would be small—just their parents and the Carlitzes. Neither the Waterses nor David's parents had ever been abroad. Barb Carlitz and Alice went shopping for a wedding dress at the boutique of the famous British designer Biba. "A beautiful mauve crepe," Alice reminisces.

But one day, David and Alice looked at each other and realized that, as Alice puts it, "Somehow we just didn't connect."

What had happened? Barbara Carlitz remembers Alice telling her at the time that it was David who "had gotten cold feet." Years later, when Barb raised the same recollection to Alice, "She looked at me like I was nuts."

Lindsey Shere believes it wasn't a breakup at all: "I'm pretty sure that the real breakup happened after she came back from England, because I remember talking to her in our garage. She was quite upset—it had clearly just happened. I don't remember what she said except that it was David's idea, because he was unhappy about something."

Says David himself, with a shrug, "We were like teenagers. We just changed our minds."

And Alice says, "David's exactly right. We were too young."

On the surface, it was just that casual. But their whole generation was deeply suspicious of established institutions, and not getting married was truer to the do-your-own-thing ethos of the time than long-term commitment would have been. Alice to this day is wary of personal attachments that entail obligation. Her idea of friendship or of love is the voluntary exchange of affection between independent individuals.

Alice and David continued to spend as much time together as possible. After Alice's Montessori studies concluded, they headed for Paris for two weeks of serious eating.

David flew home to California in midsummer 1969. Alice, meanwhile, found a new friend in another American woman studying at the Montessori Centre, Judy Johnson, and together they bought an Austin Mini Cooper and set out across the Continent, on a beeline for Bulgaria. Another friend had introduced Alice to Bulgarian music. "We thought we were going to listen to Gypsy music in Bulgaria, and smell rose essence, or something. And, of course, we found kind of a military state.

"Well, we got to Turkey, and we drove into the interior, and we hooked up with two French guys. They followed us in their little Citroën Deux Chevaux, and we'd set up tents together side by side. It was a great thing, because two women couldn't get into anyplace without men."

In an essay she contributed to a collection called *The Kindness of Strangers,* Alice recalled how deep an impression Turkish hospitality made on her.

We ran out of gas. . . . A shy, big-eyed boy appeared, and he mimed that there was no gas to pump. And we counter-mimed that we supposed we would have to wait. . . . Then, fingers pointing to mouth, where would we get something to eat?

. . . Solemnly the boy leads us indoors and into the back room where there are benches against the wall covered with beautiful old rugs, a brazier in the corner made out of an old gas can, birdcages hanging from the low ceiling, and a baby brother. Clearly the parents are away and the big brother has been left behind to babysit and turn away customers, and to offer us the imperative hospitality of rural Turkey.

The boy builds us a fire out of pinecones, puts on a kettle, and makes us tea. Then he produces a small piece of cheese and painstakingly cuts it into even smaller pieces, which he offers us gravely.

. . . He has given us everything he has, and he has done this with absolutely no expectation of anything in return. A small miracle of trust, and a lesson in hospitality that changed my life forever.

"We went down along the coast and into Greece, and ended up in Corfu. It was like the Garden of Eden," Alice muses. "You just went out and picked things off the tree. We tenderized octopus by throwing it against the wall. We cooked every day. We'd have this beautiful feta cheese with ouzo, and beautiful olives and olive oil. I'd never had olive oil like that. We never used a watch. The people had these big pig roasts, with everybody dancing. There was a certain poverty, certainly, but it was a beautiful way they lived their lives in spite of it. And then we went to Venice, and I fell in love all over again. I'm still in love with Venice."

HER MONEY GONE, Alice returned to Berkeley in the late summer of 1969, now fully qualified to teach at the Montessori school there. She moved back in with David Goines, in a new apartment he'd found on Channing Way. They seemed to their friends to be just as attached as ever. They just didn't want to get married.

A French couple named Claude and Martine Labro had recently moved to Berkeley from Vence, in the south of France. Claude, a mathematician, was teaching at the university. Like David, Martine was a graphic artist—as well as a serious cook, like Alice. A mutual friend urged a meeting, and Alice took to Martine immediately. Alice's notions of French elegance were somewhat general; Martine's were highly specific. Martine knew how to draw the perfect warm bath, just the right temperature, with a perfect little vase of flowers on the windowsill. She knew how to arrange the curtains so that the light filtered through just so. Martine had learned from her mother to search through the *marchés aux puces* for the thing unanticipated but just right, and now she and Alice began to haunt the Bay Area's flea markets together. Martine loved American patchwork quilts, and so did Alice. Martine loved antique dresses of fine and much-worked cloth, gathered, shirred, beaded, pleated, sheer-layered, softly draping, pastel. Alice began to wear such dresses. Martine thought Alice looked fabulous in a beret or a tightly wound cloche. Alice wears such hats to this day.

"I guess you could say I'm extremely impressionable," Alice says. "I've gotten something important from a great number of people in my life. Martine was very important in my whole aesthetic. She was very definitive. About lighting—that was one thing I got from her, an obsession about lighting. I also learned from Martine a certain kind of frugality. I'll never forget Martine serving a chicken for ten people. I bought one chicken for, you know, two or four. That's the American way. And she bought one chicken for ten. I was astonished that she could imagine there would be enough food. She made the most beautiful dinner, and everybody had plenty of everything. It was just that they had a small amount of chicken."

That winter, Alice and David parted again, this time for good—although they have remained close friends ever since. It is in fact a nearly universal principle in Alice's life that any man who has ever been her lover will be her friend forever. No strings, no obligations, no entanglement, no mutual responsibilities—such is Alice's ideal setting for the free exchange of admiration, attraction, affinity, love.

The late sixties and early seventies were the heyday of the French cinema, and the Telegraph Repertory Cinema in Berkeley was a favorite night out for Claude and Martine. They had become friends with its young manager, Tom Luddy, and early in 1970 they introduced him to Alice.

Alice fell hard for Tom Luddy, and for French movies. She moved in with Tom in his little one-bedroom house on Dana Street. She still cooked with Lindsey and Charles Shere, and now Martine and Claude Labro were joining in as well. Frequently, they turned out elaborate, multicourse feasts.

Dinner, cooked by Alice and company, would often be followed by a movie that Tom had brought. "Tom would show maybe a political documentary, or a Bresson film, or some old American film that we had never seen," Eleanor Bertino recalls. "Film was the art form of the moment. And Tom knew so many interesting people. Susan Sontag, Huey Newton, Agnès Varda, Abbie Hoffman, Jean-Luc Godard—Tom was Godard's agent in the United States. If they were in town, they would be invited over to the house. It was, like, this fantastic salon, in this incredibly modest house. Then Alice would serve Cognac and a little French tart in the latter part of the evening. She was completely obsessed with food by that point. I always say that the best year of Chez Panisse was the year before it opened."

Tom took Alice to see the classic trilogy of films written and directed by Marcel Pagnol (and derived from his own stage plays of the same names), *Marius, Fanny,* and *César.* "Alice just cried and cried, cried her heart out, she was so moved," he recalls. All three films revolve around a little bar-café on the Old Port of Marseille and its motley habitués. The Bar de la Marine is an island seemingly outside of time, with its own crusty ways, genial spirit, complex affections, and long afternoons of card games and ancient arguments. César is the irascible but golden-hearted owner of the bar; Marius, his passionate, ne'er-do-well son; Fanny, the lovely and innocent girl whom Marius impregnates and abandons. The emotional climax of the films comes when the much older Honoré Panisse offers to marry Fanny and raise the coming child as their own. The generosity, the sheer goodness, of Panisse struck a deep chord in Alice, and the easy familiarity, trust, and benevolence shared by the waterfront community reawoke her old conviction that a restaurant could exemplify those values.

Through Tom's friends Alice now had had a peek at the world in which things really got done and weren't just dreamed about. As she began to imagine the food, the lighting, the feeling, the communitarian ethos that her restaurant would embody, Alice knew, at last, what she wanted. The Montessori way—direct sensory experience, experimentation, optimism, confidence—would be the way of her restaurant. As for the practicalities, she had no specific ideas. She had never heard of a business plan. She had only faith that things would fall into place.

Alice had good reason to believe there would be a public for her cooking. Nearly everyone who had come to dine at the little house on Dana Street said that hers was some of the best food they'd ever tasted. Even Tom's French friends, not as free-handed with praise as Americans tended to be, called her a genius. The university, with its cosmopolitan and well-traveled faculty, could provide a ready customer base. Many other restaurants in the East Bay—and, for that matter, the majority in the supposedly great dining capital of San Francisco—compromised shamelessly on the quality of ingredients. At many, the service and welcome were indifferent at best. And the cooking ranged from occasionally competent to consistently poor.

Alice's first hope, an inspiration that had come to her in 1969, was for a tiny storefront in an alleyway off Telegraph Avenue, where she would serve the buckwheat crêpes she had loved in Brittany. But a businessman friend of David's did a projection of the best possible financial scenario and showed Alice that in so small a place—especially with people hanging out for hours as she intended they would do—even breaking even, never mind making a profit, was out of the question.

All through the spring, summer, and fall of 1970, Tom and Alice and Claude and Martine tried restaurant after restaurant "to see what we could learn from them," Tom explains. "Usually it was learning what not to do."

Then, in the little town of Bolinas, on the Pacific coast not far north of San Francisco, they discovered the Gibson House. It was a converted Victorian farmhouse, surrounded with flowers, where the chef—a woman—produced such exotic fare as roast duck garnished with nasturtiums from the restaurant's own flower beds. There were flowers everywhere inside as well, and patchwork quilts on the walls, and mismatched china and flatware, and, as Alice remembers the scene, "Nobody cared if you wanted to stay at your table playing poker all evening. I loved the idea of a restaurant in a house. I loved the flowers. I loved that you could stay as long as you liked."

By the end of 1970 Alice knew that her dream could be realized. There were long discussions with Tom Luddy and others about what to name the restaurant. Eventually, they agreed to find a name somewhere in the Pagnol trilogy, but they couldn't agree on what it would be. Then it came to them all at once: The restaurant should be named not after one of the major characters but after sweet old Panisse. Chez Panisse!

Years later, in her foreword to an edition of Pagnol's pair of memoirs *My Father's Glory* and *My Mother's Castle,* Alice wrote that she chose the name "to evoke the sunny good feelings of another world that contained so much that was incomplete or missing in our own—the simple wholesome good food of Provence, the atmosphere of tolerant camaraderie and great lifelong friendships, and a respect both for the old folks and their pleasures and for the young and their passion." There was also the charming fact that a *panisse* was a chickpea-flour fritter sold since time immemorial in the streets of Marseille.

There would be a restaurant downstairs, and a little bar upstairs. You could come for just a cup of coffee, a dozen oysters, a sandwich, an ice cream cone, a bottle of Champagne, a six-course feast. Chez Panisse would be utterly informal, anyone would be welcome, and the food would be superb.

Tom understood that Chez Panisse would have to be an actual business, requiring capital, planning, and discipline. "Among the friends who used to come over for the films," he recalls, "was Paul Aratow, who was a graduate student studying Italian at Berkeley and married to a woman named Connie. They had a little money in their family, and they lived in a nice house, while we were more the poor, starving types. Sometimes we'd also show movies at Paul and Connie's house, and Paul would cook."

At the University of Florence, Paul had learned Italian cooking from some of the faculty wives. "He made pasta from scratch!" Alice says. "That was unheard of." When Connie had a Fulbright to study in Paris, Paul mastered French cooking too. He had no professional experience, but he exuded self-confidence. He also owned a collection of French copper cookware manufactured for Dehillerin, from whom Escoffier himself, the father of modern French cuisine, had bought his pots and pans. Tom told Paul that Alice was looking for backers for a restaurant. Would he be interested in coming in as a partner?

"And I said, 'Why not?' Not knowing then"—his voice trails off. Paul persuaded Alice that Chez Panisse should be open nearly around the clock, like La Coupole in Paris, serving breakfast, midmorning snacks, lunch, tea, ice cream, dinner, and late supper.

Paul also brought in Rosemarie Harriot, who supposedly had some accounting experience. By the time the partnership came together, Paul's marriage had come apart, but he had a girlfriend, from whom he borrowed six hundred dollars to put into the deal. There were several limited partners as well—Alice's old family friends Barbara and Michael Carlitz, the rock critic Greil Marcus and his wife, Jenny, and other friends.

1517 Shattuck Avenue, 1971

There were also some necessarily silent partners—drug dealers. These were not the scary Glock-wielding gangsters one associates with the term *drug dealer* today. These were ordinary gentle Berkeleyites who happened to make their livings by supplying a network of friends with pot and other "soft" drugs. "Well, of course, they were the only people who had money," Alice says. "The only sort of counterculture people who had money. We couldn't get it from a bank, God knows."

Early in 1971, Paul found a two-story down-at-the-heels old stucco house in Berkeley. Alice thought 1517 Shattuck Avenue was perfect.

"It looked like a rundown hippie crash pad that had fallen on bad days from too many students living there," Tom Luddy remembers.

Originally, the two lawyers representing the partnership intended to invest as well, but at the eleventh hour they pulled out. Instead they bought the building, which was a solid, lawyerly, salable asset; they would then lease it to the restaurant, which was a highly speculative asset at best.

Alice's parents mortgaged their house in southern California, to the tune of ten thousand dollars, and put it all at Alice's disposal. Paul Aratow and Alice's dad insisted that the lease include an option to buy the property in two years.

As construction proceeded, friends came and went, hammering, sawing, kibitzing. Paul and his brother learned to hang Sheetrock, put in pipes, build a brick patio. Frequently, the workers' compensation came in the form of lunch, cooked on a grill in the backyard.

Alice thought that Paul's international training and seamless confidence would make him the perfect chef. But as construction progressed, the reality of the unforgiving hours of drudgery that are the sine qua non of a chef began to sink in. When he learned what his salary would be, his mind was made up. Cheffing at Chez Panisse was not to be Paul Aratow's career.

Alice, superb cook though she had become, could not picture herself behind the stoves. She wanted to be in the dining room—with people, personifying the open-hearted hospitality that she saw as fundamental to the restaurant's identity. She also wanted to determine the menus. She would certainly be in the kitchen as well. She alone would dictate how every dish was to be prepared, down to the finest touch of technique: how brown a particular sauté should be, how many shallots to sweeten a sauce, how finely chopped. She knew exactly how she wanted everything to taste, to look, to smell, to feel.

By the spring of 1971, Alice was seeing Chez Panisse as a gestalt: Food would be the center of attention, certainly, but the experience as a whole would depend on a complex of sensations. The room must look a certain way—casual, offhand, warm. From Martine Labro she had learned that light was the key. "Martine," says Tom Luddy, "was the kind of Frenchwoman Alice really admired—not some bourgeois Frenchwoman but an artistic one, not some snobbish Parisian. She was somebody from the south of France who loved the Berkeley scene, as much a bohemian radical as Alice but also very feminine, very artistic. And you know Frenchwomen all have a sense of light. The restaurant has to look good, women have to look good in the restaurant. My wife is French. They're all that way. Women have to look beautiful." Martine recommended that there be many small sources of light, and gilt-framed mirrors to reflect it, so that there would be a warm, seemingly sourceless glow.

Alice wanted every guest to feel welcomed and, most of all, comfortable. There would be no snobbery, nor fawning, none of the fussy formality that characterized most French restaurants in the United States. There would be both waiters and waitresses—at that time, a rarity. They wouldn't even wear uniforms.

"Just something nice and neat" was the extent of Alice's expectation. It would be some years before Chez Panisse would settle on the minimalist "uniform" that persists to this day: plain white shirt, plain black pants or skirt, plain black shoes.

In the flea markets, all through the summer of 1971, Tom and Alice and Martine shopped for mirrors, lamps, cutlery, china, and glassware—much of it Victorian, none of it matching. All of it, however, felt good in the hand. Covering the tables would be red-and-white-checkered oilcloth, not white linen. The tables themselves would be oak, and of various shapes and sizes. The chairs would be oak as well, straight-backed, simple. The oak floors would be polished and uncarpeted. The plaster walls would be painted a soft ivory. The trim would be the most classic of California woods, redwood. The windows facing west would be uncurtained, so that the intense afternoon and sunset light that glittered off San Francisco Bay would pour in unhindered. Alice wanted fresh flowers everywhere, with an enormous, blowsily spilling bouquet given a table all its own (a table, Paul pointed out, that might otherwise have accommodated four paying customers).

The ventilation had to be such that the cool breezes off the Bay would scent the dining room even as the warm aromas from the kitchen curled in from the other direction. The play of fragrances would make entering diners pause and notice, and having paused, they might then see how extraordinary the flowers were. Each bite of the food would be something to savor, something to slow the eater down. Every nuance of the experience would be sensuous, every detail thought through. The surfaces had to be such that voices were clear, while sharp noises were muffled. When she realized that booted feet on the stairs produced a bone-jarring thunder (heavy boots were big in Berkeley in the seventies), Alice started shopping for an Oriental runner.

Her most momentous decision was that the dinner menu would offer no choice whatever. "I wanted it to be like going to somebody's house. Nobody gives you a choice about what to eat at a dinner party." The menu would be new every night, seven nights a week.

Elizabeth David had exerted the strongest influence on Alice's conception of the individual dishes. Richard Olney, the American food writer long resident in the south of France, inspired the Chez Panisse approach of sequencing the dishes into a harmonious whole. In *The French Menu Cookbook,* published in 1970, Olney had written, "A menu composed of preparations that are not themselves French may remain totally French in spirit, for it is the degree to which a menu is based on a sensuous and aesthetic concept that differentiates a French meal from all others. It may be served under the simplest and most intimate of circumstances, but its formal aspect is respected, and its composition—the interrelationships and the progression of courses and wines—is of the greatest importance."

In August 1971, Alice started hiring. There were no job descriptions. Experience was not required. Alice simply knew that she would know who was right for Chez Panisse. One of the first applicants, for a waitress position, was Sharon Jones, who is still a close friend of Alice's. Alice, washing salad greens, didn't even turn around to look at her. As Sharon stammered through her qualifications, which were slim at best—a little waitressing in college—Alice asked her no questions, just listened. At length Alice turned around, gave Sharon a quick look up and down, made intense, searching eye contact, and told Sharon she was hired. Sharon wanted to work part-time, because she was studying theater. Fine, said Alice.

In fact, nearly everyone who applied for work at Chez Panisse was doing something else—poetry, filmmaking, graduate school, pottery—and Alice willingly made room for whatever it happened to be. If you wanted to work every other Thursday, fine. If you needed to take a couple of weeks to go meditate in an ashram, no problem.

The story of another of the original waiters, Jerry Budrick, is prototypical Chez Panisse. Jerry was just the kind of character Alice delighted in. "I was in the used fur coat business, just kind of hanging out in Urbana, Illinois," he recalls, "and this fellow came hitchhiking through from New York back to Berkeley. We stayed up late at night smoking marijuana and singing songs and having a great time, and he said, 'I'm pushing out to California.' I said, 'How are you going to get there?' And he said, 'I'm going to hitchhike.' I said, 'There's a foot of snow outside, and it's zero degrees! Are you crazy?' He said, 'I don't have enough money to pay for a ticket.' I said, 'Well, I can get us a car that somebody wants taken somewhere.' So I got us a drive-away GTO. Thirty-two hours later, we were in Bakersfield. We went on to L.A. in a Cadillac and eventually to Berkeley. He was a drama student at Cal. His housemates became my buddies. They were all graduate students in various departments there. I met this wonderful woman, and she and I took a trip up to Vancouver, Canada, together. She was going to see her boyfriend, but she ended up becoming my wife instead. We took a long trip to Europe and then drove across to India and Nepal and then drove back to Europe. We came back to this little town in Austria, and I got a job as a waiter for about a month and a half in the summer. I spoke enough German to get by, and they needed someone who spoke English. Then we came back to the Bay Area. One of my old friends was a guy named Bob Waks, who ran this cooperative on Shattuck Avenue called the Cheese Board.

"Well, Bob was walking down the street, and I was walking down the street, and he said, 'Where have you been for the last two years?' I needed a job, and I thought, Well, being a waiter might be a good thing to do. Bob told me about this new restaurant that was opening across Shattuck from the Cheese Board. So I went over there and got interviewed for a job at Chez Panisse. This was August of '71. I started the first night."

"He just had a style," Alice reminisces. "I think I hired him because I thought he was an Austrian waiter. He had this fancy wallet that folded out—one of those change wallets that European waiters have. I was so impressed with that wallet. He came for his interview, and he was wearing a black vest and a white shirt, and he just looked like a ready-made European waiter. So I hired him."

Alice's hiring for the Chez Panisse kitchen, following her instinct for who "got it" or didn't, harvested an impressive array of advanced degrees and highly trained intellects. When Paul Aratow declined the invitation to be chef, Alice chose instead Victoria Kroyer, a U.C. Berkeley graduate student in philosophy who had never worked in a restaurant but who had cooked Alice a superb audition meal. Alice persuaded her friend Lindsey Shere, with her Berkeley degree (like Alice's) in French cultural history and her faultless instinct for fruit, to be pastry chef. Charles Shere, the composer and critic, would work in the café upstairs part-time, tending bar and making sandwiches and ice cream cones. Most of the rest of the kitchen brigade had similarly high qualifications for jobs other than the ones they would actually be doing. Alice felt sure that with all those brains, what they lacked in knowledge they could surpass in imagination. What they lacked in experience, Alice would make up with sheer numbers.

As the days ticked down toward August 28, it became clear that Chez Panisse was not going to be ready. Construction on the upstairs café was halted. Alice and her partners were out of money. People were working on the basis of trust, or hope, or desperation.

"Well," says Alice's sister Ellen, "her whole personal approach had always been chaos. We used to say she spent money like Waters. She thought if somebody called her with a credit card offer with a ten-thousand-dollar credit limit, that meant she had ten thousand dollars."

Friends and the staff-in-waiting walked around Berkeley passing out flyers and got an enthusiastic response. The dinners that Alice had been cooking with her friends for the last several years had become a local legend, and people wanted to know if the food could possibly be as good as the hearsay held it to be.

On August 27, 1971, construction and painting began at dawn and continued far into the night. All day August 28, the half-panicked finishing continued. The fragrance of simmering stock mingled with the sharp scents of sawdust and wet paint. Carpenters were still nailing up shelves as six o'clock approached, amid hurrying cooks, jostling waiters, worrying backers, and an exceedingly anxious Alice Waters.

5.

VERY BERKELEY

1971–1973

As the first days and weeks passed, Alice was happy but not satisfied. The yellow-gold light shed by the 1920s Pullman car candlesticks she had found in a flea market seemed to nearly anyone else a marvel of refinement, but Alice didn't like it. "The light on the food should be white," she insisted, "so that it looks the beautiful colors that it is. I didn't like the whole idea of separate tables, either. I'd rather have had just one big table, with the food served from big bowls. But I also loved the idea of a couple of shills in the corner, a couple we'd hire to eat there every night and say, 'Ah, this is the best meal ever!'"

She didn't like the noise that shoes made on the bare wood floor. When the young French waitress Brigitte clomped through the dining room in her wooden clogs, it was deafening. That was not the only grievance against Brigitte. One elderly female customer complained that the young lady was quite clearly not wearing any underwear. Alice didn't care what Brigitte wore or didn't wear.

Above all else, what Alice wanted was that Chez Panisse should be warm, its aural atmosphere a lively but civilized flow of conversation punctuated by the sounds of popped corks and softly clinking cutlery. But she didn't want rugs; spilled food stuck in them. "I wasn't sure I liked the square-cornered tables, either. A circle's such a nicer shape."

The lack of choice on the menu was in part the product of Alice's desire to compose meals like music, and in part an expression of familiality. "But frankly," she says, "it was also a little bit of laziness. And ignorance. I really didn't know how other restaurants turned out all those dishes for so many people all at once."

In Alice's vision, Chez Panisse would never be grand, but it would never compromise on quality. The utmost in craftsmanship and effort would characterize its every creation. If the staff worked as hard as she did, and with the same meticulous care, they would be well rewarded; if they did not, they would not last. It was simple: "No corners cut," she told everyone. "Ever."

Ingredients of the quality that Alice insisted on were expensive. "I was looking for the food that I'd eaten in France. I was on a quest. I remember buying four cases of Kentucky Wonder beans and just taking the little ones out of the bottom and pretending those were haricots verts. I threw all the rest into the compost."

She knew nothing about business and didn't give a damn. If she wanted a certain ingredient, truffles, say, she declined to notice the price. Shaver in hand, she would stroll through the dining room snowing truffles left and right, no charge, "just to see the delight on their faces."

Bills were accumulating on the floor of the grungy little office, mingling with still-unpaid construction bills. Nobody knew what was coming in, how much was going out, and in whose hands or into whose pocket. On September 12, 1971, when the restaurant had been open for all of two weeks, Alice and her partners distributed a memo to the staff reading, in part, "We cannot meet the current payroll. . . . We have $500 to disburse, which is 10% of the payroll, so we are paying 10% of the wages due to each employee. Everyone will have to be paid off as we correct the financial situation. If anyone wants to return his partial payment, it will be put into a fund and redisbursed to other needy employees. . . ."

Alice outside Chez Panisse, 1971

"I had nightmares all the time," Alice recalls. "It was a train out of control, a wreck about to happen."

THOUGH CHEZ PANISSE seemed unable to overcome what seemed to be continual financial crisis, the restaurant gradually began to come together. The food came to the customers within a reasonable time, most of the time. It was more consistently good, often very good. The menu began moving away from three-day stocks and Escoffier. The La Coupole concept died unmourned. "Paul Aratow's idea had been for us to be open twenty-four hours a day. Eventually he settled for seven-thirty in the morning until two a.m., seven days a week. I was very insecure," Alice admits, "so I went along with it. But that didn't last very long. Nobody came before noon. Only dinner was successful at all."

Alice combed through her cookbooks every day, and her half-imagined conception of pastoral France was taking clearer shape. "I always came back to Elizabeth David. Asparagus vinaigrette, cauliflower soup, roast pork with whatever. It definitely was French in spirit, and kind of simple-*sounding*. Not so simple to *do*, in fact."

The first menu that anyone saved was that of Sunday, October 31, 1971. It was rendered in Alice's own calligraphy, which she had learned from David Goines, and in her own dauntless franglais:

hors d'oeuvres variés, including homemade terrine

❧

boeuf en daube provençal

❧

salade

❧

fresh fruit tarte

❧

$4.50
à la carte: desserts .75, coffee .25, tea .30, espresso .30
dining room open 6:00 pm–10:30 every day

For Friday and Saturday nights, the price was raised to $6.00. In Berkeley, California, in 1971, that was not cheap. The amounts equivalent to $4.50 and $6.00 in 1971 are about $22.00 and $29.00 today. But that would still be much less expensive than now: Dinner prices at Chez Panisse in 2006 ranged from $50.00 on Monday nights to $85.00 on Friday and Saturday.

Alice wanted to keep the prices as low as possible, but her native extravagance, and her insistence on the best in everything, sometimes trumped her generosity. When she didn't like the flowers, which she had been buying and arranging herself, she found the equally perfectionist Carrie Wright. Carrie's arrangements might include grasses, dead branches, shriveled berries, old baskets, strange, menacing jungle flowers, but they also spilled forth in profusion, expressing everything Alice loved about abundance, vitality, and finding grace in the unexpected. With Alice's devil-may-care carte blanche, Carrie's artistry was also stunningly expensive.

"We were always scrambling," Alice says. "The menu was decided by what meat we could get on what day. You'd know that one day the sweetbreads came in at Such-and-such Meats, and the freshest ducks were available on Tuesday and Thursday at some place in Chinatown. I was driving all over the place. And the bills, the bills—we just lost track. We were headed for catastrophe."

For help, Alice called on the only friend of hers who had ever actually run a business: "Gene Opton. She ran a store called the Kitchen, in Berkeley, one of the early fancy kitchen equipment stores," Alice says. "I knew her because I went there when I first got back from Europe. I was looking for little *baba au rhum* containers and little porcelain cups for chocolate mousse. She was the one who gave me Elizabeth David's book."

Gene agreed to take a look at the financial situation. "At that time there was a little run-down shack behind the house," she recalls, "with a refrigerator where Lindsey could keep butter. They also had a stand-up freezer back there. All just family-type equipment. There was a desk, and in the middle drawer were receipts from hardware stores and other places where materials had been bought. No one had ever sorted them or added them up. Or paid them."

Having given up the notion of being chef, Paul Aratow was acting as a sort of general manager, though everybody knew that no management decision, no matter how small, would be made by anybody other than Alice. "It was a madhouse," Paul remembers. "Nobody, none of us, had any real experience. We would have heated discussions about putting in more tables. Alice would say, 'No, it has this lovely atmosphere, not too crowded.' And I would say, 'We're losing money! We're turning people away! We could serve another twenty meals a night and break even if we put three more tables in!' She was very stubborn. And we were equal partners, so there was no way that one of us could do anything the other didn't want. Alice had a very pure vision, and she didn't really have the business sense to get the thing off the ground."

When somebody showed up with a bushel of perfect garden-grown radishes with dew still wet on the leaves and soil still clinging to the roots, it was the form at Chez Panisse not so much to pay for them as to make a reciprocal gift—free dinner, for instance. This sort of thing is what people in Berkeley call "very Berkeley." Alice and the waiters were giving away desserts, Champagne, whole dinners, left and right.

"There was too much, too many," recalls Claude Labro, laughing. "Too many friends. Too many service, much too many cooks."

Rosemarie Harriot, the third general partner, who was going to run the business end of things, lasted less than two months. One day in the fall of 1971, she simply disappeared, never to be heard from again— though to this day her name remains on the restaurant's monthly Pacific Gas and Electric bills.

"I knew it was going to be hard work," Alice says. "What I guess I didn't know was that I wouldn't be able to get control of it somehow. I thought, since we had all these people, surely we'd be okay—and because Paul seemed to know so much more than I did. But then, of course, he left."

"I had no idea how complicated it would be, and how difficult it would be to get help that would work. We were really floundering," Paul said years later. "Besides, I'm a filmmaker, and I had never intended to spend the rest of my life at Chez Panisse."

It's hard for Alice or anyone else to say how much the general craziness, including the blithe disregard of financial reality, may have had to do with recreational drugs, because they were so thoroughly integrated with the rest of the Chez Panisse experience. It was quite unremarkable for a waiter lofting a tray to suck back a last-minute toke before plunging through the swinging door to the dining room, exhaling as he plunged. It was hardly remarkable to the customers either, many of whom had arrived already ripped to the gills themselves.

Wine was popular too during work hours. The first time someone bothered to tote up the loss, in 1972, less than a year after the restaurant's opening, thirty thousand dollars' worth of wine was unaccounted for.

Gene Opton recalls, "Alice would say in this overwhelmed way, 'We just really need help.' There was no system for keeping track of the hours. When I said there should be a time clock, it was taken as a really mean-spirited, bureaucratic intrusion on the style that Alice had hoped would be okay. There was talk about running it as a commune. The Cheese Board was successfully setting up its commune across the street, which was a most amazing enterprise. But they understood that the people who belong to the commune have to bring in the equivalent of capital."

One of the most remarkable mysteries in the history of Chez Panisse is how this careless, sometimes intentional ignorance of fiscal discipline persisted through the years, as the restaurant's excellence and reputation rose and rose. It was not until it was nearly thirty years old that Chez Panisse began to behave truly like a business.

"Alice had no interest in these facts, basically," Gene Opton avers. "It's not the way she thinks about things. They were serving meals for four-fifty that cost a minimum of six dollars to prepare, and they had borrowed to cover the construction and hadn't paid that off. But my husband, Ned, thought they were a worthwhile undertaking nonetheless, and he said, 'Why don't we see if we can get involved with this, and make them a loan?' Part of the agreement was that I was named the manager of the restaurant—a combined CEO/CFO. We had a very formal document stipulating that all the financial matters were to be decided by me and paid by me. I mean, physically writing the checks. I was to hire and fire all the personnel. And a plan would be arrived at that would make the restaurant sustainable. For a considerable time I wasn't paid, but then eventually I was paid six hundred a month, as was Alice."

Alice signed the agreement, and then continued to do exactly as she wished. If she wanted truffles, she bought truffles. New china? Hire another friend? Give away bottles of Champagne? No document was going to stop Alice Waters from building Chez Panisse according to her dream. She did not own a majority interest in it, and never would. But no matter what the legal papers said, Chez Panisse, from day one, was Alice's, to be operated, populated, decorated, redecorated, reconceived, fussed over, fiddled with, and loved as Alice saw fit. Nobody else had her zeal, her imagination, her inexhaustible energy, her innate authority.

"If Alice got stubborn," Jerry Budrick remembers, "there was no way to shake her. She would just ramrod things through. But she always had a keen eye, and her palate has always been so wonderful. I'll never forget the time she was invited to participate in a tasting of twenty different foodstuffs that had been frozen. The frozen food industry was having this panel come to taste to see if they could actually freeze things and then claim that they tasted as good as fresh. So they had twenty of the same thing, some fresh and some frozen, and they put them into various dishes and disguised them. Alice got all twenty. Nailed them all."

People meeting Alice for the first time would be struck by her shyness, her uncertainty, her unfinished sentences, the childlike tone her voice often fell into. Her familiars, however, knew that behind Alice's diffidence lay an indomitable will. She drew people out, asked their ideas, freely gave credit for all she'd learned from her worldlier friends—the Sheres, the Labros, Eleanor Bertino, David Goines, Tom Luddy—but once she had made up her mind about what was right, what was best, what was to be, that was that. If Alice said the salad looked tired, Victoria knew not to argue. It didn't matter if it was five o'clock—Victoria threw the salad out and managed somehow to find something better in the hour remaining

Alice, Lindsey Shere, and Victoria Kroyer, 1972

before the tables began to fill. If Alice ran her finger along a molding and frowned, she didn't even have to speak—someone would come running with a damp cloth to dust it. When she moved the big vase of Carrie's flowers a quarter inch to the precise center of the table, someone would be watching and would get it right tomorrow. The cooks would mock Alice behind her back, plucking an infinitesimal leaf from a plate and sniffing, "Too much lettuce!"

SLOWLY, a modicum of discipline asserted dominance over slapdash passion. Lindsey Shere set the tone. Having grown up on a farm in Sonoma County, daughter and niece of food-loving Italians on her father's side, daughter of a pastry-loving German mother, Lindsey had been baking since the age of nine. The farm had a big orchard—prunes, walnuts, peaches, pears, plums, nectarines, figs, Sonoma's celebrated Gravenstein apples—and Lindsey had a passion for perfect fruit. Eight years older than Alice,

Lindsey nonetheless also looked like a girl, wide-eyed, quick to smile. She was consistently calm and meticulous, the epitome of cheerful discipline. Her domain was the little shack behind the restaurant. When it rained, she had to rush her tarts under an umbrella to the kitchen.

Lindsey's desserts looked so simple, and they were. They were also the first dishes fully to embody the elegance and unassuming perfection that were Alice's ideals for Chez Panisse. An unobservant eater could gobble down a slice of Lindsey's pear *tarte Tatin* without a thought, and might also find the serving a bit on the small side. The diner attuned to nuance would feel the puff pastry melting unctuously across his tongue, would recognize the heady essence of pear caught at its fleeting moment of lushest aroma, would sense the precise balance of the fruit's texture between softness and resistance. Gifted with palates of exquisite sensitivity—to a degree perhaps incomprehensible to those who do not possess such power of discrimination—Lindsey and Alice could communicate almost without words. *"Mmm,"* Alice would murmur over something hot from Lindsey's oven, swaying as if to faint. "Oh, Lindsey!" And Lindsey would merely smile.

Lindsey was farm-girl frugal. "If sixty customers were expected," says Alice, "Lindsey would make sixty desserts, and woe to the waiter who dropped one, or, worse, gave in to it."

· LINDSEY'S ALMOND TART ·

What I start with is just a regular short-crust pastry. Basically, flour and butter and a little bit of sugar and a little bit of water and flavoring—grated lemon peel or a little bit of vanilla. The crust gets rolled out thin and put into a nine-inch tart pan and chilled thoroughly. Keep back a little bit of dough for patching later. While that's chilling—you can make it well ahead if you want, and freeze it—the filling is made with three-quarters of a cup of whipping cream, three-quarters of a cup of sugar, and a teaspoon of Grand Marnier. Mix those in a stainless steel saucepan, and then put the saucepan on a moderate burner. Stir till the filling comes to a full rolling boil and it looks thick and bubbly. Then you add a cup of sliced almonds—unpeeled almonds, raw—and set it aside for about fifteen minutes.

Then you prebake the shell in the top third of the oven at about three seventy-five, till it's golden, twenty or twenty-five minutes. You want to bake it all the way, because it won't cook any more once it gets that liquid filling inside it. If there are any cracks that go all the way through the crust, here's where you should patch them, because otherwise the filling will just run out.

Put a piece of foil in the top third of a four-hundred-degree oven, because the filling is probably going to bubble over. Put the dull side of the foil up, because the shiny side can mess up your oven thermometer's sensor.

When you pour the filling into the crust, make sure that the almonds are evenly distributed. Spread them around with a spatula.

Put the tart in the oven and start checking after about fifteen minutes. At a certain point it'll start to make big, thick bubbles—which is what you want it to do—and if the almonds start popping up to the top, push them down into the cream with a spatula. Keep doing that until the top starts to brown. Continue baking till it's a really nice caramelized brown color, with maybe a very few creamy-looking spots, about thirty or thirty-five minutes.

Set it on a rack to cool for about five minutes. Then you need to push the bottom up and free the sides of the tart. If you don't, it'll glue itself to the sides of the tart ring. If you want to take the tart off the tart pan bottom, it's easiest to free it when it's cooled some more, so that it's thoroughly set but not completely cool. If you want to take it off later, you can put it over a burner just enough to melt that layer of sugar and cream.

> I would serve it like cookies, basically, because it really is not a fork dessert at all. You want to pick it up and eat it.
>
> You could serve it as a cookie, or with a fruit compote. Whipped cream I can't even imagine, or ice cream—that would be just too, too much.

Lindsey was as frustrated as Alice at the poor quality of ingredients they often had to settle for. It was during those first few months that Lindsey's husband, Charles, observed the growth of what he called "the hunter-gatherer culture of Chez Panisse," which still persists. In an essay called "The Farm-Restaurant Connection," published in 1989, Alice looked back on these days. "Not only did we prowl the supermarkets, the stores and stalls of Chinatown, and such specialty shops as Berkeley then possessed, but we also literally foraged. We gathered watercress from streams, picked nasturtiums and fennel from roadsides, and gathered blackberries from the Santa Fe tracks in Berkeley. We took herbs from the gardens of friends. We also relied on friends with rural connections. The mother of one of our cooks planted *fraises des bois* for us, and Lindsey got her father to grow the perfect fruit she wanted."[1]

This was something that no American restaurant had ever done. Chez Panisse imbued its food with the aromas of its locality, the textures of its place. The French use the word *terroir* to denote a food's or wine's evocation of the whole of a place—the minerality of its soil, the roughness or smoothness of its landforms, its heat or cold, the fragrances carried on its breezes. Alice did not know the word, but her food's expression of its *terroir* was foremost among the qualities that from its earliest days set Chez Panisse apart.

Tom Luddy knew that there was nothing else like Chez Panisse, and he believed that it deserved to be better known. His Telegraph Repertory Cinema programs and his work with the San Francisco Film Festival drew people from worlds beyond Berkeley. Soon he would become director of the prestigious Pacific Film Archive. "Most weeks," he recalls, "I'd have two or three great filmmakers visiting. There were the old masters—Howard Hawks, Douglas Sirk, Satyajit Ray, Akira Kurosawa, Roberto Rossellini—and young masters—Jean-Luc Godard, Werner Herzog. And the up-and-coming American directors—Francis Ford Coppola, George Lucas. Actors and actresses too. I always took them to dinner at Chez Panisse." These worldly visitors recognized that something was going on here unlike anything else in America—amateurish, perhaps; inconsistent, certainly; but nearly always delicious, unique, and fun.

There was fun behind the scenes as well. The kitchen's discipline extended to cleanliness, civility, impeccable technique—but it was never meant to hinder creativity or the high spirits that Alice prized. If a waiter, or even a busser, wanted to try cooking something, that was fine—though it would never appear in the dining room unless it passed Alice's unsparing review. Often Alice came running to Victoria, excitedly waving a recipe she'd found in one of her obscure cookbooks. Alice herself had never made the dish, neither had Victoria, nor had anyone else in the kitchen, but Alice would decree it to be next Monday's main course—a full-dress performance without a minute's rehearsal. The regulars knew to expect the occasional failure, and knew too that if they complained, the kitchen would invent something else on the spot.

Alice brought the Montessori ideal of learning-by-doing to every activity in the restaurant. "I always believed you can't ask somebody to do a job when you don't know what's involved in it. Say you're asking somebody to wash dishes. You can't know how hard that is, or what it's really worth, what people should be paid or how it should be set up, unless you experience it yourself. So when somebody new would start, I'd take them into every little nook and cranny. They'd have to go into the narrow closet to see how narrow it was. They needed to go outside and see how we took care of the garbage. They needed to go into the refrigerator and see how cold it was, and the big carcasses of meat. I wanted them to understand the things that the cooks were using. How hot it was in front of the ovens. How it all felt."

Years later, a longtime Chez Panisse employee reflected on the far-reaching effects of Alice's Montessori indoctrination: "Every single person who works here, including the dishwashers, loves to eat. Go to the Berkeley farmers' market on a weekend, and you see everyone from the restaurant shopping. And these people don't make a lot of money, but they all have dinner parties, and they're spending their money on traveling, and we're all comparing cheap travel notes. It's a common view of life, I think. It's really family-oriented. You just don't find restaurants where people have as many kids as they do here. And where people have solid marriages, and have been married a long time."

The menus for the week were posted every Monday. Lots of people, the clientele still being largely local, just strolled by, took a look at the hand-printed bill of fare in the picture frame on the front of the building, perhaps came in and discussed it with Alice or a cook, and made their plans accordingly.

"You ate what was there," Greil Marcus recalls, "and often it was something you had never had, or cooked in a way that you had never imagined. Very quickly Jenny figured out that the wrong way to go to Chez Panisse was to see what the menus were and pick something you thought you would like. The best way was to pick something that you thought that you didn't like or you had never heard of. We loved having people come from out of town, and taking them to this extraordinary place that didn't meet anyone's expectations of a good restaurant. It wasn't fancy, there were no pretensions, there were no choices, there were none of the dishes associated with fancy restaurants, or very few, and it was just thrilling."

The kitchen staff met early every afternoon. The first order of business was to compare what was on the published menu with what was actually in the house. If salmon was scheduled for Friday night and the salmon that had come in that morning was, in Alice's opinion, anything less than pristine—well, did anyone have a suggestion? A cook might volunteer that she'd seen some excellent halibut at the Japanese market, though it seemed awfully expensive. Alice never asked the price. The staff could eat salmon for the next two days. Someone might then ask, "Wouldn't the halibut go just as well with the chanterelles, garlic, and chervil butter we'd planned for the salmon?" Others would start chiming in. Maybe a vinaigrette instead of butter, to spike up the somewhat tamer flavor of the white-fleshed fish? Maybe shallots instead of garlic?

The new menu would grow through shared creativity and Alice's firm decisions. Alice declared the peas too starchy, but a cook had noticed some beautiful little purple artichokes in a basket someone had dropped off. There weren't enough for a whole course, but someone then suggested they be braised with potatoes and spring onions. Someone else had heard that one of the neighbors up the hill might have spinach in her backyard. The cook made a quick phone call, and the spinach arrived, just picked, at five. The main course had now become halibut with chanterelles, garlic, and a chervil vinaigrette, accompanied by baby artichokes braised with potatoes and spring onions and by a spinach purée.

Alice would write out the new menu. Sometimes the dish would change even in mid-evening, if someone—most often Alice—had a better idea.

At the end of each meeting, there would be a conversation to decide who was going to do what. Members of the kitchen brigade were not classified as sauciers and prep cooks and line cooks and grill cooks. All of them could do anything, or at least were eager to try. Sometimes Alice expressed a preference that a certain person should cook a dish to which Alice thought he was particularly well suited; more often, the cooks worked it out among themselves.

This approach set Chez Panisse radically apart from traditional high-end restaurants. There was no apprentice at a cook's elbow to sharpen her knives, chop her shallots, sweep up her spillage, wash and dry and steam her twenty pounds of spinach and hand-grind it through the food mill. Nobody had to stand at a permanently assigned station wearily flipping the same four things night after night. Every dinner was a new challenge. Certainly cooks pitched in to help one another, but basically the person who chose to do the halibut was expected to butcher it, make the stock, pick through the chervil, emulsify the vinaigrette, and clean up afterward. Whoever volunteered to do the spinach purée had sole responsibility for it.

So if Alice didn't like some tiny something about one of the dishes— and very often she didn't—she knew whom to talk to about it. "The spinach is sandy," she might say, and walk away. Humbly, whoever was doing the spinach would dump it in the compost, find another batch of acceptable spinach, clean it, and start again. Alice would taste it again. "A little lemon?" she might suggest, and that, almost unfailingly, would be just what it needed.

Friends of Alice's were guinea pigs for the kitchen's experiments, and in return they were often the recipients of her generosity. If someone had foraged a few morels, not enough to put on the menu, Alice would just appear at a friend's table and set down a plate of morels fried in butter, saying, "Just something to pick at." When Barbara Carlitz (having moved from London to Palo Alto) brought in her new baby, Alice puréed carrots *à la grecque* for little Natasha.

Alice never went so far as to say that the customer was always right, but she did bend to the reality of some of her customers' insufficient enthusiasm for the likes of sweetbreads, tongue, or kidneys. In November 1971, a little squib was added at the bottom of the otherwise still firmly fixed menu:

steaks and chops

Alice didn't like it when people rejected her chosen menu, so she usually didn't keep the steaks and chops on hand. If a customer ordered one, somebody from the kitchen would be hastily dispatched across Shattuck to the Co-op or to Lenny's meat market.

Change was constant. When seven nights a week proved too wearing, Sunday dinner was dropped. Alice opened a private dining room, then closed it. Toward the end of 1971, the dispiriting sight of people waiting two hours for dinner led her to accept a formality she had hoped to avoid: reservations.

In February 1972, after desultory carpentry and finish work through the fall, Chez Panisse finally opened a modest, kitchenless café upstairs, serving sandwiches, ice cream sundaes, and drinks till midnight. Downstairs, the dining room started serving an informal, modestly priced lunch four days a week. In April 1972, $2.50 would buy the *plat du jour*—perhaps poached chicken with aïoli, blood sausages with apples, or quiche lorraine.

Breakfast soon reappeared as well, very French, evocative of Alice's junior year in Paris—croissants, café au lait in bowls, *pain au chocolat*. In April 1972, concerned that some of her friends couldn't afford Chez Panisse, Alice introduced a cheaper weeknight dinner menu, comprising an appetizer and a main course only, for $3.75, while raising the three-course version by a quarter, to $4.75. House wine was 60 cents a glass, $2.25 a bottle.

In the spring of 1972, an aspiring young restaurateur named Tom Guernsey and his wife, Nancy Donnell, visited Chez Panisse, seeking inspiration for a place of their own. After hearing Tom's ideas, Alice hired him on the spot. Tom established a stylish Sunday brunch in the café, offering a set menu at $2.75. The first:

English chicken & bacon pie

ꝏ

homemade Bath buns

ꝏ

citrus fruit cup

ꝏ

café noir or café au lait

A certain spirit was taking hold at Chez Panisse that spring. The kitchen was turning out delicious food, the service was gracious and precise, and the dining rooms felt effortlessly comfortable. The camaraderie and the sense of belonging among the staff were like nothing any of them had known in their lives. The feeling of belonging extended well beyond the employees, too. Not only they, but also the suppliers and the regular customers, seemed to be thinking of the Chez Panisse circle as a whole, a tribe, a family. Restaurant kitchens were notoriously noisy, uncivil, profane places, but the kitchen at Chez Panisse was orderly, polite, almost serene. Trust and charity and generosity were the norm. Even at the height of service, with everybody working at maximum effort, a newcomer, astonished, might hear:

"Could you hand me that butter, please?"

"Certainly."

"Thank you."

"You're welcome."

Not many new people, as it happened, were coming aboard. The staff in the earliest days had been much too large for the tasks at hand, and gradually, those who didn't quite get it drifted away. The core members of the *famille Panisse* could not imagine leaving. This was a family worth being part of.

Within the first year of the life of Chez Panisse, Alice had created a little world, and peopled it with like-hearted creatures, and now it was alive. After the last customers were gone, some of the staff would stay, usually in the café, to wind down, talk, drink wine, smoke some dope, flirt, maybe fall in love. They would push the chairs and tables to the edge of the room, crank up the rock 'n' roll, and dance. "I've always loved to dance," says Alice, "and oh, we did dance."

For all the fun, however, Alice was driving herself to exhaustion. One night, Tom Luddy arrived at the restaurant to take Alice home, and found

Tom Guernsey dancing with Alice

her in the kitchen sitting on an upturned pot, sweaty, bedraggled, head down.

"What's wrong?" he cried.

"I can't see," answered Alice. Her nervous system had shorted out, and, albeit momentarily, she had gone blind. This happened to her from time to time, and her vision would always return, so it was not cause for a trip to the emergency room, but it certainly upset Tom Luddy.

He waited until Alice could come with him to the car. He walked her up the stairs and into their house, and Alice, once inside, collapsed on the floor. Tom picked her up, undressed her, and put her to bed.

Alice had Sunday off, but for her it was virtually never a day of rest. More and more often, some friend of hers, or would-be friend, would plead, "Oh, my daughter's getting married, and we thought it would be a dream if you'd cater the wedding," or the benefit, or the kid's birthday party, and Alice, again and again, would accede.

Tom Luddy was going out of his mind. "Alice, you have to say no," he said over and over, "learn to say no, you just have to. You can't do it. You just have to say no, say no, say no, say no."

And Alice in her littlest voice would plead, "But I can't. I can't. They're such good customers, they're such good friends. How can I say no?"

Finally, Alice had to choose between Tom Luddy and Chez Panisse. No one was surprised when she and Tom parted ways—she was married to the restaurant, and both she and Tom recognized that she could never give him the time and attention that he (like any other man) required. No one was surprised that Alice and Tom separated without rancor. Nor was anyone surprised that they stayed friends, or that Tom and his movie pals would continue to come to the restaurant, often, down through the years. A pattern was being set: Alice's ex-boyfriends would nearly always remain close to her.

Kermit Lynch, a wine merchant and importer, and a longtime friend of Alice's, remembers, "Right next to my wine shop was a restaurant called La China Poblana, which served Mexican and Indian food. Sometimes Alice would come there bleary-eyed, so tired it was hard to get her out of the car, and then she'd drink a couple of Bohemias and eat some spicy food, and *bang*, she was bright-eyed and ready to go back to work."

Gene Opton and her husband, Ned, had continued to pay off the restaurant's debts as those debts rose and rose. Gene was reviled by some of the staff, who had a very Berkeley disdain for the squalor of mammon. But she did know what she was doing. Although Paul Aratow and Alice Waters were, on paper, the owners of Chez Panisse, they owed considerably more than the restaurant's net worth to Gene and Ned Opton. In effect, the Optons now owned Chez Panisse. And it was eminently clear to them that Chez Panisse was not, and was not likely to become, a profit-making enterprise.

In April 1972, Chez Panisse had its first review, in a mimeographed newsletter called *À la Vôtre,* published anonymously by Serena Jutkovitz in San Francisco. "There are so many aspects of this new restaurant that are almost touchingly admirable," she wrote,

> that what faults there are seem somehow more tolerable than they might elsewhere. Unfortunately the warm mood is disrupted by chilly drafts.
>
> The soup was called *purée de poix* [*sic*] and, though piping hot and interesting, suffered from what struck us as the only mildly troublesome aspect of the restaurant—talented amateurism. The soup had no pea taste, but was permeated with the flavor of— probably—Madeira.
>
> Our second dinner began with *hors d'oeuvres variés,* each portion of which was brought out and served separately from a platter, a charming though seemingly inefficient system. First came a delicious mixture of marinated broiled green pepper and fennel (!), then a cold lentil salad which was delightful. There were also hard-boiled eggs with homemade mayonnaise and a tasty substance on a buttered crouton that seemed like lamb marrow, but no one could identify it for sure since that particular cook had gone.

In May 1972, the Bay Area's leading restaurant authority, *Jack Shelton's Private Guide to Restaurants,* gave Chez Panisse its first rave:

Right now in an unassuming, circa 1900 wood-frame house on Berkeley's Shattuck Avenue, an exciting experiment in restaurant dining is being carried out. That is how I view Chez Panisse—as a vibrantly alive, ongoing experiment, not always meeting with un-qualified success, but never anything less than stimulating and often positively exhilarating.

Shelton's praise went on for three densely typed pages:

novel and diverse repertory . . . eager efficiency . . . relaxed friend-liness . . . a complete delight. . . . What other restaurant is willing to refute the lengthy menu dictates of the general public and offer an uncompromising, set daily menu? What other restaurant displays the daring of offering such an intriguing variety of dishes over any short span of time? . . . Chez Panisse, even if I found your cooking disappointing, I would openly admire your courageous stand! . . . Don't lose your marvelous aura of adventuresome experimentation, don't bridle the dining room staff's enthusiasm and camaraderie with the patrons. Keep striving to improve and to experiment, but don't change, whatever you do!

Exhorted never to change, Chez Panisse promptly changed. Jack Shelton's ink was barely dry when Victoria Kroyer quit. "I left to go live with a person I thought I was going to marry, in Montreal," she says. "It was one of those serious miscalculations of youth."

"I never wanted to be chef," says Alice, "but there I was. Luckily, I had Barbara Rosenblum, Victoria's sous-chef, who knew what she was doing."

As chef, Alice delved deep into the provinces of France for recipes hardly ever seen on this side of the Atlantic: *cou de canard,* duck neck stuffed with duck meat and foie gras; *jambon en saupiquet,* a very old recipe, ham in a vinegar-piqued cream sauce; *cassoulet,* the laborious white bean casserole with duck or goose confit; *aïllade de veau,* veal stewed with tomatoes and lots of garlic, the sauce thickened with bread crumbs; *ris de veau à la lyonnaise,* scallops of sweetbreads with a sauce of chopped hard-boiled eggs, mustard, capers, *cornichons,* and chives; *choucroute garnie,* the steaming heap of juniper-redolent sauerkraut piled with pork loin, ham, bacon, preserved pork belly, and an omnium-gatherum of sausages; and, with a frequency attesting to its popularity with the Chez Panisse crowd, Victoria's archetypal Parisian bistro dish *lapin à la moutarde.*

There was so much friction between Gene Opton and Alice over Alice's free-spending ways—and so much resentment of Gene by the restaurant's freethinking staff—that Gene's effectiveness was declining toward zero. Basically, nobody was listening to her anymore. As Gene's star waned, Tom Guernsey's rose. Everybody liked him, and his gentle manner was very Chez Panisse.

Tom's marriage to Nancy Donnell had foundered as Tom allowed himself to realize that he was gay. In his self-discovery, Tom seemed to blossom. Nearly everyone who knew the early days of Chez Panisse remembers Tom as the exemplar of its unique esprit. He was the person to go to when something wasn't working right, when a supplier was delivering late, when you were troubled, when you wanted more money, when you wanted out. "Tom was the glue," says Alice. "I was always out on one limb or another, and Tom held the center together. He was friends with the dishwashers, he knew all the gossip, he knew everybody in the restaurant. He had a great good spirit, and had wonderful taste. A really elegant guy. Very sensual. I was in love with him. There were lots of gay men that I fell for. Fritz Streiff, who came later to cook, I fell in love with him too."

"Alice falls in love," says Fritz. "This is the story of Alice's life. She falls in love with a dish. She falls in love with a lamp. She falls in love with a bowl of cherries. She falls in love with a man. Alice loves men." Fritz went on from cooking at Chez Panisse to being a waiter, a host, and ultimately an occasional ghostwriter for Alice. Introductions to her books, the phrasing of recipes, her speeches, even her letters would begin with Alice talking through her ideas as Fritz simply listened. Then he would write up the ideas. Then Alice would edit. Fritz would rewrite. Alice would re-edit. And so on till it was just right.

Alice soon fell in love again. "The first anniversary came, August of 1972," recalls Jerry Budrick, "and that night we had a big party. Everybody had a great time. At the end, it came down to just me and Alice, and Alice seduced me, right there in the restaurant. And we began an affair that went on for eight years."

"One reason the story of Chez Panisse is so complex," says Barbara Carlitz, "is that Alice was involved with so many of the men. And if she wasn't involved with them, then someone else in the restaurant was. Oh, boy."

"Alice's life is driven by passion," says her erstwhile transatlantic shipmate Tim Savinar. "At bottom, I think, it's sexual passion, which sometimes she lets overwhelm her and sometimes she sublimates in the food of Chez Panisse."

IN OCTOBER 1972, Victoria Kroyer's Montreal sojourn ended. "It didn't suit me one little bit. Either Montreal or the guy."

"There was a very unpleasant altercation when Victoria came back," Gene Opton recalls. "I said to Alice, being this terribly literal person—and it is a shortcoming, I am very literal—that if Alice was being paid to do the cooking, there was no money to pay Victoria to do it. We were still running in the red. We weren't anywhere close to getting out of it. I said, 'You're supposed to cook here.' Then Victoria and Barbara Rosenblum came to my house and confronted me. Victoria was quite irate."

Victoria wanted to be chef again, and Alice was more than glad to step aside—but at no reduction in salary.

Victoria promptly resumed her place at the stoves, with Barbara as sous-chef. Alice had won another round. But the Optons still owned the business.

Jerry remembers: "Gene was going to buy Paul out and get Alice as her partner—but a minority partner—and was going to set the direction of the restaurant in a different way from what we had established that first year, which was this joyful place. I went and I talked to Charles Shere first, because I thought of Lindsey as an important member of the group, and I could tell that she didn't like being ruled by somebody either. I said, 'Charles, we can't let this happen. Here's what I think the plan should be. It should be that the principal players in the restaurant become the own-ers, and we go out and find the money that it takes to pay Gene back out of this.' We needed like thirty-five thousand dollars to do that. I thought it should be Alice, me, Lindsey and Charles as one partner, and Tom Guernsey and Nancy Donnell as one partner, plus the chef."

"It was a great deal more than thirty-five thousand," Gene Opton maintains.

"Anyway," says Jerry, "Gene was pretty resistant to being bought out. But we convinced her. It wasn't easy, because she really believed in what she was trying to do. Here's a typical problem we faced. One of the first things that Paul Aratow had insisted upon, and one of the great things— I'm not sure it was so great, looking back—was that we had to taste the wines. Everybody should be able to talk about the wines to the customers. So we had tastings. Well, it ended up we were drinking a substantial por-tion of the wine inventory by doing that. You open a bottle from every case, that's eight and a half percent of your wine gone. Gene wanted to abolish that. And then there were the giveaways. That kind of thing was difficult to sustain, but I believed in it. It was a sharing attitude. We were bustling, and we didn't think of ourselves as starving, so we could share it."

"Alice had already made it clear," says Gene, "and I knew enough at that point, having worked with her for a year and a half, that she found me unacceptable. So it became a matter of just extricating myself without additional hassles or hard feelings. What happened was that when the new partners assumed control, we were given a note that was paid off over a period of time at a really modest interest, something like eight and a half percent. Which for a risky loan at that time was very low."

Charles Shere's take on the history of Chez Panisse is often one of amusement. "So we were exercising our option," he quips, "while exorcis-ing our Opton."

The dining room, 1972

FOR ALL THE TUMULT behind the scenes, Alice Waters and Chez Panisse continued to innovate, to surprise, to dazzle. The restaurant's second New Year's Eve dinner, December 31, 1972, was a sharp turn away from the country dishes that Alice and Victoria usually favored. This menu was all Victoria's, and an exercise in pure classicism:

Pâté de poisson à la Guillaume Tirel

❦

Consommé royale à l'oseille

❦

Pigeonnaux farcis, choux rouges braisés

❦

Fromages variés

❦

Gâteau Moka, Paris-Brest, ou tarte aux oranges

❦

Bonbons assortis "Chez Panisse"

The first course was a fish pâté in the style of the chef to the French royal courts of the latter fourteenth century. Guillaume Tirel was also the author of one of the first cookbooks ever written, *Le Viandier*, published under the pen name Taillevent—now the name of one of the greatest restaurants in France.

The soup was a classic of nineteenth-century banquets. It was one of those things that may look easy to the untrained eye, and in many a restaurant may be, entailing little more than opening a can. This consommé was the culmination of hours of preparation—a long-cooked chicken-and-vegetable stock, clarified with egg whites and decorated with tiny floating cutouts of egg custard. At the last minute, Victoria added ribbons of sorrel, a lemony-sour leaf that grows wild in lots of places but was then little known in America.

The main course was roast squab (baby pigeon), another delicacy beloved in France but at that time seldom seen here, its flesh rich, dark red, and liverish, stuffed with its own innards and accompanied by braised red cabbage.

Lindsey Shere's glistening orange tart exalted the only decent local fruit available in the depth of winter. Her second dessert, the Paris-Brest, was a crown-shaped ring of cream-puff pastry, sliced horizontally in half, filled with praline buttercream, and sprinkled with chopped almonds. For the *gâteau Moka,* Lindsey sliced *génoise* cake into thin layers and interleaved them with mocha buttercream, the whole swathed in mocha icing. The chocolates that followed were all handmade by Lindsey as well.

"The price," notes Alice, "was the highest Chez Panisse had ever charged: twelve dollars."

To raise the money to buy the Optons out, Alice turned to a few of her closest friends—Greil and Jenny Marcus (who were already partners), Daidie Donnelly (also one of the original investors), Nancy Donnell (Tom Guernsey's ex-wife), and Barbara and Michael Carlitz. Henceforward, they would be shareholders in a corporation named Pagnol et Compagnie. Up to that point, Paul Aratow and Alice had owned Chez Panisse fifty-fifty.

(It may be more accurate to say that what they owned fifty-fifty was their debt to the Optons.) Paul now sold all but a 10 percent interest to the new stockholders, and with his retained 10 percent, he became another stockholder. Mary Borelli, whom Gene had brought in as bookkeeper, also bought a block of shares. The senior shareholders would constitute the new board of directors of Pagnol et Cie. They would be the people who ran the restaurant: Alice Waters, Jerry Budrick, Charles and Lindsey Shere (acting as one partner), Tom Guernsey, and "the chef"—an ambiguous definition, since Alice had been chef, and Barbara Rosenblum still was chef, and now Victoria was back.

"We decided," says Jerry, "that we had to choose between Barbara Rosenblum and Victoria Kroyer, and we chose Victoria. We told Barbara that she was, I guess, fired, for want of a better word."

"It's not like lowering the boom on someone," says Greil Marcus, the writer who has been a partner in Chez Panisse since the beginning. "Letting someone go is a process. It's usually not like Dr. Doom comes and gives somebody the bad news. But when we've had to, we have cut people loose, we have forced people out, we have bought people out, we have gotten rid of people with utter ruthlessness and boldness. And it's been the right thing to do. Sometimes I marvel at the way we have closed ranks and gotten rid of people who, despite their long involvement with the restaurant, despite the fact the restaurant wouldn't be here, perhaps, if they hadn't done what they had done, when the time came that they became a threat to the stability of the future of the place, we got rid of them."

Alice herself has virtually never been the ax wielder. Someone else would start with a subtle hint or two that Alice wasn't entirely pleased. Sometimes it took a few more hints. Alice's hands were clean: A major dismissal was nearly always voted on by the board. The dismissee, nonetheless, nearly always believed the decision had been Alice's. In many cases that was quite true, and the vote of the board had been just a formality. In this case, anyway, Barbara Rosenblum got the message. The generous spirit of the *famille Panisse* went only so far.

"And, well," recalls Jerry Budrick, "Victoria said, 'You can't fire my best friend! I quit.'"

Victoria soon found a job as personal chef to the director (and Chez Panisse regular) Francis Ford Coppola at his grand mansion in San Francisco.

"So we needed a chef," continues Jerry, "and we put an ad in the *Chronicle*. We couldn't believe it. We had, like, four people come."

Then came a fifth applicant, who would turn Chez Panisse from a very good restaurant into a great one.

6.

JEREMIAH

1973–1975

Jeremiah Tower looked, spoke, moved, and dressed like no one Alice Waters had ever met. His pale cheeks had dark pink rougelike accents at the cheekbones. His thick strawberry-blond hair was swept back from his forehead in a carefully tousled swirl. His head and shoulders were massive, but his hands and feet seemed tiny. He wiggled his fingers as he talked, his words rapid, breathy, florid, in an accent Alice couldn't place. There was something feminine in the way he tossed his hair back, something aggressively masculine in his forward-leaning carriage. There was in his bright blue eyes the jaded look of an old roué, though he was barely thirty years old. If Jeremiah had ever known humility, he did not betray it. He made sure Alice knew right away that he'd gone to Harvard.

What was somebody like this doing answering a classified ad for a chef?

Well, he simply *adored* food. (He did not add that he was flat broke.) He had been cooking forever. He had been taught, he said, by an Aborigine to roast barracuda and wild parrots on an Australian beach; by his mother, in Jean Patou suits and Cartier jewels, to dine in grand hotels and on ocean liners; by an aunt, a Philadelphia Main Line ex-debutante, to love art galleries, emeralds, and no restaurants but the finest; by the head-waiter at London's Hyde Park Hotel to slice smoked salmon paper-thin; by a tweedy English lesbian to smoke a cigarette in an ivory holder and drink gin; by six years in a British boarding school to detest bad food, crave fresh fruit, and love boys; and by a decidedly louche teaching fellow at Harvard to revel in candlelight, drugs, and Champagne. He had been making nasturtium sandwiches at the age of five.

Jeremiah's first job after graduating from Harvard College in 1965 had been as chef of the Horse and Groom, a pub in Surrey, near his parents' former house. He was soon sacked for forcing French food on the shepherd's-pie regulars.

He tried a girlfriend, and a farm in Massachusetts. On the girlfriend's family's island in Maine, he read Euell Gibbons's *Stalking the Wild Asparagus* and gathered mussels, duck eggs, and wild greens. It was there that he saw for the first time beyond fancy cooking to the indispensability of the freshest, most vivid-tasting ingredients.

A return to Harvard in 1967, to study architecture at the Graduate School of Design, offered another opportunity to *épater la bourgeoisie*. In his memoir *California Dish*, Jeremiah writes that for his assignment on public housing, he "decided on a multimedia effort: cooking, film, music, and drugs. My presentation was called 'Champagne While the World Crumbles,' and consisted of a film loop of the atom bomb going off amid footage of the worst public housing projects and urban sprawl I could find. The music was Lou Reed, the food a huge platter of marijuana cookies." He got his master's degree in 1971.

He worked in garden design, and wrote a memoir. For "the World's Fair in Hawaii that I had heard would be on the water," he designed a pavilion that would be half above and half below the ocean surface. In the summer of 1972, he drove with his pavilion plans to San Francisco, where architects turned him away. There never had been going to be a World's Fair in Hawaii, aquatic or terrestrial.

"On my thirtieth birthday," Jeremiah writes, "I was down to twenty-five dollars." He managed, nevertheless, to make himself a New Year's "feast for one": boiled garlic mashed with beef marrow on toast, accompanied by a bottle of Château d'Yquem, the outlandishly expensive sweet white wine.

In January 1973, a friend of Tom Luddy's told Jeremiah about the job opening at Chez Panisse, and asked Tom to introduce Jeremiah to Alice. Jeremiah had eaten there once, and remembered "the most perfect slice of raspberry tart I had ever tasted."

Jeremiah presented Alice with a sheaf of eighteen sample menus—omitting the desserts, which he knew to be still Lindsey Shere's domain. Among the dishes he proposed were *gougères* (Gruyère cheese puffs); *matelote à la normande* (a mélange of several varieties of saltwater fish, poached, then served with a sauce of cream, fish stock, cider, and Calvados and garnished with mushrooms, mussels, oysters, crayfish, and heart-shaped croutons); *cervelles de veau froides à la crème* (cold calf's brains in cream); and "haricot" of oxtail Alice B. Toklas (which despite the name has nothing to do with beans: it is a seventeenth-century dish in which the jointed oxtail is stewed with turnips, chestnuts, and spicy sausage). He also brought Alice an azalea with peach-colored blossoms.

Alice was charmed. It was his panache and his menus that got Jeremiah Tower hired, but the Chez Panisse legend is the soup that Alice asked him to taste and correct.

"I turned to the biggest aluminum pot I had ever seen, twenty gallons, full of a liquid purée of some kind. I stuck a finger in and tasted it. All it needed was salt, but I added a bit of white wine and cream, to show off."

"I, of course, immediately fell madly in love with him," Alice says. "And that was a problem. Yes, he was gay, but that didn't ever stop me from trying. He was incredibly handsome, and he had taste. I was in love with the way he thought about food, the way he handled food, the intellectual approach he had, and the guts. He wanted to make an artistic statement. You know how when you're in love with somebody, you really learn things in a way that you never forget, and you learn everything because you're so interested in that person? We had a collaboration, and I loved that. I would seek out better and better ingredients—he would say, 'Oh, let's do it with live fish!' and I'd find live fish for him. Or go out to Dal Porto Ranch for the little baby lambs he wanted. 'Go get me some wild fennel!' and I'd go find the wild fennel. He was a perfectionist, and so was I, and that's why it worked."

Jerry Budrick says, "I told him, 'Well, there's one rule here. I'm already here, and I'm Jerry'—because he was Jerry Tower. 'What's your real name?' He said, 'Jeremiah,' and I said, 'Okay, do you mind if you become Jeremiah instead of Jerry?' And he said, 'No.'" For Jerry Budrick there was an undercurrent of discomfort in this exchange, despite the fact that it came out as he wished; for Jerry Budrick was still Alice's boyfriend (though they had yet to live together), and her infatuation with Jeremiah Tower was plain.

According to plan, Jeremiah was allotted five hundred senior shares in Pagnol et Cie. As chef, he was paid four hundred dollars a month, which, adjusted for inflation, would be a little over seventeen hundred dollars today. Chefs were not stars in 1973. They were laborers. Jeremiah, however, steeped as he was in the lore of the tyrannical rulers of the French kitchen in the great hotels and manor houses of the nineteenth century, didn't let his puny salary get in the way of his grandeur.

His first sous-chef was a bearded, Brillo-haired renegade hippie and artist named Willy Bishop, who thought that anyone who looked and acted like Jeremiah "could only be an asshole." But Willy, too, in due course, was charmed. To Jeremiah's swagger Willy made an ideal foil—acid-witted, hard-working, hard to gull, resolutely blue-collar.

Willy had been a department store window dresser, a record shop clerk, a poster salesman, a bartender, a drummer in a band, a fruit salad maker, a dishonorable dischargee from the Air Force, and finally a Chez Panisse dishwasher. He would always be a painter. But he had soon shown cooking talent, too. Alice and Jeremiah both loved his raffish style. When Jeremiah's intellectualism and sophistication got "too Harvard," Willy—who had grown up in New Haven in the shadow of Yale without a thought of ever going there—was a ready, foul-mouthed antidote. For the first year and more of Jeremiah's tenure as chef, he and Willy alone prepped and cooked nearly everything that came out of the kitchen except Lindsey's desserts.

Jeremiah began his transformation of Chez Panisse immediately. Loud Led Zeppelin was banned from the kitchen stereo; opera replaced it. Classic stocks were simmering for days once more.

Willy Bishop and Jeremiah Tower

With a modest remodeling, the café upstairs became an extension of the dining room, adding some twenty-five seats to the fifty downstairs. In addition, there was a private room, called the *cabinet,* pronounced as in French, "cabeenay," with a table for six.

Jeremiah was especially fond of dishes that anyone but a French-born historian of gastronomy would have to ask a waiter to explain: from his first week alone, *poulet à la limousine* (chicken stuffed with sausage and roasted with chestnuts), *caneton à la rouennaise* (roast duck stuffed with its own liver, with a bordelaise sauce thickened with duck liver), and *pissenlit aux lardons* (salad of dandelion—"piss-in-bed" in French—with bacon).

Alice continued to write out the menu in French in calligraphy, but in late March 1973, in response to the perplexity that Jeremiah's dishes occasioned, that sheet now came attached to a second, in English, typed. *La flammiche de Flandres* could now be understood as "brioche cheese tarte," *aïgo bouido à la ménagère* as "Provençal tomato and garlic soup," *oeufs durs au gratin Boulestin* as "eggs with mushrooms and tomato sauce"—named for Marcel Boulestin, the world's first TV chef, whose program *Cook's Night Out* began appearing on the BBC in 1937.[1]

"Jeremiah would try anything," Willy Bishop remembers. "It was not that we were confident but that we didn't know better. When we first did chateaubriand, neither he nor I knew which way to cut the top sirloin roast. If we turn it this way, the grain goes this way. How much do we trim the fat? And one end would always be gristle and rind and all that. That was for the well-done people.

"Fuckups? We had a few. More than a few. I remember Jeremiah trying to make fish quenelles. He didn't get the batter right, and of course you're supposed to turn them with spoons and make these little kernels and float them. Well, they kept falling apart in the water, and I didn't know what to do, and he didn't know what to do.

"Another big disaster was a *brandade de morue,* which kept separating. We had hot towels under our mixing machine, the bowl that Lindsey used to make pastry. The bowl was big, and it was thick, and you could not keep the thing hot inside, warm enough so that it would coalesce—the cod and the potatoes and shit—and so it just looked like mashed potatoes. But what can you do? The menu is printed, and there's nothing else in the house, and there you are. Screwed.

"Still, he was such a perfectionist. We had braziers under the work-table, burning charcoal. He would throw spices or herbs on it, and we had to go around with this little mister with rose water. It was theater, in his mind. Of course, he was insecure about what he was doing, so it made him a nervous wreck. But showtime was showtime. Very disciplined. Sometimes we'd run out of food, because Alice would overbook. She couldn't say no."

"Jeremiah was Escoffier," says Alice, "with the whole extravagant, decadent thing. We used to go out after work and have Champagne and caviar, and he'd order the best, spend all our money. Little by little we dressed up the dining room. We were never able to afford very much, but we certainly went from oilcloth to linen.

"I believed in his fantasy, his myths about himself and about the food. And I sold it to the customers—the whole fantasy. Once we were doing grilled salt cod, and he didn't know to soak it. He put it on the grill, and I took it out to the dining room. The first customer said, 'This is inedible.' Jeremiah was dictatorial: 'Tell them to wash it down with a glass of wine. It's supposed to be drunk with red wine.' So I would go right out to the dining room: 'That's the way the chef intends it. Drink lots of red wine with it.' And who knows? They did or they didn't, but I made them believe that's the way it was supposed to be."

Chez Panisse was moving very quickly away from the cozy, easygoing model of Pagnol's Bar de la Marine. Not yet two years old, struggling from paycheck to paycheck, utterly unprofessional at every level, Chez Panisse was becoming a Great Restaurant in spite of itself.

Alice and Jeremiah began seeking out better and better provender to match their ever-more-ambitious cooking. They would rattle across the Bay in Alice's asthmatic 1966 Dodge Dart for ducks and fish in San Francisco's Chinatown. In the Italian delis of North Beach, they bought olive oil, olives, and anchovies. At the wholesale meat market, Jeremiah would plunge his arms into drums filled with blood and calves' livers, picking out only the blondest livers, as the butchers looked on both aghast and impressed. Fishermen would offer them "trash fish"—perfectly good but noncommercial species—with which Alice and Jeremiah would eagerly experiment. Foraging friends would bring in wild mushrooms from Mount Tamalpais, huckleberries from Point Reyes, a better egg from some old farmer's lost race of chickens, an incomparable plum varietal from somebody's brother's backyard.

There were now, and would be thenceforth, two formal seatings: For the first, diners arrived between six and six thirty; for the second, between eight forty-five and nine fifteen. Everyone seemed to object to what in California amounted to a choice between a too-early dinner hour and a too-late one. People are still objecting, but most seem to accept the system as just another Chez Panisse eccentricity. The homey provincial fare that was Alice's hallmark often gave way now to *consommé de veau aux cerises* (veal consommé with cherries), *bouchées à la reine* (sweetbreads, chicken, and mushrooms in Madeira cream sauce, served in a vol-au-vent pastry cup), *meurette bourguignonne* (freshwater and salt-water fish poached in red Burgundy with brandy and leeks, served with garlic croutons).

Ruth Reichl, who would go on to become the restaurant critic of the *New York Times* and editor in chief of *Gourmet* magazine, was a waitress at another restaurant in Berkeley. She remembers:

My parents came to visit my husband, Doug, and me when we were living in Berkeley, and my mother said brightly one night, "You know, I've read about this little restaurant." This was in '73, and we had no money, and the idea of going out to eat was really exciting. This was still in the days when if you didn't like what they had on the menu, you could have a steak. And my mother ordered a steak, and Alice came out and really tried to talk her out of it. I realized later that the steak was frozen and she wasn't proud of it. It was very interesting to me to see these very determined women facing off. Alice was absolutely determined that my mother was not going to order this steak, and my mother, having decided that the steak was more valuable than the *blanquette de veau,* was determined she was going to have the steak. Alice is not used to losing an argument. My mother, however, never lost an argument, and she won this one. For years, my parents sent me twenty-five dollars on my birthday for Doug and me to go to Chez Panisse. It was the one restaurant meal that we had every year.

Alice did find ways to assert her own, simpler taste. For the second birthday of Chez Panisse, August 28, 1973, she instituted the first of many special dinners that emphasized the restaurant's heritage in rustic, non-Parisian cooking. Her ex-lover and still-close friend David Goines designed the menu-cum-poster. That was also the beginning of a tradition of original posters for special occasions at Chez Panisse, many of them, over the years, created and printed by David. The menu, in Alice's distinctive jumble of English and French, read:

Cassoulet

ɞ

¹/₂ litre of wine & salad

ɞ

$5.25

ɞ

Also un film de Marcel Pagnol

Seasonality was not yet a Chez Panisse ideal. Alice was serving the wintriest, heaviest imaginable dish at the height of summer. The price was generously lower than the usual $6.00, but the very next day, regular weeknight dinners rose to $6.50, weekend dinners to $7.50.

On September 4, 1973, at the even stiffer price of $8.25, Alice and Jeremiah presented their first regional French special dinner, in tribute to Alice's beloved Brittany. The menu, as was customary now, was bilingual:

Huîtres
(oysters, on the half shell)

ɞ

Crêpes de moules
(mussel crêpes)

ɞ

Canard nantaise
(roast duckling with baby peas)

ɞ

Salade cressonière
(watercress salad)

ɞ

Fromage Pont l'Évêque

ɞ

Le gâteau Bas-breton aux amandes
(almond cake with almond paste and crème Chantilly)

ɞ

Special regional wines

More than one hundred people came, half again more than the week-night average. On November 27, 1973, the nightly menu began to read, CHEZ PANISSE: FRENCH COUNTRY COOKING.

Two nights later, it was Jeremiah's favorite region, Champagne, that was the focus of another special dinner. The menu was a long way from "country cooking"—and cost an unprecedented $10 a person—but the dishes reflected Jeremiah's researches in old French cookbooks, and they were authentically *champenois:*

Boudin de lapin à la Sainte Ménehould
(white sausage of rabbit, breaded and grilled)

❦

Truites au bleu au Champagne
(fresh trout poached in Champagne)

❦

La brioche de ris de veau au Champagne
(sweetbreads in a brioche pastry with a Champagne sauce)

❦

Salade verte

❦

Plat du fromage[2]
(cheeses from the Champagne region)

❦

Sorbets de poire et de cassis
(fresh Comice pear and black currant sherbets)

Properly done, *truites au bleu* are rather shockingly blue, and for the trout to come out that way, the cook must have not just fresh trout but live ones. A living trout is covered with an invisible, slimy film that protects its skin from infection, and that film begins to deteriorate within seconds of the fish's death. Perfect technique—instantaneous death and evisceration, the gentlest of handling—will yield a trout that on contact with boiling liquid turns bright blue.

The Champagne dinner's trout came from a hatchery in Big Sur. "We brought them back in barrels," says Alice. "We thought we could keep them alive if we aerated the water in the sinks in the kitchen." Jeremiah borrowed a compressor from a garage across the street, "but of course we didn't consider what kind of water was in those sinks. Chlorinated. So the trout were jumping out of the sinks. We were hitting them on the head and gutting them through the throat and throwing them in this pot of court bouillon. The whole kitchen was full of water and trout on the floor. It was exhilarating. Just unbelievable. And they did turn blue."

FOR ALL THE FLUBBING and seat-of-the-pants improvisation, Chez Panisse was setting standards that not only had never been met in America but had never even existed. What Alice and Jeremiah were doing resembled in many ways the French approach to food, but they were doing it without the historical precedent, the formal training, and the infrastructure that made fresh, seasonal food second nature to the restaurateurs of France.

In France, chefs had it a lot easier. Alice had roamed the markets at Les Halles in Paris, marveling over what to her were miracles of freshness and variety and to the French nothing more than how things were supposed to be. "They always had this local distribution system," she explains. "So much wonderful food came from nearby, less than an hour away."

When the restaurateurs or their agents began their daily rounds before dawn at Les Halles, the fish were gleaming with life just departed, skin redolent of Mediterranean reef, deep Atlantic, cold swift river, or alpine lake. There were greens just cut from their stems in the cool of the late afternoon; ripe fruit picked one piece at a time and laid gently in straw; whole infant lambs from the salt marshes of the southwest; quivering whole foies gras from Quercy; blue-legged chickens that had grazed their way slowly to maturity in the open pastures of Bresse; wild mushrooms and strawberries gathered in the forests of the Massif Central; little cheeses from

Burgundy, the Pays d'Oc, Alsace, Normandy, Savoie, a hundred, a thousand places, each cheese an individual voice of an individual place, made on a farm by a person with a name. Could Chez Panisse ever be what she wanted it to become, Alice wondered, in the absence of a system like that?

It was the same virtually all over Europe, all over Asia, indeed in much of the world, where farms were still small and "agribusiness" was unknown. "But not here. Not in Berkeley, not in San Francisco or New Orleans or New York"—not anywhere in the cities of the world's leading industrial nation, the biggest producer and exporter of food on the planet.

"Some good things you could get in some places," Alice remembers. "Great beef in New York, fresh fish there and in some other port cities. There were roadside farm stands in the summer with lovely fruit and vegetables. There were the Chinatowns and other little ethnic enclaves."

Fancy French food, of a sort, could be had in most big American cities—at the Blue Fox or Ernie's in San Francisco, Quo Vadis or Le Pavillon in New York, the Maisonette in Cincinnati, the Pump Room in Chicago, Locke-Ober in Boston, Antoine's in New Orleans, Justine's in Memphis. Restaurants such as these worked hard to find decent ingredients, and the food there could be excellent. "Ah!" Alice sighs. "La Bourgogne in San Francisco! I loved that place. They had Dover sole flown in, and Maine lobsters cooked live, and Grand Marnier soufflé with two sauces, and the most fabulous Swiss waiters that you fell madly in love with."

But at a good many expensive French restaurants in the United States, the foie gras in the tournedos Rossini might well reek of tin, and the truffles were likely to have no taste at all. One could get *escargots bourguignonne,* but the snails were canned. Some of the most popular dishes were flamed with liqueurs—steak Diane, bananas Foster, (canned) cherries Jubilee—triumphs of spectacle over savor.

Even then, the customer often had to surmount the untranslated French of the menu and the leather-clad *carte des vins.* The *froideur* of the waiters intimidated more customers than they charmed. Then there were the mysteries of multiple tipping: of the captain, the waiter, the sommelier, the coat-check lady, maybe the bartender, maybe a bathroom attendant, sometimes a cigarette girl—and, worst of all, the magisterial maître d'hôtel, especially if one preferred a table out of olfactory range of the toilets. More often than not, these masters of condescension were French, and, says Alice, "They'd have been out of work in a week if they'd acted like that back home in France." What was worse, these restaurants were staggeringly expensive—two or three times the price of a meal at Chez Panisse.

Good, honest, even splendid meals could be had in a few Chinese restaurants if a party insisted emphatically enough that they liked real Chinese food. A few other old-fashioned ethnic restaurants produced authentic versions of the food of the old country—though more often it would be Americanized beyond the old country's recognition.

"You could also eat very well if you were lucky enough to get in on a midday dinner at an old-fashioned family farm," says Alice, "where the ham and the greens and the okra and the peaches in the cobbler had all been grown on the place and the homemade bread was hot out of the oven."

And thanks to Julia Child on TV, Craig Claiborne in the *New York Times,* James Beard's syndicated columns, and *The Joy of Cooking,* more than a few Americans were starting to cook serious food at home. Like-minded people were finding one another, giving long, leisurely dinner parties with plenty of good wine (which was blessedly cheap).

If one was fortunate enough to live near one of the serious food shops springing up in the largest cities—such as Balducci's in New York's Greenwich Village—fine olive oil, a wide range of cheeses, artisan bread, and imported pasta could now be had. Their produce would definitely not have been organic, and it was as likely to be out of season as in. Pesticide-laden fruit and vegetables imported from Mexico and Chile were common, but at least they were fairly fresh, and the shops took good care of them. A few of the great old downtown markets remained—such as the Reading Terminal Market in Philadelphia and Pike Place Market in Seattle—where local farmers and fishermen sold their wares directly to the public.

In most of America, however, the prospects for good food were getting worse. The family farms were dying off. The children of the immigrants who knew what good food was were growing up detesting the old-country stuff. "Little family restaurants that might have had a few good simple things were being plowed under to build McDonald's," Alice says.

Even in the moderately expensive restaurants, portion control—a rigid formula governing the amount of each item served—was becoming the order of the day. Chicken Kiev and shrimp "scampi" could be had in frozen heat-and-serve vacuum packs, and an innovation called the microwave oven could have the food out the swinging door in a few minutes flat. Frozen inventory meant nonspoiling inventory. Mass purchasing and mass marketing empowered the rise of chain restaurants above and beyond hamburgers, fried chicken, and pizza, with national brands for every niche—Benihana Japanese steakhouses for dinner-as-theater, Red Lobster and Captain D's and their heaps of deep-fried seafood, T.G.I. Friday's custom-tuned to the drinking crowd, Denny's to the nondrinkers, Bonanza and Ponderosa for cheap steaks, the International House of Pancakes and its many colors of syrup twenty-four hours a day. All these companies used sugar and fat in amounts much higher than in home-cooked food. Crabmeat and clams no longer needed to taste like themselves; in fact, they no longer needed even to be crabmeat and clams, as long as their simulacra were well-breaded, deep-fried, salty, and hot. America's journey toward obesity had begun. "It just made me want to cry," says Alice. "But mostly I just kept my head down. It wasn't till years later that I really saw what was going on."

For people who wanted to cook seriously at home, the raw materials available were also declining in quality. There was an increase in the range of choice, especially of packaged, processed foods. Fruits and vegetables that had been available only in season were now in the supermarkets year-round—grown half a world away; treated with pesticides, fumigants, and preservatives; refrigerated sometimes for months; leached of nutrients and of flavor. All this had been made possible by the consolidation of agribusiness companies, which controlled growing, shipping, marketing, and retailing: Their flawless-looking but half-dead produce was highly profitable, in part because it underpriced any competition from local, small-scale farmers, whose produce might be less perfect-looking but was certainly better-tasting. The proliferation of choice was an illusion. "If you wanted a peach that tasted like a peach," says Alice, "you pretty much had to grow it yourself."

Such was the culinary landscape outside the charmed refuge of Chez Panisse. "When I traveled"—which was rarely—"I had to bring food with me," Alice recalls. "My life-support kit. A bottle of olive oil, a bottle of vinegar, a loaf of bread, a little bag of salad, and some cheese." She would not darken the door of a McDonald's, either for irony's sake or as opposition research.

She was well aware of the decline in how America ate, but as yet she saw no hope of changing it. "All I knew was that Chez Panisse could be better than it was." If there were no farmers in northern California raising chickens comparable to the blue-legged beauties of Bresse, perhaps Alice could persuade a farmer to raise some old, nearly lost noncommercial breed of American chicken. There was no bread to compare to Poilâne's in Paris, but, Alice recalls, "We had a busboy on the staff who decided he was going to keep making bread till he got it right. Steve Sullivan. And he did get it right. We're still serving his bread. We lent him money to start up Acme Bakery." (In its four Bay Area bakeries, Acme now has sales of twelve million dollars a year, producing several dozen kinds of bread and selling them to some four hundred restaurants and retail businesses.) There were hippies raising goats up in the hills of Marin and Sonoma beginning to learn to make chèvre as beautiful as the small-farmstead cheeses of France. But of course they never advertised. They had to be found. Alice and Jeremiah were finding them—farmer by farmer, artisan by artisan. "We were starting to reach outside our own little circle, telling them, 'You can do this too.'"

The Chez Panisse ideal was coming to fruition—French techniques pepped up with jazzy improvisation, bright-flavored and utterly fresh California ingredients, purity of flavor, simplicity of presentation, seasonality: This was the birth of what came to be called California cuisine.

AS JEREMIAH EXPLORED the little-known masterpieces of the golden age of French cuisine, and Alice began to codify her complementary doctrine of seasonality, freshness, local sourcing, and unfettered creativity, gastronomy in France itself was moving in similar directions. It is safe to say that virtually no one of culinary importance in France had heard of Chez Panisse, but "we did have some notion of what was going on over there," Alice remembers, "through what we'd read and what our friends could tell us. I'd still not been back there." The most influential chefs of France were reaching at once back into forgotten classics and forward into experimentation—just as Alice and Jeremiah were doing.

The early 1970s in France gave birth to what the French restaurant critics Henri Gault and Christian Millau had dubbed *la nouvelle cuisine.* From the summit of their epicurean Sinai, Gault and Millau proclaimed ten new commandments:[3]

1. *Tu ne cuiras pas trop:* Thou shalt not overcook.
2. *Tu utiliseras des produits frais et de qualité:* Thou shalt utilize fresh, high-quality ingredients.
3. *Tu allégeras ta carte:* Thou shalt lighten thy menu.
4. *Tu ne seras pas systématiquement moderniste:* Thou shalt not be inflexibly modernist.
5. *Tu rechercheras cependant ce que t'apportent les nouvelles technologies:* Thou shalt nevertheless explore new techniques.
6. *Tu éviteras marinades, faisandages et fermentations:* Thou shalt avoid marinades, the hanging of game, and fermentation.
7. *Tu élimineras sauces brunes et blanches:* Thou shalt eliminate traditional brown sauces and white sauces.
8. *Tu n'ignoreras pas la diététique:* Thou shalt not ignore nutrition.
9. *Tu ne truqueras pas tes présentations:* Thou shalt not gussy up thy presentations.
10. *Tu seras inventif:* Thou shalt be inventive.

The chefs favored by Gault and Millau—Paul Bocuse, Alain Chapel, Jacques Pic, Michel Guérard, Jean and Pierre Troisgros, among others—were rather selective in their obedience to the commandments. Bocuse could not resist antiquarian presentations such as bass stuffed with lobster mousse, baked in pastry sculpted to look like the fish within, and sauced with beurre blanc, which, because it was not thickened with flour, did not, in his view, officially count as a white sauce. Chapel still loved such thoroughly non-light classics as chicken cooked in a pig's bladder with copious cream and truffles. Chapel also stuffed a calf's ear with sweetbreads and truffles and sprinkled it with fried parsley, and combined in one dish morels, crayfish, and the cockscombs and kidneys of young roosters. Jacques Pic was among the first to offer a *menu de dégustation*, a tasting menu—he called it his Menu Rabelais—consisting of eight courses plus cheese and dessert. None of these was anything like "lightening thy menu."

But Michel Guérard decamped from what he deemed the toxically froufrou atmosphere of Paris to build a luxurious weight-loss spa in the clear-aired southwest of France, where he perfected his low-in-fat, high-in-vegetables, visually stunning *cuisine minceur,* as well as his own take on the nouvelle cuisine, which he dubbed *la cuisine gourmande.* The Troisgros brothers were dragooning kids to hunt for snails, encouraging local farmers to grow things to the restaurant's specifications, insisting on absolute freshness, serving only what was in the prime of its season, and truly not gussying up their presentations[4]—precisely the practices of Chez Panisse.

"Jeremiah kept up with all the new styles and ideas coming from France," Alice states, "and I loved all that, and I couldn't wait to try it at the source."

While the French press and intelligentsia debated the philosophical implications of the nouvelle cuisine, most of the rest of France continued along in its sturdy bourgeois way, with its tradition-bound, delicious dinners at home or in its thousands of bistros, where the same clear notes rang again and again—Muscadet; Beaujolais; just-opened oysters; calf's liver with long-cooked onions; sole *meunière*; roast veal; thin pan-fried steaks with a little reduction of red wine, shallots, and butter; a little salad; a little cheese; a piece of fruit. To some American tourists, the servings seemed penuriously small, the hours spent at table painfully long. Conspicuously absent from many of the bistros' menus, but conspicuously abundant in French homes, were vegetables, nearly always local, fresh, and plainly cooked. "When I was first there," Alice says, "which was what? forty years ago? the poorest people always ate well, always had a salad and a beautiful soup with beans and cabbage and lovely things. It always tasted good."

. . .

"IN OUR BEST MOMENTS," Alice recalls, "Jeremiah would think of a menu, and I'd say, 'Well, I think maybe this would be better.' And he'd say, 'Oh, yeah, let's do it like that.' And then I'd say, 'Oh, God, you need to put a vegetable with that because *dadadada*.' It was like that all the time. It was a collaboration. It was fun for us. I was in the dining room, and I knew what things people were really liking, or how they were reacting to special little things that we'd try for just a few people, and I would feed that back to him. Sometimes I'd bring in something that I'd tasted, or some recipe I'd found, and Jeremiah and I would work through it, making it better, trying this and that accompaniment, till we were both satisfied. And we were both not easily satisfied. It was important for the sort of spiritual life of the restaurant that we be a little daring, that we not get too set in a path."

Alice and Jeremiah were attempting a difficult, even paradoxical expansion of the Chez Panisse experience: They wanted to maintain the restaurant's easy informality, its gemütlichkeit, and now to that they wanted to add a sense of festivity, of occasion—and more profit. That meant more special dinners, more-breathtaking cooking, more panache. "We cooked a wild boar outside, on the sidewalk in front of the restaurant, that we had gotten from Big Sur," Alice explains. "Jeremiah had some friends down there, and somebody had hunted this huge object. I think it was about four hundred pounds, and somehow we spitted this thing, and then it started to rain, so we rigged up a tent. The spit was turned by hand. It did draw quite a crowd."

Festivity also meant special consideration for the most festive members of the Chez Panisse circle. Tom Luddy's movie people were especially valuable. No matter how crowded the restaurant, no matter how late the hour, Alice would always have a table for them. The clientele was subtly changing. Chez Panisse was becoming chic.

"They were all so sexy," Ruth Reichl remembers. "Jerry Budrick was very sexy. I had a huge crush on him. He was really arrogant—and delicious. There were all these really good-looking people at the restaurant. In many ways, Jeremiah and Jerry were very similar—you know, bad boys.

Jeremiah Tower

And Tom Luddy also. The Swallow [a collective restaurant where Ruth worked as a waitress] was in the Pacific Film Archive, and Tom would come swanning through with Martin Scorsese and all these people with a sort of entourage. People who weren't important, he would bring to the Swallow. When it was someone important, you'd know they were going to Chez Panisse. We were earnest, Earth shoe. They were glamorous."

Jeremiah was feeling mounting pressure—much of it self-generated, but no less stressful for that. "Chefs have a reputation for bad behavior," he writes in his memoir *California Dish*, "in part because they have to play so hard to counteract the daily pileup of tension and fatigue. . . . For many of us, it was about how many oysters and great wines we could fit into a few hours and still get some rest before the work began again. . . . The mental onslaught was never-ending, even in sleep. . . . And drugs were easier to organize than sex, unless it was casual, which usually meant with one another."

Eleanor Bertino recalls, "Lindsey, of course, had this little shed in the back, and she'd go home at four o'clock. So at night there was nobody working there. I think there was a bed in there at one point."

During the week, living on oysters, wine, and the tiny bites he would taste at the restaurant, Jeremiah was half-starving himself. Then on his one night off, he would pig out at Trader Vic's in Oakland or Vanessi's in San Francisco, often till very late. On the verge of cracking up one night at Chez Panisse in January 1974, he suddenly burst into tears and announced that he had to have a vacation. He promptly fled to the Caribbean, not specifying a date of return.

It was just then that Anne Isaak appeared. (Here again is an example of the curious pattern in Alice's and others' recollections of the history of Chez Panisse. The right people seem simply to "appear" at just the right moment. It can be presumed that people who might have been right happened to appear at wrong moments, and hence never entered the history.) Anne had worked in professional kitchens—including a good one, with highly competent Chinese cooks, and also "the worst kitchen in the world, Elaine's in New York." Everything about Chez Panisse appealed to her. When she went to ask for a job,

there was nobody in the restaurant, and I went into the kitchen. There was this woman at a large sink, cleaning trout. Alice. She said, "Well, I'm cooking right now, because Jeremiah is away, but we're going to be trying people out for a sous-chef job soon." I went for a tryout, and she hired me just like that. She said, "The problem is, I'm only here temporarily, and you're going to be working with Jeremiah, and he doesn't like women."

My first job was to chop parsley, and I had had this great experience with the Chinese, learning how to chop parsley with two knives. No one was professional at Chez Panisse, so they were very careful about picking parsley off the stems, and everything was done kind of slow, and nobody had their own knives then. But I had my own knives, and they were sharp, unlike all the other knives in that kitchen. So I got all the parsley together and I went *hrruuummmm*. That gave them the impression that I knew something.

While Alice and Willy and Anne Isaak manned the stoves in Jeremiah's absence, Jeremiah's Caribbean vacation—with margaritas delivered to his hammock on the quarter hour, as he has recalled it—set his brain sizzling with new ideas. The regional French dinners were popular, and profitable, but he wanted now to build festival dinners on the work of the historic chefs of France—Escoffier, Prosper Montagné, Henri-Paul Pellaprat, and Urbain Dubois—and then lead up to the present with the British apostle of Mediterranean simplicity Elizabeth David and the American Richard Olney, who also espoused a style of French cooking considerably pared down from the liver-challenging classics Jeremiah had tended to favor.

After a few more weeks, Jeremiah came back to Chez Panisse eager to be doing new things. Elizabeth David and Richard Olney were all very well, but what really turned him on was when he could "go big, outlandish." For the hundredth birthday of Gertrude Stein, February 3, 1974, he took both text and recipes from *The Alice B. Toklas Cookbook* (Toklas was Stein's lifelong companion, and a San Francisco native). Willy Bishop designed the menu card, portraying Gertrude Stein as a stove with Alice B. Toklas in her oven:

Dining. Dining is west. **Mushroom sandwiches**
upstairs.
Eating. Eat ing.
Single fish. Single fish single fish single fish.
Sole mousse with Virgin Sauce. I wrote it for
America.

Everyone thought that the syringe was a whimsy.
Mousse and mountain and a quiver, a quaint statue
and a pain in the exterior and silence. **Gigot de la
Clinique** a cake, a real salve made of mutton and

liquor, a specially retained rinsing and an
established cork and brazing

Wild rice salad. She said it would suit her.

Cake cast in went to be and needles wine needles
are such. Needles are. **A Tender Tart.** That
doves each have a heart.

Nobody ever followed Ida. What was the use of
following Ida.

Cream Perfect Love.

Though tempted, Jeremiah refrained from putting hashish in the after-dinner cookies.

He had been avoiding marijuana since an incident involving the new, much more powerful pot coming onto the market. Egged on by the waiters, he had taken one puff from a fat joint. He then walked through the swinging doors with the intention of joining Alice and eight food writers at a table, but he made it only three steps before passing out cold. A quick glass of Champagne, administered by Willy Bishop, revived the hopelessly stoned chef.

For her birthday, in April 1974, Alice took off two weeks, to return, at last, to Europe. "That was when I really started to get it about French food, I think. I realized how relentless and how careful the scrutiny of everything was in the best places—and I don't mean necessarily the most expensive places. It was about caring."

Lindsey and Charles Shere went to Europe for their first time in the summer of 1974. For six weeks they immersed themselves in every manner of French restaurant, from the plainest to the fanciest. "Alice felt that people should be able to take these trips, to have time off to educate themselves. And it was an eye-opener for me," says Lindsey. "We went to the Auberge of the Flowering Hearth for the first time, and we went back and back and back. The cookbook that Roy Andries de Groot wrote based on the food at the Auberge was a tremendous influence on Chez Panisse. They were cooking regionally and seasonally before we were." The inn is no more, but the book *The Auberge of the Flowering Hearth,* while not well known, is a masterpiece. It informs the cooking of Chez Panisse to this day.

THEN CAME THE RESTAURANT'S first glimmer of national recognition. Marion Cunningham, then a food writer for the *San Francisco Chronicle,* brought James Beard to the restaurant. "And he," Alice recalls, "was the first one to say that this was really not like anything else."

"We went for lunch," Marion remembers, "and the first sentence Jim said was, 'This is not a real restaurant, Marion.' Meaning it was a home that took in money for food."

Characteristically, Beard's praise in his syndicated column was acidulated by a dash of reproof: "Recently, while dining in a fascinating small restaurant called Chez Panisse, in Berkeley, California, I had a perfectly cooked duck with green peppercorns, a lovely blend of flavors—but the peppercorns were floating around in the sauce. Had the peppercorns been crushed to a paste before being added, you would have savored their special flavor without having to bite into the peppercorns themselves, which is not as pleasant to the palate."

The complexity and the difficulty of Jeremiah's food were on a steep upward trajectory, and so was the labor required to produce it. Jeremiah and his staff were often at the brink of exhaustion. Then, in 1974, an effective (or so it was thought at the time) antidote to the pressure arrived at Chez Panisse: "It was cocaine that became the fuel for the energy that changed the way America dines," Jeremiah writes in his memoir.

"After work, we would drink until the bars closed, and then I would go home and be able to paint and go to bed at six or seven and go to work at one or two," recalls Willy Bishop. "And I was turning forty at the time, and they were all under thirty. I think the exuberance overtook everyone, and with coke you were able to do things you couldn't really do. Nothing was daunting.

"On Sundays, it was always slow. There were just three of us. Jeremiah and me and this boy whom Jeremiah was in love with. A pretty. He went off to Reed College in Oregon. We were doing nitrous oxide, the chargers. You could pass out. That kid fell down once. After that, he didn't do it anymore. I remember the time one of the busboys came through the door and fell down. He had stuffed opium up his ass. Too much. He just fell right down. That's the way to do it—it bypasses the digestive system, and that way it doesn't make you nauseated. The mucous membranes absorb it.

"We'd do acid on Sundays too. These were purple barrels. The purple barrel is a mild acid like a purple tab or windowpane. It was more like MDA [3,4-methylenedioxyamphetamine, a stimulant that made people so euphoric, and so benignant, that it was called the love drug]. Everything is good and happy, and you just work."

"You've got to remember that drugs were everywhere in those days, especially in the restaurant business," Alice asserts, "and we were no different. Actually, we were probably a little more disciplined, most of us. We all got into it, some more than others, but that period was very short. Certainly for me it was very short."

The year 1974 also brought Chez Panisse its first house wine, of an unofficial sort. Jerry Budrick had been making banana wine at home for several years: "It was quite good, light and fruity, shall we say, and almost free." That fall, a friend of his from Amador County suggested that Jerry try making real wine. The next thing he knew, his Amador buddy had presented him with five hundred pounds of zinfandel grapes.

"We had a big garbage can and some bricks that went down in the bottom of it, and then another garbage can at the bottom with holes drilled in it," Jerry explains. "My feet were too big, but Alice's were just fine. So she crushed, and we made wine from these five hundred pounds of grapes. And it was delicious. We let it age for a month or two, and then we bottled it. I used to bring a bottle when I knew some dignitaries were coming to the restaurant, some wine people, just to fool them. Darrell Corti is a famous wine guy from Sacramento. I said, 'I'd like you to try this wine. I'm not going to tell you what it is, you tell me.' He swirled it around, did the whole thing, and he said, 'Well, this is an Amador County zinfandel, and I've never had it before.' I said, 'How did you do that?' I was blown away. We've been friends ever since."

FRIENDSHIP, romance, casual sex, and serious commitment swirled through the population of Chez Panisse, in such complexity that sometimes the categories were hard to distinguish. Alice was still semiofficially the companion of Jerry Budrick, though not his cohabitant. "We never got to live together," Jerry recalls. "First I had a house with my wife in it, and that wouldn't do. Then in '74 I got divorced, and I bought another house, a fixer-upper that was in such disrepair that Alice couldn't stand it. She just wouldn't live there with me. She lived in lots of places. She lived in a garage for a while."

"Well, I mean, I did fix it up," Alice says.

"She lived in a ship captain's mansion."

"With a turret!" Alice exclaims. "Just like London, but much grander. It was a sensational house, historic. I had the whole first floor."

"Then there was that house on Delaware that she ended up sharing with Jeremiah," Jerry recalls, pointedly.

"Jeremiah wasn't my boyfriend," says Alice. "It was a very odd thing. I mean, no. He was interested in every young guy at the restaurant. But he indulged me to a certain extent. We always danced together. We always went out at night. We went on trips together. We had this whole romantic way of being together. I always wanted to dance with Jeremiah."

Alice and Jeremiah traveled to Nice, and drank Krug Champagne, he writes, "on the terrace of Venice's Gritti Palace in the moonlight." They were perfectly, dangerously balanced—in their level of aesthetic refinement, in their ambitions, and in their desire to be in charge of Chez Panisse.

Rivalry, romance, Champagne—whatever the Alice-Jeremiah elixir was concocted of, it was powerful. In those halcyon days, they seemed to see no limit to what they could accomplish together. In February 1975, Chez Panisse mounted a three-week festival of special dinners honoring a French gastronome and writer whom both Alice and Jeremiah delighted in—Maurice Edmond Sailland (1872–1956), who was known by the single-barreled pseudonym Curnonsky (a curious hybrid of Latin and Russian, roughly meaning "Whynotsky"). *"La cuisine, c'est quand les choses ont le goût de ce qu'elles sont"* was Curnonsky's most famous dictum: "Fine cooking is when things have the taste of what they are."[5]

Though Curnonsky is best known for his celebration of the provincial cooking of France, his masterpiece, *Cuisine et Vins de France,* published in 1953, goes in rather less for rustic *cuisine grand-mère* ("grandmother cooking") than for haute cuisine at its loftiest heights. Accordingly, Jeremiah and Alice's menus for the three weeks of Curnonsky featured such extravagances as *tarte à la moëlle périgourdine,* translated on the menu as "tart of beef marrow, butter, Madeira, and veal essence"; *canard farci aux huîtres,* "fresh duck stuffed with shallots, fresh oysters, and the duck livers, braised with aromatic vegetables"; and, on the last night, the *timbale épicurienne de Curnonsky,* "the great extravagant seafood 'timbale,' including, in one dish, cooked together, fresh Maine lobster prepared *américaine* (with veal essence and brandy), fresh shrimp *bordelaise* (with red wine, shallots, and beef marrow), oysters poached in white wine, cream, shrimp butter, and truffles."

About the Curnonsky dinners Jeremiah told San Francisco *City* magazine, "French food is family food. Even though it's an incredible amount of work, each thing in itself is very, very simple. That seafood timbale, for instance, was actually a very simple thing, even though it took a week to prepare, and unbelievable labor. When you opened the casserole, you could see immediately that there were oysters in their shells on top, with cream and white wine sauce, and then prawns and lobsters underneath, in their sauce. But that's simple—in a way."[6]

THE WINE WRITER and importer Gerald Asher represented an estate in Provence called Domaine Tempier, whose wine was made under the appellation of Bandol. This appellation was hardly known in the United States, and it had not been much better known in France until the Peyraud family took over at Tempier and began to produce some of the deepest-flavored, best-balanced wines ever to come from the south of France. When Lucien

Alice, 1975

and Lulu Peyraud came to visit Gerald Asher in San Francisco in the spring of 1975, he recalls, "I wanted them to eat at Chez Panisse. Alice loved them immediately, and wanted their wine." Much more would come, in due course, of this meeting.

The menu for Thursday, June 5, 1975, shows how far Jeremiah and Alice would go in those days for an "ordinary" weeknight dinner at Chez Panisse:

Gratin de queues d'écrevisses
(the classic, expensive, very time-consuming, and now rare dish
of shelled crayfish tails sautéed in Cognac,
covered with a cream and crayfish butter sauce and gratinéed)

Consommé de chou rouge
(duck consommé with puréed red cabbage and
sliced red cabbage cooked in walnut oil)
🍃

Selle de porc sur le gril
(marinated loin of pork roasted over a charcoal fire with fresh herbs,
served with a fresh herb butter sauce)
🍃

Salade chaude d'épinards
(salad of spinach wilted in olive oil and sherry vinegar)
🍃

Fruit and cheese
🍃

Crème Carême
(cherry sherbet)
🍃

Coffee or tea
🍃

$9.00

That's $34 in today's money.

Less than two weeks later, Chez Panisse served a British dinner, to commemorate the Battle of Waterloo. The menu was in English, archly accompanied by "a special translation for non-English-speaking diners":

Salmon cooked in white wine, pounded with butter,
then preserved in ramekins
(saumon braisé au vin blanc mélangé avec du beurre en ramequins)
🍃

Either: veal kidneys cooked in butter, cream, and port
OR soup of veal, beef, lamb, and pigs' ears with vegetables
(soit rognons de veau braisés au beurre avec crème et porto
OU potage de pieds et oreilles de cochon)
🍃

Roasted leg of lamb with pickled mushrooms
(gigot rôti avec champignons marinés)

✾

Salad of greens, herbs, radishes, and spring onions
(salade verte aux herbes, radis, et oignons nouveaux)

✾

Stilton cheese to eat with port
(fromage Stilton)

✾

Custard with maraschino and "cuirasseau" with sliced almonds
(crème anglaise parfumée au Maraschino et Curaçao)

✾

$9.00

IN JUNE 1975, Alice's old Berkeley friends Martine and Claude Labro had returned to their home in the Provençal town of Vence. A friend of theirs, Nathalie Waag, ran a quirky little restaurant there called Au Hasard (best translated as "Serendipity"), where she served whatever she happened to feel like cooking every day. Nathalie's boyfriend, a mathematician, was going to an IBM conference in San Francisco, and bringing Nathalie. The Labros told Nathalie that she absolutely must look up their great old friend the restauratrice Alice Waters, who also served whatever she happened to feel like cooking every day. "My first thought," Nathalie recalls, "was about the name of the town, Berkeley, which seemed so funny to me, because in French, *beurk!* is the noise in cartoon strips to mean throwing up. In any case, I went. When I met Alice, she was running out of the restaurant. I asked her if she knew Alice Waters, and she said, 'Yes, why?' And I said, 'I am a friend of Claude and Martine.' So she grabbed my arm and said, 'Come with me. I'm going to buy fish.' And then she said, 'Come for dinner tonight.'"

The dinner that night epitomized the what-the-hell over-the-topness of Jeremiah at his most extravagant and eccentric. Every course was accompanied by a Sauternes, the intensely sweet Bordeaux white wine that,

according to custom, was considered appropriate
indeed only with certain desserts, or with foie gras. And the
any Sauternes. These were among the rarest wines, of any
able anywhere. It can safely be said that no other restaurant in
America or France would have dared to present so voluptuous, s
sybaritic a meal. "This was pure Jeremiah," Alice says. "I had nothing to
do with it."

Jambon de Virginie aux pruneaux
(ham from Culpeper, Virginia, braised in Sauternes and served
with prunes stuffed with green olives)
1947 Château Caillou
❧

Colombines de saumon Nantua
(quenelles of salmon with crayfish butter sauce)
1949 Château Climens
1949 Château Doisy-Daëne
❧

Entrecôte de boeuf
(sirloin of beef, roasted,
potatoes cooked in butter and duck fat with mushrooms)
1967 Château d'Yquem
1955 Château d'Yquem
❧

Pommes Chez Nous
(green apples filled with berries, served with crème fraîche)
1959 Château Guiraud
❧

Salade Alice
(salad of greens, herbs, radishes, and spring onions)
❧

Tarte chaude de fruits
(hot deep-dish fruit pie)
1959 Château Suduiraut

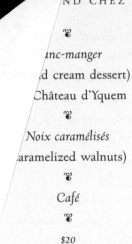

nc-manger
d cream dessert)
Château d'Yquem

❦

Noix caramélisés
aramelized walnuts)

❦

Café

❦

$20

Three vintages of Yquem! It was, and remains, one of the most expensive wines in the world—though all wine prices were far lower then, including Yquem's. (Today a Château d'Yquem of an age and quality comparable to that of the 1922 in 1975, the 1953, goes for between $1,000 and $2,000 a bottle.)

Alice sat at the table with Nathalie throughout the Yquem dinner, each delighted with the other. Alice was looking for a farmhouse to rent in France that summer. Nathalie adds, "And I said, 'Well, there's my farmhouse in Bonnieux.' And she said, 'Yes, but will you be there?' And I said, 'I don't know.' She said, 'Is it big enough so that Claude and Martine could come?' And I said, 'Ah-hah! and we could play poker!'" The Labros had fallen in love with American poker during their sojourn in Berkeley, and had played a lot of it with David Goines and Alice. "Then she said, 'But how much?' And I had no idea. I had never rented my farmhouse. But I ended that beautiful evening with a lot of dollars in my pocket and a new friend. And I spent three or four weeks that summer in the farmhouse with Alice. She wanted me to be there too.

"I remember very well that on the twelfth of August [1975], she went to visit Richard Olney, and I acted as her driver." Richard was the author of one of Alice's culinary bibles, *The French Menu Cookbook,* and he lived only a few minutes' drive from Domaine Tempier, and was a close friend of the Peyrauds'. (Years later, when Lulu was known as one of the best home cooks in France, Richard would write the cookbook *Lulu's Provençal Cuisine.*) Through Alice, Nathalie too would come to be a friend of Lulu and Lucien Peyraud's, as would Claude and Martine Labro. These interlocking friendships assured for the future of Chez Panisse a permanent connection to that little corner of Provence.

Alice was entranced with Lulu's primitive kitchen and the glories Lulu produced in it. From that visit forward, Lulu Peyraud would serve as Alice's mentor, soul mate, and hero. Alice loved the simplicity of Lulu's food, and its dependence on the most perfect ingredients, as exemplified here in Alice's words:

· LULU PEYRAUD'S TAPENADE, SEA URCHIN TOASTS, AND SARDINES ·

Lulu always serves tapenade toasts as a little *amuse-bouche,* with those little Niçoise olives and garlic that are just pounded together in a mortar. Actually, sometimes she sneaks and does it in the blender. I still don't even know where the blender is in that house. But I always do it with a mortar and pestle. Garlic, olives, and olive oil—that's it. Lulu sometimes puts some savory in it.

My favorite thing that she does—well, I have two favorite things. One is that she gets her son to go down and get sea urchins in Cassis, fresh ones, dive for them. She'll have little pieces of a brown bread, and she'll spread them with butter and then take out the roe from the sea urchins and put it on the buttered bread, raw, absolutely raw. And you eat it right away.

My other favorite thing is her sardines. She'll just fillet the sardines right on the spot, and sometimes she puts them on a little plate, raw, with salt and oil. Or she'll just put them on a piece of buttered bread or a crouton, raw, or just slightly cured. She fillets the sardine right there, and you don't wait. Oil, salt, and lemon juice, that's it. You don't put any parsley on.

At Chez Panisse, we get sardines fresh from Monterey Bay. They're not quite like hers. I mean, hers are still alive, and ours aren't quite that perfect, but we do get them within twenty-four hours. At the most.

AFTER THE SAUTERNES DINNER, Chez Panisse staged its own vacation, a figurative one. On the first of July 1975, the menu touted *TROIS SEMAINES DE VACANCES DANS VOTRE ASSIETTE:* A THREE-WEEK GASTRONOMIC TOUR OF FRANCE FROM YOUR DINNER TABLE. In those three weeks alone, there were special dinners featuring the regional dishes of Brittany, the Auvergne, Languedoc, Picardie, the Touraine, the Lyonnais, Champagne (again), Normandy, Alsace, Burgundy, Gascony; the Dauphiné (typified in *"truffade:* potatoes and tomatoes cooked as a cake in bacon fat"); Bresse, the Dombes, Bugey, and the Pays de Gex (*"caneton au beurre d'écrevisses:* roast duck served with a crayfish, brandy, and butter sauce"); Nivernais, Morvan, and Bombonnais (*"saupiquet des Amognes:* slices of ham sautéed in butter, served with a sauce of juniper berries and shallots reduced with vinegar enriched with butter and sour cream"); and Provence (*"Berlingueto:* hard-cooked eggs stuffed with fresh basil, anchovies, garlic, bread crumbs, parsley, and black pepper, set on a bed of the stuffing and browned in the oven with olive oil").

Immediately after that onslaught of butter, cream, and other fats, on July 22, 1975, the menu announced, *"Trois semaines de vacances ne suffisent pas—il nous faut quatre semaines (au moins):* A three-week vacation is not enough, so—a fourth week to more distant places." That single week took Chez Panisse to Switzerland and Savoie, to the county of Nice, to Corsica (*"la polenta de castagne:* chestnut pancake with heavy cream"); to Saintonge, Aunis, and Angoumis (*"la Migourée de Matata-Meschers:* various saltwater fish browned in butter and olive oil, heated in the sauce of butter, white wine, garlic, onions, and shallots"); and at last to Morocco and Tunisia ("*Shlada dyal Feyjel ou Lichine:* salad of oranges, radishes, orange-flower water, cinnamon, and romaine lettuce").

A sensible observer might have concluded that the Chez Panisse kitchen could not possibly get any more extravagant. A sensible observer, as happens so often in this restaurant's history, would have been wrong. After what he describes in *California Dish* as "a surreal holiday in Mustique," where he says Lord Colin Tennant tried to persuade him to stay as Princess Margaret's chef, Jeremiah was ready for more. He and Alice staged a two-week festival, beginning at the end of September 1975, in honor of "the divine Salvador Domenech Hyacinthe Dalí," the surrealist painter, who had published a cookbook of his own—a very strange one—dedicated to his wife, Gala. From it, the kitchen of Chez Panisse produced, among many other equally Dalíesque delicacies, "*un cannibalisme parfait de l'automne:* a prawn-cold parfait of crushed prawns with cream and garlic, served with hot sausages in pastry"; "*un atavisme des oxyribonucléique sans truffes:* a salad not composed by Alexandre Dumas of beets, celery root, and Maxim's sauce"; "*un délice petit martyr sans tête:* toast of avocado, brains, almonds, Mexican liquor, and cayenne"; "*un Spoutnik astique d'asticots statistiques:* love's apple consommé: frog and tomato consommé with Royalist flourishes"; and "*l'entreplat drogué et sodomisé:* leg of lamb injected"—by hypodermic needle—"with Madeira and brandy, roasted with garlic and herbs."

Fireworks like these could not fail to be seen from across the Bay, and from farther. Despite the Dada antics and the artery-clogging sauces and the narcissistic bravado, Chez Panisse was eliciting serious praise. In the combined Sunday edition of the *San Francisco Chronicle and Examiner* of September 7, 1975, Wade Holland wrote,

> Chez Panisse can be criticized for overly casual service, for culinary experimentation that does not always meet with universal approval, for refusing to give the guests a choice of menu items, and I suppose for simply being "too Berkeley." But after four years, it also just happens to be in my estimation one of the very best French restaurants in all of California and certainly the most innovative. . . . Chez Panisse's inestimable stature owes to unremittingly superb

quality in food preparation, innovativeness in menu planning, purchase of the finest of ingredients, and resolute attention to even the smallest culinary details.

Also in the fall of 1975, Alice and Jeremiah hired another young Harvard graduate, Fritz Streiff, who had been learning the fine points of the nouvelle cuisine at Jacques Manière's Au Pactole in Paris. Fritz was eccentric, brilliant, charming, deeply cynical, and just as sentimental. He fit in perfectly. Fritz was partial to white linen suits and bow ties. He wore round-lensed vintage thirties glasses. He was always depressed, though in his telling his depressions were often rather funny. He loved to see the bad side of everything. He remembers with pleasure disillusioning his bosses about the immortal Auguste Escoffier: "Escoffier was on the take!" Fritz told Alice and Jeremiah. "He and César Ritz cheated the Savoy Hotel [where Ritz was manager and Escoffier chef] out of a bunch of money. Escoffier was taking money on the side from suppliers. They both got sacked."

The restaurant sought out wine to match the swagger of the staff and the ambition of the cooking. Jerry Budrick had been so pleased with the homemade zinfandel that Alice's own feet had pressed that he proposed to make his next batch of it the official Chez Panisse house wine, and Alice agreed. He promptly contracted for six tons of grapes from Amador County and went looking for a winery to do the vinification. Unfortunately, the one he had counted on was fully booked. Because Pagnol et Cie's board of directors had declined to put up the money, Jerry owned those six tons of grapes. Then Bruce Neyers, the business manager of the brand-new Joseph Phelps Winery, came to dinner with his wife, Barbara; and Jerry, as he loved to do, fell into conversation with them. Both Phelps and the Neyerses would go on to fame as winemakers, but at this time they had plenty of excess capacity. And sure, they'd be glad to make some wine for Chez Panisse. They vinified some of Jerry's grapes in the then-popular style of Beaujolais Nouveau—fresh, fruity, unaged, and good for only a few months—while the rest became a sturdier, barrel-aged, longer-lasting wine. For a restaurant to have its truly own wine—not just a bottle of somebody else's with a custom label slapped on—was yet another first. It was good wine, too.

. . .

THEN CAME THE REVIEW that overnight elevated Chez Panisse t
fame. In the October 1975 issue of *Gourmet* magazine, Caroline
wrote:

> Chez Panisse is joyously exploring *la vraie cuisine française* in all its
> vigor, freshness, and variety. . . . One evening some months ago,
> while diners in restaurants the length of California were facing that
> unholy trinity of onion soup, duckling à l'orange, and crème cara-
> mel, we were occupying a window table in the enclosed porch off
> the dining room at Chez Panisse and discovering a ramekin of mush-
> rooms in the style of Quercy, roast duckling with fresh basil, and an
> almond tart surely made in heaven.
>
> Like many creative young chefs in France today who have turned
> away from the pretensions of *la grande cuisine,* [Jeremiah Tower]
> strives for the simplicity and directness that characterize French
> provincial food, with its emphasis on fresh ingredients and the in-
> tegrity of each taste.

"Well," says Alice, "that was when we knew we'd arrived. Really arrived. I wish I could say I felt better about it. Mostly what I felt was dread.
Everybody and his mother were going to want to come in and see what
all the fuss was about. Coming in with a chip on their shoulder. One of
my dearest friends sent us a funeral wreath."

The review in *Gourmet,* just as Alice had feared, brought a whole new
crowd of doubting, demanding customers to Chez Panisse. "In the last two
months," wrote San Francisco's *Bay Guardian* in November 1975, "the
modest Panisse has suffered two critical blows which have left the staff
shaken and staggering.

"Since the reviews appeared in the *Chron* and *Gourmet,* Alice Waters
calculates that near on sixty percent of the customers have been out-of-
towners. . . . There have also been phone calls coming in at an average of
one every two minutes, flooding Panisse's two lines. Unfortunately the

a mixed excess of diners—Alice Waters esti-
venty no-shows per night."

other restaurants could only have dreamed
with big spenders, Chez Panisse was doing
e its ascent to national fame.

cklash was inevitable. The *Berkeley Gazette*
dollars for "pork and beans"—the restau-

cassoulet.

Willy Bishop was outraged. "That *cassoulet!* My God! We had to make goose confit. We had to make lamb stock, and duck stock for the beans. We worked probably twenty hours before we put it in the oven. Different-size casseroles—one for two, one for four. Different timing for each casserole, so it would be ready exactly on time. Perfect timing. Perfect bread crumbs on top. Oh, my God! That *cassoulet* was so rich and so fine! And that fucking guy called it pork and beans."

All through the fall and winter of 1975, Jeremiah's temper had been flaring more often and more nastily. Once, when he noticed that a busser had his fingers in the food as he headed for the dining room, Jeremiah's reproach was "What is it about 'keep your fingers out of the food' that your little cockroach mind can't grasp?"[7]

For Jeremiah, this was an opportune moment for a little sabbatical—and a chance to seek out Richard Olney in France. Richard was a culinary saint to him as much as he was to Alice. Perhaps more important, he was just the sort of whimsical, stylish, gay, and alcoholic sybarite Jeremiah adored. They shared an almost inconceivable capacity for wine. After a great banquet of the gastronomically elite Club des Cent in Paris in mid-October 1975, Jeremiah accompanied Richard to his house at Solliès-Toucas. "The long winter nights were filled with single-malt whiskey, old French music hall records, and talks about food," Jeremiah writes in *California Dish.* "All this talk of eating and love made me want to do a festival at Chez Panisse in celebration of [Richard's] new book, *Simple French Food*"—a book that would move Chez Panisse back toward its roots in the French countryside. Together Richard and Jeremiah planned a series of menus for a California Zinfandel Festival, to come the next fall. For the menus, Richard encouraged Jeremiah to think not only of French food but of the possibilities inherent in some traditional American cooking.

Richard also introduced Jeremiah to Domaine Tempier. Lulu Peyraud's cooking was rustic, highly aromatic, strong, and personal. She didn't care how anybody else did anything. She had her own, fiercely elemental way. She still cooked nearly everything on a wood-fired hearth (though she did have a tiny two-burner stove and oven in another room).

Jeremiah returned to Berkeley in December 1975, in time to concoct a New Year's Eve dinner worthy of Olney's sumptuous gourmandise.

La salade de Bugey, Lucien Tendret
(salad of lobster, chicken breasts, black truffles, squab breasts,
mushrooms, and shrimp, with a mustard vinaigrette)

❦

L'entrecôte de boeuf, sauce périgourdine
(prime sirloin of beef with truffles,
roasted and served with a truffled Madeira sauce)

❦

Le purée verte et la purée blanche
(purée of green beans and purée of turnips, leeks,
and potatoes, with garlic)

❦

Le granité de Champagne
(Champagne sherbet)

❦

Tartelettes de fruits
(fruit tartlets)

❦

Bonbons Chez Panisse

THERE ARE A NUMBER of veterans of Jeremiah's time at Chez Panisse who dispute his memories. Kim Severson, reviewing *California Dish* in the *San Francisco Chronicle*, wrote, "To make it through former superstar chef

Jeremiah Tower's memoir, the reader has to suspend disbelief and accept three basic premises: 1) Everything was his idea. 2) Any culinary and financial reversals weren't his fault. 3) Everyone wanted to sleep with him."[8]

Patricia Curtan, the artist who has been part of the life of the restaurant for some thirty years, was particularly outraged, and she has good authority as a witness. She was a student of David Goines's in the mid-seventies as well as the lover of Willy Bishop. She worked as a bartender and occasional cook at the restaurant, and eventually became, like David, a designer of menus and posters for special occasions at Chez Panisse. She says that in *California Dish,* Jeremiah "took a story that was rich and nuanced and interesting, and he reduced it down to just this one version of himself at the center. It just diminished everything. He portrayed himself as this incredibly hardworking genius who worked twelve, eighteen hours a day, and that wasn't true either. There were so many people working really hard propping him up. Willy was an incredible workhorse. He didn't buy the prima donna act."

Greil Marcus, the writer who has been a partner in Chez Panisse since the beginning, also remembers the Jeremiah years as less than halcyon: "There was a time, maybe two years or so after Jeremiah started, when we didn't feel comfortable there, didn't feel welcome. It had become extraordinarily insular. A lot of the clientele were dope dealers. A lot of people were eating there for free. I remember saying to Alice any number of times, 'Alice, if we don't feel welcome there, and we're part of it, how do you think the general public is going to feel?' Jeremiah had a good deal to do with that, because that's his whole way of being in the world, to divide the world into those who count and those who don't."

Alice's former lover Tom Luddy, though he continued to dine at Chez Panisse and to bring his visitors from the movie industry, says, "I always felt that the food Jeremiah was cooking went against the philosophy of Chez Panisse, and Pagnol. It was getting back toward this Parisian, over-ripe, overrich, decadent, French high-class food that I never liked. I think Alice was intimidated by Jeremiah. Alice, God bless her, is not an egotistical, overconfident, arrogant soul. She's easily intimidated, and Jeremiah knew how to intimidate her."

Ruth Reichl, today the editor of *Gourmet* magazine, recalls, "Jeremiah had a much more sophisticated vision of what the food should be. And Alice was entranced by that. But she was influenced by other people too. It was a time when everybody was learning from everybody else. But I think that the uncompromising quality, the purity of the ingredients, is her. Jeremiah did not bring that to the table. For me, the epitome of the food at Chez Panisse was not the great Sauternes dinner, it was when you misread the menu and you thought you were going, you know, for some squid-ink fantasia, and it turns out to be chicken, and you're disappointed because it's not the meal you want, and then it comes out and it is the best piece of chicken you've ever had in your life. And that's not Jeremiah."

ONE NIGHT IN 1975—she does not remember quite when—Alice was savagely attacked in her home. "It was a huge, shocking, awful thing," she recalls.

I was living in a little cottage behind my friend Suzy Nelson's house, in a garage that I had made into a little studio. I was sleeping on a loft. I had thought many times that if somebody broke in, I would throw myself out the window. I had always thought up little scenarios. But I never imagined being awakened by somebody with his hand on my mouth in the middle of the night. I had always thought that I'd rather be raped than killed. But it turns out that's not true. I was willing to fight that hard. It was a real revelation about myself. I screamed bloody murder. I fought up to the point that he choked me until I passed out. I don't know how long I was out, but when I woke up, he was still there. When I thought about it later, I was pretty sure that he had lost his knife and was looking for it. He didn't rape me. I think he was looking for his knife, and he felt insecure without his knife. And he couldn't find it, and so he said, "Give me some money." And I said, "I don't have any, but I have a restaurant, I'll go." He was behind me. I never saw him. Then he said, "Well, go up to the loft." And I remembered my exit strategy. As soon as I got up there—he was holding on to my foot—I just threw myself with all my weight out the window. And he let go of me. The window was only one little story from the ground—probably eight or ten feet. I was down somehow, and I started running. And I escaped.

Alice was now afraid to be in the cottage alone. She quickly found another house, and Jeremiah gallantly offered to move in. Alice was grateful for his protective company, at least initially. "Ultimately," she says, "that's how it all kind of fell apart, with his moving into my house—and taking over my house. And the restaurant likewise. I just couldn't stand to be around him at that time." She had been so shaken by the attack that for some weeks afterward Alice exerted much less control over Chez Panisse than was her custom, and Jeremiah accordingly took up more psychic space in the restaurant, and she felt crowded out. In her home he had arrived as her protector, but she found his presence more irritating than comforting—so irritating that she moved out. "I just camped out with friends," she remembers, while Jeremiah continued to live in her new house.

Finally, Alice reached the limit of her patience, and one night, when Jeremiah was out, she reoccupied her house. Conveniently, Jeremiah had left his key there, and Alice locked him out.

7.

LAST
BIRTHDAY?

1976

In January 1976, in *City* magazine, Alice's old political mentor Robert Scheer wrote, "As a result of recent writeups in *Gourmet* and other magazines, the Orinda crowd has swamped the place and the regular trade of drug pushers and movie types is in danger of being squeezed out. . . .

"It is the best restaurant in the Bay Area. . . . Since my ratings include price in the judgment, a restaurant as expensive as Chez Panisse ($10 prix fixe) had better be extraordinary. . . . If an offering seems odd, as with the pig tails and ears last week, then we must assume that our sensibilities are still too limited." Scheer awarded the restaurant his highest rating, four stars.

Jeremiah took umbrage at a review that would surely have delighted any other chef, and on January 16, 1976, he wrote a letter to Scheer, reading in part:

*Overcoming a desire to demand a proxy apology for [the] clientele of
Chez Panisse who reside in Orinda (for since when has the resident area
of anyone been a civilized reason for public condemnation?), and rising
above a desire to punch you in the nose for describing in slanderous fashion*

the "expensive ($10)" Chez Panisse as a hangout for "drug pushers" (who
would probably feel the restaurant far too inexpensive) and movie types
(for greater artists than you, Mr. Scheer, like Nick Ray and Kenneth Anger,
the restaurant could never have been a haven were it at all expensive or
did they mind the "Orinda crowd"), yes, putting these desires aside, I would
prefer to point out that there is no greater bore than the offense of a snob
who is uninformed, uneducated and cannot walk the fine line between
rudeness and a well brought-up and healthy contempt.

Alice and Jeremiah in the fall of 1975 had hired a young Frenchman, Jean-Pierre Moullé, to serve as sous-chef. Jean-Pierre was lean and graceful, strikingly good-looking, with a strong-cheekboned facial structure, shaggy hair, a ready, roguish smile, and an unlimited store of charm. His manner was confident, but without arrogance. His formal French culinary training brought a new professionalism to the Chez Panisse kitchen. "Jeremiah was inspired, and he inspired me," says Jean-Pierre. "I was his tech support. He had no formal training, you know. To get from point A to point B or A to Z he was going zigzag. I said, 'Well, you can do it this way.' We worked well together."

Drugs and alcohol on the job were the curse of American restaurants in the 1970s and well into the 1980s. And while they made the late, long hours fun, they were a bad influence on the cooking. "I did enjoy it too," says Jean-Pierre. "I love Champagne. Cocaine, Jeremiah did a lot. I did it for a year or two, and then I quit, because when you get tired, you get more tired. It was bad. I remember once we were doing tastings and asking everyone 'Okay, who's going to taste the dish?'—because with cocaine, nobody could taste. And you're not hungry."

And so the Chez Panisse kitchen barreled along, heedless of burnout, heedless sometimes, too, of the dining room, where impatience, irritation, and disappointment were making themselves felt to Alice and the serving staff. "There was a lot of carousing in that kitchen," remembers Lindsey Shere. "And not even necessarily after hours. A lot of stuff went on in the kitchen even during service, a lot of drinking and arguing. Often there was a question about whose idea was whose. Jeremiah and Alice were definitely on a collision course."

Alice did not fire Jeremiah, but their relationship remained tense. In midwinter of 1976—not long after his intemperate letter to Bob Scheer—Jeremiah returned to France to join a gastronomic tour that Richard Olney was leading.

In Jeremiah's absence, Alice took over as chef. Two months later, when his money ran out, Jeremiah was ready to come home. Meanwhile, Willy Bishop had quit for good. "After it got written up," Willy says, "the food weenies came, the people with expectations and snobbery and criticism. After those reviews, the pressure just got to be too great. But it also brought an influx of new talent willing to work for nothing. Alice has always had a way of making people want to help her, do things for her."

Jeremiah returned from France with a host of new ideas. He proposed that Chez Panisse offer not one but four set menus every night, ranging from ten to twenty-five dollars a head. Since Jeremiah's advent in 1973, the former café upstairs had functioned as an extension of the main dining room on crowded evenings; now he wanted to establish a real café there, with its own full menu, simpler and cheaper than downstairs and offering a range of choices. Another inspiration from France was to offer a selection of special dishes that could be ordered a week in advance.

Alice's response to Jeremiah's café idea was that if guests were offered all that choice, the kitchen's focus would be diffused, and the unique identity of Chez Panisse would be at risk. She turned down all of his proposals flat, and stood ready for the consequences. Jeremiah decided he would finish out 1976 and leave.

While he remained, however, his ambitions continued to mount. He convinced the board of directors to raise the price of Friday and Saturday dinner from ten to twelve dollars. Though his departure was nine months away, he was already planning to go out in glory. At the beginning of March 1976, the restaurant posted this notice, in Jeremiah's unmistakable voice:

The last three weeks in March will celebrate a great master, a great pupil, and their followers. First, a week of Escoffier, who introduced the twentieth century to great French cooking and vice versa; followed by two weeks of menus devised for Chez Panisse by Richard

Olney, who renewed the passion and updated it. If the price for a particular dinner sometimes seems a bit stiff for the apparent humbleness of the ingredients, it is because of the immense care and labor involved. Following these three weeks, we will experiment with an à la carte grill-type menu and concept, emerging from Escoffier's innovations, so that the public may evaluate the two distinct styles.

And why did Alice, having already deflated Jeremiah's hopes for broadening the menu, ever allow the last statement to appear? "I guess he sort of sneaked it through," she says now. In any event, no "à la carte grill-type menu" ever came to pass.

The only change from the traditional set menu was a return to the *hors d'oeuvres variés* of the restaurant's earliest days. Jeremiah's versions, of course, were very different from the simple appetizers of 1971. On one menu he wrote, "The various hors d'oeuvres will include fish salads, mushroom brochettes, calves' brains vinaigrette, grilled kidneys with mustard, oysters sautéed in butter, duck livers, eggs with avocado, crab mayonnaise, and many others." He also provided diners with a densely typed page of Auguste Escoffier's culinary philosophy and a second page presenting capsule biographies of the legendary chefs Escoffier, Marie-Antoine Carême, Prosper Montagné, and Philéas Gilbert.

On April 1, 1976, Alice brought in an important late-night guest, Robert Finigan, the Bay Area's most authoritative restaurant critic. Finigan had been a classmate of Jeremiah's at Harvard, though they had not met there. He had bought *Jack Shelton's Private Guide to Restaurants* and had kept the name, though it was now Bob Finigan who wrote the reviews. By the time Alice and Bob and two others arrived, that evening's main course, roast leg of lamb, was down to three decent servings and a few trimmings that Jeremiah remembers as "some crisp bits that were delicious but totally unpresentable to paying customers." Jeremiah sent the waiter to ask if steaks would be okay. No. Alice had promised Bob Finigan lamb.

"I was entertaining three guests on this occasion, and their three portions were picture-book perfect slices of rosy meat," wrote Finigan in his newsletter of May 1976. "But mine had been assembled from inordinately gristly pieces hacked inexpertly from the leg. I quietly instructed the waiter to ask the chef for more appetizing slices. He was back in moments, the same plate in hand. 'The chef says, "Tough s——,"' he announced."

As occasionally happened at Chez Panisse, the waiter was just a friend of somebody's, not a pro at all, and it had not occurred to him that you shouldn't pass along remarks from the chef such as "tough shit" to a customer, especially if (a) he was a restaurant critic, and (b) Alice was at the table.

Finigan reported the incident, but his review ended, astonishingly, with this: "When I reflect on the pressures that weigh on Chez Panisse, I am amazed not that it stumbles occasionally but that it does not stumble more often. . . . The Chez Panisse experiment must be judged overall a resounding success."

A number of the faithful regulars of Chez Panisse who had predated Jeremiah had been gradually falling away throughout his four years there. His food struck many of them as fussy, overbearing, and excessively formal, and it seemed to them to be getting more so. Because of its growing fame, the restaurant continued to do good business, but many of the customers now were tourists, and many of them were more demanding than the local regulars, colder, sometimes even rude. The jovial egalitarianism, the camaraderie between staff and clientele that had defined Chez Panisse as much as its exquisite food, had deteriorated badly, and the mood of the staff was darkening. The longtime waiter Steve Crumley, for example, had taken to calling Jeremiah by Benito Mussolini's self-bestowed sobriquet— "Duce." (Others, apropos of Jeremiah's lofty, sometimes prissy manner, called him the queen of England. For the restaurant itself, one wag coined the nickname Cheese Penis, which was quite popular for a while behind the scenes.)

Despite the discontent among the staff, the food had never been better. Somebody with a better head for business, thought Alice, might be able to make good money here. Chez Panisse was not yet five years old, but Alice was sick of the whole thing—the arguments, the lame-brained new clientele, the eroding spirit of the place. She conferred with the other directors—Jerry Budrick (still her boyfriend as well), Tom Guernsey, Charles and Lindsey Shere, and Jeremiah—but they could not come to an agreement. Eventually, however, Alice prevailed. She wanted to sell the place and get out.

On May 26, 1976, the *San Francisco Chronicle* reported rather quietly that Chez Panisse was for sale. The price was half a million dollars, not including the services of either Jeremiah Tower or Alice Waters.

And yet, such now was the restaurant's reputation that Jean Troisgros— co-owner, with his brother Pierre, of the Restaurant Troisgros in Roanne, one of the best restaurants in the world—asked if his nephew Michel might come to work in the kitchen at Chez Panisse. In *California Dish,* Jeremiah wrote, "I said to Michel, 'I should be studying under you.' And he said, 'Oh no, no, no, no. You've got it the wrong way around, because . . .' you know, because I didn't know any of the bad habits of the French." With Fritz Streiff and Jean-Pierre Moullé already there, the majority of the *brigade de cuisine* would now be French or French-trained, just at the moment when Chez Panisse had begun in earnest to Americanize its food.

It was typical of Chez Panisse that French and American influences would first oppose each other and then find a creative mutual accommodation. Jeremiah had been inspired by the Four Seasons restaurant in New York, the first fine-dining establishment since the nineteenth century to elevate American food and wine to parity with French, and Alice and Jeremiah were still seeking out more and better sources of local fruit, vegetables, and seafood. (Meat was still a problem, the wholesale market at that time being under the near-total control of the big national packing houses.) Spurning the American bicentennial, over which the rest of the country was making such a fuss, Chez Panisse decided that its next special dinner would be—very Berkeley—in honor of Bastille Day, the French equivalent of the Fourth of July. Every course would be based on garlic—a notion that would have repelled any French chef or gastronome. Only Americans would propose such a menu as that served at Chez Panisse on July 14, 1976.

Champignons à l'ail aux feuilles de vignes
(whole garlic and mushrooms baked with olive oil in grape leaves)
❦

Purée d'ail rôti, cuisse de poulet
(roast garlic puréed and served with baked chicken legs)
❦

Aïoli aux haricots verts et pommes de terre
(garlic mayonnaise served with green beans
and little red boiled potatoes)
❦

Nouilles fraîches, sauce pistou
(fresh pasta served with a paste of garlic, basil, pine nuts,
olive oil, and parmesan cheese)
❦

Tripes au pistou
(beef tripe with basil and garlic)
❦

Bourride aux tomates
(fresh fish poached in a fish stock with tomatoes,
with garlic mayonnaise thinned with the broth)
❦

Gigot rôti, sauce à l'ail saintongeoise
(leg of lamb marinated with garlic and wine, stuffed with
prosciutto, and served with a sauce with mint,
garlic, and wine that's simmered for hours)
❦

Purée de pommes de terre à l'ail
(potato purée with garlic-infused cream)
❦

Figues, fromage blanc, et miel à l'ail
(fresh figs, white cheese, and garlic honey)
❦

$15

It was a roaring success, to return by popular demand every summer thenceforward.

THERE HAS BEEN a sort of manic-depressive oscillation throughout the history of Chez Panisse, and despite reviews, new and unpopular customers, and never-ending staff conflicts, the *famille Panisse* was recovering its *joie de vivre*. Through the summer and into the fall of 1976, the dance of French and American influences went on. Chez Panisse continued to serve French dishes with French names, but increasingly derived inspiration not from Alice's and Jeremiah's forays into obscure old cookbooks but directly from the bounty of northern California's soil and waters. In August, when summer squash, green beans, basil, eggplant, and tomatoes were coming in, the accent was French, but the language was American.

"We were doing some of the simplest food we'd ever done, and I loved it," Alice says. "And the customers loved it. We had tomato soup with

David Stewart, a waiter since the earliest days
of Chez Panisse, and Alice

basil. Beet and red onion salad. Fresh pea soup. Steamed clams. Roast duck with bacon and onions. Salmon with beurre blanc. Virginia ham, all by itself on the plate. Vegetable salads. Avocado with walnut oil and lemon juice. Chocolate cake with ice cream."

Alice had always preferred local food sources, but Jeremiah's extravagant creations had sometimes required long-distance importation. With the new simplicity, however, both Alice and Jeremiah were discovering local resources much finer than what had been available to them just a few years before. "We were really foraging, and finding the most wonderful things," remembers Alice. "Crayfish raised in California. Wild salmon that was caught just outside the Golden Gate. People gathered wild mushrooms for us, and we just grilled them wrapped in grape leaves—Napa grape leaves. We were getting our oysters from Tomales Bay [just north of San Francisco]. More and more of what came out of that kitchen was about the fruits and vegetables that grew within just a few miles of the restaurant. Avocados, peaches, watercress, peppers, beans. We got rabbits from Amador County, squab from Sonoma, live trout from Big Sur. This was when the farmers' markets were springing up all over the place, and we got such beautiful things from them that we barely had to touch them."

From that summer of 1976 on, farmers' markets would be a fundamental element in not only the food but also the philosophy of Chez Panisse. The markets connected the cooks directly to the land. Alice's description of putting together a typical salad from the market demonstrates how ingredient-driven her culinary creativity had become.

· FARMERS' MARKET SALAD ·

I start by looking for really good textures and colors. In spring, I'm certainly going to have radishes in the salad, either shaved or quartered, and I'm going to have all those little spring greens. I'll get them from different vendors, from whoever has the best little wild rocket or whatever. I love those tiny little onions in the spring that are so small they're almost like a little chive. I'll put those in whole. The radishes can go that way when they're tiny as well. Fennel for sure. I love fennel in salad. You can chop up the little fennel leaves—they're beautiful when they're just new. And I like mustard flowers as a garnish. I might get farm eggs and put in some hard-boiled eggs that are halved.

Hard-boiled eggs are wonderful when they're really done right. I bring the water to a boil, and then I put in the eggs. And then I boil them for—well, it depends on the size of the egg—maybe eight minutes. The way I tell that they're done is I take an egg out of the pot and I'll just crack the shell slightly and press, and you can just tell. If it's too soft, you put it back in again. Just firm, and you know that it's done, and you rinse it in cold water.

I've had raw asparagus in a salad like that, but for vegetables, usually I'll make a plate that is more of a spring aïoli plate. I'll cook asparagus and artichokes and potatoes and carrots and fennel, and then make some green garlic aïoli with it. I crush the green garlic—the green and the white parts both—in a mortar, and then blend that into a homemade mayonnaise. Little piles of each of the vegetables, separate, not seasoned—dead plain. It's a beautiful lunch. It's my favorite lunch to make for friends—some variation of vegetables with either vinaigrette or an aïoli, and maybe with a tapenade and some toast.

For any salad greens, you're looking for the ones that have just been picked. Ones that have an aliveness about them. Ones that don't have any little discolored ends. I don't mind the ones that have a little dirt on them because they just came out of the field. They didn't even have time to wash them. You'd be surprised where you can find greens like that. If I lived on the Upper West Side of Manhattan, I would make friends right away with a gardener who was part of one of those community gardens.

The restaurant's fifth birthday, August 28, 1976, featured "oysters, roast pig, composed salads, pasta, our own pastry and ice cream, and other gastronomic treats; the Louisiana Playboys and late-night jazz perhaps; the Marcel Pagnol movies *Marius, Fanny,* and *César;* a new poster by David Lance Goines; et cetera." David's poster proclaimed "Fifth Birthday Celebration," in English, but the specially printed menu, also designed by David, was headlined with the ominous French words *dernier anniversaire*—"last birthday." It wasn't a joke.

The restaurant may have recovered its spirit, but Alice had not recovered hers. "I was just fed up," she recalls. "These new customers, if they decided not to go, they'd just not go—and not call. Of course that was costing us money. What was worse was the wasted food. Seeing our beautiful food go into the garbage! And empty tables—we weren't used to that at all. There's a particular feeling when everybody's in there together, and a big empty table absolutely spoils that."

As the far horizon of Jeremiah's tenure came into view, and with buyers bearing half-million-dollar checks so far nonexistent, Chez Panisse found itself in an identity crisis. Even if Jeremiah had been going to stay, it's doubtful how much longer the restaurant could have endured as a living museum of bygone French cookery, or as a madcap laboratory of surrealism, experiment, and irony. "We'd been the obstreperous teenager about long enough," says Alice. "It was getting time to try to grow up a little.

"One of the ways we were doing that was by simplifying, and by focusing more and more on what was local. We had a stronger sense of who we really were as a restaurant. We did a special dinner that fall that really showed what we were about. Looking back now, I can see that that was when our style was really finding itself. This could be a menu from last week as easily as thirty years ago." There was nothing clever about the title, nothing fancy about the food. The menu was all in the plainest of English—"and all Jeremiah's," says Alice.

NORTHERN CALIFORNIA REGIONAL DINNER
October 7, 1976

Spenger's Tomales Bay bluepoint oysters on ice

❧

Cream of fresh corn soup, Mendocino style, with crayfish butter

❧

*Big Sur Garrapata Creek smoked trout steamed
over California bay leaves*

❧

Monterey Bay prawns sautéed with garlic, parsley, and butter

❧

Preserved California-grown geese from Sebastopol

❧

Vella dry Monterey Jack cheese from Sonoma

❧

Fresh caramelized figs

❧

*Walnuts, almonds, and mountain pears from the
San Francisco Farmers' Market*

❧

$20.00

❧

WINES OFFERED BY THE GLASS $1.50
Schramsberg Cuvée de Gamay 1973
Mount Eden Chardonnay 1973
Beaulieu Cabernet Private Reserve 1970

Ridge Zinfandel, Fiddletown 1974
Mission del Sol, Harbor Winery 1974
Tawny Port, East Side Winery

Twenty dollars for dinner was expensive—sixty-nine of today's dollars—though certainly not unreasonable, considering the number of courses. But those $1.50 glasses of wine, adjusted for inflation, would be only $5.00 apiece today, and they came from some of California's finest bottlings. A bottle of six-year-old Beaulieu Cabernet Sauvignon Private Reserve, for example, now goes for about $80.00 retail. Restaurants typically price wine by the bottle at about twice retail, so the Beaulieu on a wine list would sell for $160.00. With wine by the glass, however, restaurants typically count on just four glasses per bottle, to allow for spillage, some spoilage, etc.—and they will price it at about two and a half times retail. Thus the Beaulieu Cabernet goes up to $200.00, which divided by four comes to $50.00 a glass!

Between 1976 and 2006, the real, inflation-adjusted price of dinner at Chez Panisse has slightly more than doubled. In the same period, that Beaulieu Cabernet Sauvignon Private Reserve has increased in price by a thousand percent, and other premium wines have risen comparably. The great Yquem dinner could not be repeated today except at exorbitant cost. Wine at Chez Panisse in 1976 was seen as one component of several that made up a nice meal, as Europeans have seen it for centuries. Rare now, however, is the high-end restaurant with more than a handful of bottles on its list selling for less than a main course, and affluent diners-out not infrequently spend as much on wine as on the entire rest of the meal.

AFTER A RESTAURANT gets rave reviews, there is usually a burst of demand, and then it slowly dies down as the many who chase the latest thing find the latest thing elsewhere. But that didn't happen at Chez Panisse. A full year after the reviews in *Gourmet* and the *San Francisco Chronicle,* the phones were still ringing all day. People were making reservations weeks in advance. The old-time regulars couldn't get a table unless they called Alice directly. "We thought for a while that perhaps we should close," Alice told *New West* magazine. "I just don't know how to express how torn we felt about the reviews, particularly the one in *Gourmet*. In a way, the review told us that this is the time to re-evaluate the way we see Chez Panisse."[1]

At Tom Guernsey's Sunday brunch, for which reservations were not taken, there were lines down the stairs, out the door, and along Shattuck Avenue, and the kitchen couldn't keep up. "One Sunday," says Alice, "I looked at Tom and asked, 'Do you want to do this?'"

"No," replied Tom.

"Well, neither do I."

And that was that. On October 12, 1976, the menu bore this note:

Two of the finest services we have provided for our amiable clientele have been our Sunday brunches and weekday coffee and croissant breakfasts. Therefore, it is with deep regret that we announce that, due to the impossibility of finding permanent employees in Berkeley who rise early and smilingly, we will not open until 11:30 a.m. from Tuesday through Saturday, and not at all on Sunday.

Tom was by now the de facto general manager of Chez Panisse, and everybody on the staff, including Alice, counted on his steadiness, his impeccable taste, and his ability to do any task the restaurant might require. Sometimes, nostalgic for Tom's brunches, Alice would implore him to make her one of his omelets. "Tom made the most perfect omelets," she says. "I'll never forget his *omelette aux fines herbes*."

· TOM GUERNSEY'S OMELETTE AUX FINES HERBES ·

First you break three eggs into a café au lait bowl. He always used a café au lait bowl. You take a fork and stir the eggs around—not too much, but a little, so you can still see separate white and yolk. Stripes. Salt and pepper. You take one nice tablespoon of sweet butter—we used an iron pan, very seasoned—and swirl it around, over medium heat. Just at the moment when it began to sizzle, he would pour in the eggs. He would move very quickly, with a wooden spoon, moving the sides in and swirling it all around. And in a minute, not even a minute, he would flip it, and then on go the fines herbes—tarragon, chervil, parsley, chives. Then he would roll it out of the pan and fold it over. He'd put just a dollop of ever-so-slightly-whisked crème fraîche on it, and sprinkle that with fines herbes all over. Sometimes he'd rub down the top with a little butter.

Sometimes we would use the recipe from *The Auberge of the Flowering Hearth.* He loved that cookbook, and so did I. He would melt sorrel and put that in the middle, and roll it out of the pan so the sorrel would be on the inside. And then he made a little whipped cream with salt and pepper and a splash of Armagnac.

There's a dramatic difference in the taste when you use good eggs, no more than a couple of days old. And it's important that the butter be sweet, not a little sour as it can get so quickly.

What to drink depends on what's inside. I like those Friulian whites. I suppose if I had something that felt very Provençal, I wouldn't mind drinking a little Bandol rosé. But then I drink Bandol rosé with just about everything. What doesn't go with Bandol rosé?

We also do scrambled eggs at the restaurant with black truffles. We truffle the eggs the day before. That is, you store the whole raw eggs buried in the truffles, so the eggs taste like truffles to begin with. Then we chop the truffles very fine and mix them in with the eggs before we cook them. We serve them with very thinly sliced *levain* bread that's grilled and then rubbed with just a hint of garlic. And a little, very wintry mesclun salad on the side.

As Jeremiah's last weeks passed, he seemed to be summing up his four years at Chez Panisse. He honored the classics: *saucisson à l'ail en brioche* (garlic sausage cooked in pastry with a butter sauce), *cotriade* (effortfully explained as "fresh fish cooked with onions and white wine in a Brittany-style bouillabaisse"), *gigot rôti, sauce madère* (roast leg of lamb with Madeira sauce). He also tipped his hat to the nouvelle cuisine, with *boeuf mariné aux kakis et aux kiwis* (beef marinated in olive oil with green peppercorns, served with persimmons and kiwifruit—the latter just beginning to be known in America), *soupe de courge Paul Bocuse* (Paul Bocuse's pumpkin soup), *truite farcie Georges Garin* (trout stuffed with a truffled sole mousseline and poached in butter), and in tribute to the *cuisine minceur* of Michel Guérard, *gigot de poulette cuit à la vapeur de marjolaine* (described on the menu as "a seemingly simple but actually complex dish of chicken drumsticks stuffed with morels, sweetbreads, and mushrooms, with a garnish of celery"). He also continued to pay homage to Alice's emergent California classicism—cold Dungeness crab with an herb mayonnaise, sautéed Monterey Bay prawns with warm fennel salad, local oysters on the half shell.

On December 31, 1976, the last meal Jeremiah Tower was to present at Chez Panisse—or so he thought at the time—was remarkably restrained. No jokes, no *tours de force* or *de folie*, (except perhaps Lindsey's *croquembouche*), just pure elegance. The menu was printed only in French, but Jeremiah translates it as below in *California Dish*.

Soupe aux truffes, Paul Bocuse
(Paul Bocuse's truffle soup, which he did for the president
of France at the Élysée Palace)

❧

Cailles rôties au vert-pré
(roast fresh quail on a bed of watercress)

❧

Fromages
(California cheeses)

❧

Croquembouche
("one- and two-foot towers of pastry-cream-filled profiteroles
stuck together with hot caramel," in Jeremiah's description,
"[the] most festive of French desserts")

❧

Gâteau au chocolat, glace au nougat
(chocolate cake with nougat ice cream)

❧

Bonbons

❧

$25.00

Jeremiah and Alice, in a tempestuous four years, had created unique combinations of ambition and simplicity, of worldliness and hominess, and of old and new. Those qualities had become, and today remain, the foundations of the Chez Panisse style.

With the end of 1976, there having been no takers in the seven months it had been on the market, Chez Panisse was no longer for sale. And the era of Jeremiah Tower had come to a close.

8.

ENNUI AND
INSPIRATION

1977–1978

In January 1977, Alice Waters for the first time assumed the title of chef of Chez Panisse. Jeremiah's departure and her own taking sole charge reinvigorated Alice. She was full of ideas, and her sous-chef, Jean-Pierre Moullé, consummately professional, could cook anything she could imagine. Together they hired Mark Miller, a superlative cook who, when he left Chez Panisse, would follow a pattern that became typical of its alumni: opening their own restaurants, sometimes in multiples, all of them taking something from the Chez Panisse spirit, but none of them entering fully into it. Only one of them—Sally Clarke, in her eponymous London restaurant—has yet dared a no-choice menu. No one cares as little about profit as Alice. Mark Miller found fame first with the Santa Fe Bar and Grill in Berkeley and later the Coyote Café in Santa Fe, New Mexico. Miller also owns restaurants in Washington, D.C., and Sydney, Australia, and is the author of ten cookbooks. Meanwhile, Alice has continued to operate the one restaurant in the rambling old house in Berkeley. Jean-Pierre has come and gone, but he has run the kitchen at Chez Panisse longer than anyone else.

"Ah, Jean-Pierre," Alice says with a sigh. "When I worked well with him was when I was doing the menus and he was helping me execute them. That was divine. That's how we started out. We worked together. I did one course, he did one course. I would put things on the menu that I knew he did really well, and he would love that. And he did those just the way or better than I would have done them. It was a great arrangement."

It was not a stable one, however. "Just like Alice was in love with Jeremiah, in a strange way, before," says Jean-Pierre, "then it was the same thing for me. She was in love with everyone who was really interesting. She had passion for people because they had something, skills, whatever. The main thing is, I was striving for recognition, because I was running that kitchen. Even if she said no, I know I was running that kitchen.

"I am a little responsible for a lot of the mess, because I was chasing girls. You know, I am French. Actually, the girls were chasing me. The first six months I was here, I would go to a party, and girls would come to me. I couldn't believe it. I messed up a lot of things in the restaurant. Starting to go out with the flower lady, going out with the waitresses. Alice didn't like it."

Beginning on June 28, 1977, the menus at Chez Panisse were no longer bilingual. Only such untranslatable items as bouillabaisse were listed in French. "When the menu went into English," says Jean-Pierre, "I think it was for Alice a period of anti-French, because of me first, and because of a lot of things. We had fights about everything."

"He was wonderful as a right arm, and more than a right arm," Alice says. "But then he wanted to be in charge, and he just didn't have the personality to do that. What he lacked—it was certainly management skills, and it certainly was communicating with me. And culinary vision. He was a great cook, but I thought the things he chose were not necessarily the things that he did best. We just had a hard time."

Meanwhile, Jeremiah Tower was finding it more difficult to tear himself away than he had foreseen. Saturday afternoons into April 1977, he gave cooking lessons in the Chez Panisse kitchen. Alice and Jean-Pierre did turn out occasional special meals—suckling pig roasted outside on the sidewalk for Jerry Budrick's birthday in February 1977; a Richard Olney menu in March featuring the great Burgundies of the Clos de Bèze; another Gertrude Stein birthday party, with a menu much subdued from the wacky version of three years back; a sixtieth-birthday lunch for the composer Lou Harrison—but Alice's focus was less now on the celebratory event and more on refining her own cooking style and seeking out ingredients of ever higher quality. "If only a few people can taste the difference, that's enough," she said.

Jerry Budrick had bought 160 acres in Amador County, in the foothills of the Sierra Nevada, and there he and Alice planned a one-acre garden to produce the hot-weather crops that the backyard gardens of Berkeley and the farms of Marin and Sonoma counties were too cool to grow. It was going to be totally organic, a concept well known to hippies and vegetarians but at that time completely ignored by high-end restaurants. What organic produce there was to be had was usually tired, bruised, and old, sold in "health food" stores reeking of brewer's yeast and dietary supplement pills. "My idea of organic was to grow everything so, so carefully," Alice says, "pulling off the bugs by hand if you had to, and bringing the food to the restaurant so fresh it was really still alive. That's what distinguishes a great salad from a good one—a great one is alive."

The Amador garden, at first, was a delight. In June 1977, Alice featured a week of menus titled SPECIAL SALADS FROM OUR GARDEN— "summer salad of fresh crab with grapefruit slices, green and white asparagus, and baby oak leaf lettuces," "fresh salmon mousse surrounded by vegetable salads," "Richard Olney's salad of various lettuces, hyssop flowers, nasturtiums, garlic, shallots, and various fresh herbs." But the delight didn't last. "That garden was a disaster," Alice confesses. "We paid a farmer and bought the seeds and really thought something was going to grow, but the gophers got there first."

That July, the Bastille Day dinner became a weeklong festival of garlic-based dinners—culminating in "roast suckling pig from garlic-fed sows from the Dal Porto Ranch in Amador County." Giving credit to the grower in this fashion came naturally to Alice. Over the ensuing years,

Alice, 1977

a bastardized version of the practice would spread across America, with dubious statements of geographic origin ("Hudson Valley apples") or virtually meaningless descriptions ("fire-roasted") giving a little tweak of borrowed prestige to tired menus. "They didn't understand," says Alice. "All we were doing was recognizing our friends for doing good work."

ALICE, for whom extended stays in the kitchen were exhausting, needed a vacation—a good, long, proper European holiday. The last dinner of the summer of 1977, including a rather daring lamb's brain salad, was served on August 27. The next day was the restaurant's sixth birthday, but it was a Sunday and there was no party. Instead, there was to be an enforced vacation, for everybody. Alice shut down Chez Panisse altogether, and the restaurant stayed closed till the end of September. "I went to see Claude and Martine Labro in Vence," she recalls, "and then all of us descended on the Domaine Tempier. Jerry came over to join us. He loved that Bandol wine. Looking back now, I see just one endless meal, outside, under the arbor, with Lulu producing the most beautiful things, dish after dish after dish. She'd always go to the docks in the early, early morning, right when the fishing boats were coming in, so she'd get the widest choice and the freshest fish. They make some very serious wines at Tempier, these noble old reds, but it was hot that September and I think only of that cool, pink, wonderful Bandol rosé."

Alice and Martine traveled a long, zigzag route to sample the newest French cooking. Alice did not relax, exactly—Alice does not relax—but, "Oh, it was a recharge, and I was so happy to be with those friends. They seem to know so much, just instinctively, about how to live, how to be happy. My French was not very good, and Lulu's English is nonexistent, but we would talk for hours. There's a special happiness that I feel only with Lulu, I think. And then with Lulu's food, well, it was paradise."

"Of course, I did have to come home. But when I came back, I didn't want to be in the kitchen anymore." Ever social, she wanted to be back among the customers. She loved to see their reactions to the food, and she drew inspiration from their enthusiasms. When a particular dish was a big hit, she would dream up variations for Jean-Pierre and his brigade to try.

Starting in January 1978, therefore, Jean-Pierre would function as chef, while Alice, though overseeing the front of the house, retained the title. Jean-Pierre was annoyed, but he stuck to his stoves. This was an early instance of a phenomenon of which many observers and former staff members of Chez Panisse have complained over the years: Alice taking credit that others think she should have shared. "History," Charles Shere observes, "is littered with the bodies of men who feel they should have gotten more of the credit than Alice."

"I've thought about this issue a lot," says Greil Marcus. "I don't think Alice would be the focus that she is if she didn't enjoy it, if that wasn't important to her. There are many ways to avoid attention. On the other hand, Chez Panisse is Alice's idea. It's Alice's values. It's Alice's standards.

To the degree that it falls short, it's because her ideas and her standards are not being met. I've said for years that if she were hit by a bus, the restaurant would close. I don't think it would sustain itself. When Alice is in Berkeley, she is at the restaurant all the time, and there is never anything that is right. She is always finding fault, whether it's with service, or food preparation, or ingredients, or the way something is cooked. That's because she has a clear idea about every aspect of what the restaurant is. And nobody else does. Nobody else has the complexity of vision that she does."

"I try to give credit where it's due," Alice says, "and I know sometimes I've failed. It's hard to be successful and not have some people be upset with you."

GRILLING HAD BEEN part of the Chez Panisse style almost since the beginning, but in the early days it was improvisational at best—a home barbecue in the backyard, or sometimes on the front sidewalk, and then a fireplace indoors with a spit that never worked properly. In January 1978, however, the restaurant closed for two weeks for the installation in the downstairs kitchen of a massive wood-burning oven and grill. "It was an inspiration from Lulu," Alice says. "Also from the Royal Pavilion at Brighton, though scaled down a little bit." When the restaurant reopened on January 13, 1978, Alice wrote at the bottom of the menu, "This weekend begins a new era in culinary possibilities for us all."

Though its finances remained chaotic and profit elusive, Chez Panisse was becoming more and more a "destination restaurant." Many people came expecting perfection—something Chez Panisse, for all its skills, rarely achieved. When so many customers will never be seen again, as was the case with the many tourists determined to eat at the great Chez Panisse just once in their lives, staffs are tempted to treat them less well than the regulars who are the true source of life for a restaurant.

In France, under the stern eye of the red-covered *Guide Michelin,* the few restaurants accorded the ultimate rating of three stars must maintain not only the highest culinary standards but the warmest of hospitality.

There was no Michelin red guide, however, for the United States, and a certain arrogance was creeping in at Chez Panisse.

The columnist Herb Caen, in the *San Francisco Chronicle* of February 18, 1978, reported an example of the decline of civility among both the clients and the staff:

> Imagine Betty Friedan, the great Fem-Libber, trying to pull rank on a sister! At crowded Chez Panisse in Berkeley Fri. night, she swept in without a reservation and demanded a table. Told she'd have to wait, she snapped at the hostess, "Look, I'm Betty Friedan!" "Uh-huh," replied the hostess, "and I'm Suzy Nelson." La Friedan stomped out.

A story often ruefully repeated concerns Jerry Budrick, who in his capacity as headwaiter sometimes greeted arriving diners. A couple approached whose appearance, for some reason, he didn't like, and he met them not with welcome but with a stream of cigarette smoke, straight into their faces.

"Jerry Budrick would always correct my French pronunciation," recalls Tom Guernsey's former wife, Nancy Donnell Lily. "He let you know how he felt about you. Not always in a gracious way—that's one way of putting it."

"We were all drinking too much," says Alice. "Especially Jerry." Jerry still considered himself to be Alice's lover, and she did not deny his claim, but the distance between them was clearly growing.

Jim Maser was married to Alice's sister Laura; both of them were very close to Alice and Chez Panisse. Jim recalls, "I went to Alice, and I said, 'Alice, how can you have this person represent you? He is so arrogant.' And she said to me, 'Well, you need to have a little bit of attitude to deal with the public.'"

"On the other hand," says Greil Marcus, "Jerry was also an enormous asset to the restaurant. He was the first person we ever knew who considered being a waiter a profession. Jerry was a fantastic presence in the dining room, and tremendously knowledgeable. He demanded respect from the customers without placing a little card on the table at the beginning of the meal saying, 'I want your respect.' Just through his manner."

"The restaurant really was a club," Ruth Reichl recalls, "and until Alice became a friend, the food was wonderful, but it was very awkward. You always felt like you were nobody. It wasn't being put in Siberia so much as I'm sure what people still feel today, which is that eighty percent of the people in the room belong to a club that you're not part of. I remember the first time after I'd gotten to know Alice, Doug and I went to the restaurant as insiders, and it was so much a better experience. It was a feeling of, Oh, now we really live in Berkeley. And we'd lived in Berkeley for about eight years."

Drinking on duty by too many of the staff was still a problem, as was the restaurant's eternally miserable financial management. But the food was as fine as ever, and again it was evolving. With Jean-Pierre in command of the kitchen, and as a result of Alice's long tour of France, Chez Panisse was becoming more French again. Though there still were California flourishes, and the menus continued to be printed only in English, there is no mistaking the French provenance of asparagus with hollandaise sauce in puff-pastry cups; Gruyère soufflé; truffled saddle of lamb; *pot-au-feu Dodin-Bouffant,* described on the menu as "an elaborate recipe from Maxim's restaurant made with larded beef, marrow bones, chicken, pork, and veal sausage with herbs, veal knuckles cooked in Burgundy wine with vegetables and garnished with duck livers." In March 1978, there was a week of specialties of the Languedoc, followed by a week and a half of dishes from the Restaurant Troisgros. Then suddenly the menus were bilingual again—French first, followed by the English translation.

For the in crowd there were parties galore—birthdays, wedding receptions, and anniversaries, each honored with a special menu. For David Goines's birthday, every table in the restaurant got a free bottle of zinfandel in his honor, and the menu—in tribute to David's scholarship in the classics—quoted the Roman poet Marcus Argentarius:

Welcome, old friend, long-necked bottle,
Dearest companion of my table

And of the wine-jar, with your soft gurgle
And your sweetly chuckling mouth: welcome;
You secret witness of my poverty
(Which you've done little enough to aid),
At last I hold you in my hand again.
But I wish you had come to me undiluted,
Pure as a virgin to her bridegroom's bed.

"In those days," says David, "there was a very strong sense of community and involvement. People would come by and shell peas and talk. When it was decided that the restaurant needed a wine cellar, I dug it with my own two hands. When garlic week came around, people would come by and peel garlic and drink wine. They'd be there for three or four days, peeling garlic and talking."

A good example of how welcoming Chez Panisse could be in the late seventies, despite its occasional bad behavior toward people it disdained, is the story of a Stanford University art-history major named Judy Rodgers. Judy had spent her senior year in high school at the home of Jean Troisgros, spending every possible moment in the Troisgros restaurant's kitchen and taking copious notes, which she brought with her when she went to celebrate her twenty-first birthday at Chez Panisse in the fall of 1977. "I showed Alice my Troisgros recipes that night," Judy recalls.

We only talked a little, but I told her that I was bereft, ever since leaving Troisgros. I said, "I'd love to just come and occasionally spend a day in your kitchen, just watching." Alice was keen on that and said yes. We kind of negotiated—no, we didn't negotiate, it wasn't a negotiation. You don't negotiate with Alice. Nothing happens like that. It's always seduction.

At that time, Alice was alone doing Saturday lunch. She proposed that I just come up and help with that, and I was thrilled. So I would drive up each Saturday morning from Palo Alto and put together the lunch at Chez Panisse. We'd always have a soup and salad combo. We always had smoked trout from Garrapata, with different flavored mayonnaise every week. My job was just doing slight variations week after week. I had to make a soup every week, always a puréed vegetable cream soup. After just a couple of weeks, Alice trusted me to do it on my own—that's one of her characteristics, to trust people. She's less worried if you don't have the competence if your heart is in the right place and you're shooting for the right aesthetic. I got in over my head, as did Chez Panisse constantly. I'd never lit a fire in a grill in my life.

Then at some point Alice proposed to me that I actually become the lunch chef. I was blown away. I was twenty-one years old. So I signed on to cook lunch during spring break. After the first two days, Alice wasn't even there, and I was in my own little world in that kitchen. Every Saturday I'd look at the prior week's menus, and Alice would talk to me about making decisions. We'd go over to the Co-op and buy some chickens, and she'd show me how to cut them in half. Sometimes she'd talk me through what to do over the phone.

I don't think anybody would pretend that everything produced by that restaurant was stellar, three-star cuisine every day. What people loved about Chez Panisse was the generosity, the spirit. It was the same thing I'd seen at Troisgros. There was so much given to you, whether it was an idea of a dish, the conception of a menu— a sequenced meal that you couldn't quite understand why it was so satisfying. That meal made you happy the way great home cooking did. It reminded me of the meals that my aunts in France made, who would uncannily fashion these simple little meals out of almost nothing—a salad with a few chopped-up hard-cooked eggs that had never been in the refrigerator, so they were warm and tender and fragrant. And a few nice seasonal walnuts with a drop of walnut oil. Alice did that same kind of thing.

Judy Rodgers would go on to her own renown as chef and co-owner of the Zuni Café. Zuni is the closest thing San Francisco has to Chez Panisse—the food is straightforward, elegant, informal, and delicious— and it's often referred to as the city's favorite restaurant.

Though modest in manner, Alice had begun to recognize her kinship with the other most celebrated people in the food world. When they came to Chez Panisse, she went all out. A good example is this seventieth-birthday menu, served on July 25, 1978, for the food writer M. F. K. Fisher, manifesting the synthesis of French and Californian cooking that the writer idealized. The titles are those of four of her books.

SERVE IT FORTH!

CONSIDER THE OYSTER
Pacific oysters served on the half shell
Billecart-Salmon Champagne

❦

MARSEILLES, A CONSIDERABLE TOWN
Fresh California snails with Pernod, tomatoes, and garlic
Bandol rosé, Domaine Tempier

❦

*Whole Pacific rockfish charcoal-grilled
with wild herbs and anchovies*
Crozes-Hermitage blanc, Bruno Thierry

❦

Young spit-roasted pheasant with new potatoes
Côte Rôtie, Bruno Thierry

❦

Bitter lettuce salad with goat cheese croutons
Bandol rouge, Domaine Tempier

❦

Three plum sherbets with orange rind boats

❦

A CORDIALL WATER
Muscat de Beaumes de Venise, Bruno Thierry

❦

Coffee & candies

At Christmastime 1977, Alice had said she didn't want to be in the kitchen anymore. A year and a half later, she wanted to be away from Chez Panisse altogether. Amid the unhappy Jean-Pierre, an intemperate dining-room staff, and her less and less familiar public, Alice was yearning again for Europe and its civilized ways. "I really needed to get out," she says. "I wanted four months. I wanted to taste, travel, take it all in, and just be away. I was uneasy leaving the restaurant for so long, but that didn't stop me. I'd been to a lot of wonderful places, but there were still so many more. So I asked Marion and Cecilia if they wanted to go."

Marion Cunningham was an early devotee of Chez Panisse who had gone on to be James Beard's personal assistant and had just finished a massive revision of the classic *Fannie Farmer Cookbook*. Having tested some seventeen hundred recipes ("Even my neighbor's dog got fat," she recalls), Marion was ready to eat somebody else's cooking for a while. Cecilia Chiang was the proprietress of one of America's first luxurious Chinese restaurants, The Mandarin, in San Francisco.

Alice, Marion, and Cecilia all agreed that it would be fun to ask Jeremiah Tower—bored stiff in the lonely wilds of Big Sur—to squire the three ladies to the greatest restaurants on the Continent. He was delighted to accept.

Then Jeremiah's mother died suddenly, and he had to drop out. Alice asked if he would like to come back to the old stand for the rest of the year. He said he would, and once more Jean-Pierre was pushed into the background at Chez Panisse.

For two weeks in September 1978, Alice, Marion, and Cecilia dined in a number of the best restaurants in Europe, often two a day. Starting in Brussels, they went to Comme Chez Soi, Galalou, The Crown, Witamers Bakery, and Ming's. In Paris, they took in Jacques Manière's Dodin-Bouffant (the successor to Au Pactole); the famed ice cream maker Berthillon; the elegant Quai d'Orsay; the very old and classicist Drouant; the beautiful, feminine Pré Catalan, in the Bois de Boulogne; the archetypal bistros Chez Allard and Au Beaujolais; the great fish house La Marée; and the paragon of three-star restaurants, Taillevent. They would travel to Alsace to experience what a long-established, seamlessly hospitable three-star in the country was like, at the Auberge de l'Ill; to Switzerland for the uncategorizable cuisine of Frédy Girardet ("The best food I had ever put in my mouth," Alice says); to the pastoral Chez la Mère Blanc at Vonnas, deep in the Burgundian countryside; to Roanne, where the Restaurant Troisgros was evolving along a path parallel to that of Chez Panisse but far above it in luxury; to Hiély-Lucullus in Avignon, where the traditional cooking of interior Provence was refined to its essence; and finally to the Champagne capital, Reims, and Gérard Boyer's Les Crayères, a magnificent château surrounded by extensive English gardens and serving the most classical of haute cuisine. "I don't know how my liver survived," Alice recalls, "but, oh, we did eat well."

For the first month of her absence, Alice had selected all of the recipes to be served at Chez Panisse, printing the menus well in advance to insure that Jeremiah stuck to the script. THE BEST OF CHEZ PANISSE, as the menu sequence was titled, was the first time that the restaurant had ever looked backward. Jeremiah's heart was not in it.

As soon as the rigid prescriptions of September were finished, however, Jeremiah tossed them aside with a flourish—free now to dish up calf's brains salad, pear soup with raspberry cream, blinis with caviar, *salmis* of quail, braised capon with two sauces, *civet* of duck with poached dried fruit, another all-Sauternes dinner. He did a week of tributes to his primary influences—Olney, Montagné, Escoffier, Elizabeth David, and "my Russian uncle." He did a week of white truffle dishes, a week devoted to Joseph Phelps's new vintage of zinfandel nouveau, a week of black truffles.

After Marion and Cecilia's departure, Alice remained and made her home base at Claude and Martine Labro's, from which it was but a short trip to Lulu and Lucien Peyraud's. Richard Olney's house was just down the road from the Domaine Tempier. Alice and Martine hit the road again. "We were still doing the three-stars," says Alice. "L'Oasis. Vergé. Les Baux. Chapel. Bocuse. But my favorite by far, after going to all of them, was still Girardet."

In October, Jerry Budrick came to Europe, leaving Jeremiah short another valuable (if volatile) veteran. Jerry, still believing in his relationship with Alice, flew to Rome with Bob Waks, of the Cheese Board, and Jay

Heminway, whose Green and Red zinfandel would succeed the Phelps zinfandel as the Chez Panisse house red wine. Alice met them in Rome, and they rented a Volkswagen for a drive through Italy.

Back in Berkeley, Jeremiah was turning out food as dazzling as ever, but he was unhappy with the state of Chez Panisse.

10/31/78

My dear Alice and Jerry,

    I am sitting here in the office on Hallowed Eve, drinking Thivin, and wondering what to say . . . what to tell you about the restaurant. . . . Now I am going to scold you, hoping that it coincides with something in your head, though I fear not. I don't think the restaurant can go on in its present way. All the trade deals, maneuverings, decentralization of responsibility, laxness (laxative) of the staff to me spells ruin very soon. . . . I do not want to incur your wrath. But I hope you come back after having very, very serious thoughts about what must happen here in the next year or two. Maybe I am just spooked with ghosts and very fatigued with two or three jobs going at once, but it's really out of my hands now and I can't do much in these few months when I am really only an eccentric visitor at Chez Panisse. It will be strong when you return, that I can say. But it ain't mine no more. I am a stranger here, except for Suzy and, believe it or not, Tom, who has been nothing but total support. How have you let these staff learn such bad manners?

    Carrie has had the same flower arrangement on the dining room mantelpiece for three weeks. DEAD LEAVES WITH BROWNING ORCHIDS. She calls every day at noon for her special order. My very sweet Alice, what have you let happen?

    It really is time to do the next thing with yourself and the restaurant— they are probably the same thing. I feel apologetic for not having a brilliant idea. My need and only idea is to go on to do something else. But I am still in love with the fact that Panisse has survived and should go on for forty years. . . .

    I feel cannibalistic, dark, Jeremaiad, and a son of the Semites. Hawk noses, smooth leather saddle bags. I smell horses in the desert when cooking,

with the obvious results: Mint is in everything. Peppers—but mostly the
varieties of the black. Melons with old Sauternes and black pepper.
Anchovies and figs with raspberries, with a tired old Margaux. . . .
And a return to the old bistro in the south of France. To the food we
did a year after I started. It appeals to me again. Fuck all this orange
peel julienne and pubic hairs of leeks. Give me some of Tempier's lunches.
Give me caviar and buckwheat and a lover of vodka-like appetite. . . .
Toast in bed in the morning with smoky tea and a hit of opium. Bitter
salads for lunch. Gin with violets at six. Guinea fowl over the coals with
pommes sarladaises, rose ice, a whipping for dessert. . . . Do enjoy it all,
do be naughty there so you can be straight here.

> *Coquilles with possum butter,*
> *Love and kisses,*
> *Jeremiah*

Meanwhile, stuffed into the Beetle, Bob Waks, Jay Heminway, Jerry, and Alice picked up a turkey in Florence for Thanksgiving, which they were going to spend at Jay's family's chalet in the Swiss Alps. Along the way there, they stopped in Turin, where they found precisely "the next thing" that Jeremiah couldn't think of.

The four had reservations for a late dinner at a fancy restaurant, but by three thirty in the afternoon they were ravenous. They stopped in at the first open place they found, a pizzeria. "We could see a fire burning inside," Alice wrote some years later, "and it pulled us in. And there I had my first pizza out of a wood-burning oven. We all thought it was the best thing we had eaten on the whole trip."[1] She asked to see how they did it. She was shown the fat oven with its firebrick floor and white-hot oak coals heaped in the corner. The temperature inside was a thousand degrees Fahrenheit. A pizza went in on a long wooden peel, was twirled once, twice, three times so that each side got the full blast of heat from the coals—"with flames swirling around under the ceiling of the oven"—and in less than two minutes it was ready to eat. "That moment was the real beginning of the café," says Alice. "Pizzas were so inexpensive to cook, and it was just so convivial, that little group of people hanging out."

A café upstairs at Chez Panisse, a simple café, with its own open kitchen and its own pizza oven. (The earliest version of the upstairs café had not had a real kitchen, and Jeremiah's recent proposal would inevitably have been fancier than what Alice had in mind now. Besides, that was Jeremiah's idea, and this one was Alice's.) It could mean the return of their friends, the regulars, the old-timers who had been priced out. There would be no compromise of Alice's standards. The ingredients would be as fine as those of the formal downstairs, and the cooking would be just as inventive and skilled, but there would be no truffles, no foie gras, no classic French sauces. The preparations would require much less labor. There would be a small menu, changing daily, according to what was best and best priced on the market that morning. You could order as little or as much as you wanted. You could hang out with your friends. It would be nothing less than the embodiment of Alice's original vision of Chez Panisse—something that from the first night forward had never really existed.

9.

CREATION AND DESTRUCTION

1979–1982

As 1978 waned, Jeremiah became more preoccupied with his own future, and Jean-Pierre was once again, though still uncredited, chef. With the New Year Jeremiah departed, this time for good, and Alice returned. The great restaurants of France had inspired her deeply, and after four months there, she determined to reproduce their masterpieces at Chez Panisse.

The menus for the first three weeks of 1979 were titled SPECIAL DISHES FROM A RECENT GASTRONOMIC TOUR OF EUROPE. From the three-star Auberge de l'Ill in Alsace came "salad of rabbit and rabbit livers cooked with truffles, served with escarole and a sauce of olive oil, lemon cream, and black truffles," and a lobster soufflé. From Troisgros there were "sweetbreads and veal kidneys sautéed with black mushrooms, served with a spicy brown wine sauce"; from Girardet, "chicken baked in a sealed crock, with black truffles under the skin, served with a leek confit"; from L'Oasis at La Napoule, "duck liver mousse dusted with black truffles and served with a Champagne gelée."

Once again, rave reviews came pouring in. Patricia Unterman in the *San Francisco Chronicle* of April 8, 1979:

> For eight years now, Chez Panisse in Berkeley has been turning out a different menu each night. That's in the neighborhood of 3000 new dishes, and they keep doing it. What is so remarkable is that the food is always exciting, very rarely poor, occasionally merely good, and usually superb. . . . The palette of foods is so varied and complex that you usually taste something you have never tasted before.

The *International Review of Food and Wine,* for its first anniversary in May 1979, held an event in New York to showcase the talents of up-and-coming American chefs, and Alice was invited to attend. She wanted Jean-Pierre at her side. She called her artist friend Patricia Curtan and asked if she'd mind stepping in at the restaurant for a week. "I was stunned," Patty recalls. "I'd never been a chef! I said, 'Well, no, Alice, I can't do that.' This is an insight into Alice: She just said, 'Well, what do you have to lose? I have something to lose here, but what do you have to lose?'"

In the *New York Daily News,* Ella Elvin described the meal that Alice and Jean-Pierre produced at the New York event:

> Coin-sized oysters taken from the sea near Seattle the day before. Whole heads of garlic, baked to a butter, that, with slight pressure, eased out of their crisp skins and became a spread for country bread with white goat cheese. Spring lamb from a California ranch, grilled to perfection . . . accompanied by a zinfandel produced on the same ranch. A salad of four-inch leaf lettuce picked just a moment before serving from garden flats carried [in Alice's lap] on the plane from California. . . .
>
> Asked how she felt about the luncheon she had just presented, Waters, ever modest, used just one word—"Pleased."[1]

Alice and Patricia Curtan in the Chez Panisse kitchen

That lettuce was in fact mesclun, the seeds of which Alice had brought back from her sojourns with Martine and Lulu and planted in her backyard. Mesclun was second nature in Provence, but at the time unknown in the United States.

The *Daily News* had found Alice in a somewhat dreamy moment, quoting her, "I'd like to have a completely self-sufficient restaurant, a country inn. I think of having a spot in the Napa Valley. That's my goal. I'd produce my own olive oil, butter, grow my own little lettuces. We could do everything."

Alice was also pleased with Patty Curtan's work in her absence, and asked her to stay on. Patty worked part-time through the summer, and with Mark Miller's departure in September 1979, she became sous-chef to Jean-Pierre. "She was so unbelievably capable, and responsible," Alice says. "She was the only one who swept the floor between seatings. She wouldn't begin to work unless the floor was swept."

Lois Dwan wrote in the *Los Angeles Times,* "In some eight years, Alice Waters has made Chez Panisse a place of pilgrimage for all serious gastronomes," and she quoted Alice saying, "It's a wonderful feeling, wonderfully exciting when at six o'clock you can just pull something out of the air and say, Oh, no, the watercress needs a little of this or that—and it becomes just right. If it looks like too much cream in too many dishes, I can just stop midstream and say, 'We can't do that.' I cooked scallops the other night, maybe fifty times, and each time it was different. There was probably one person there at the end that got the perfect scallop dish."[2]

In *New West* magazine, Colman Andrews wrote, "If you could eat in only one restaurant for the rest of your life, Chez Panisse would be the one to choose."[3]

The restaurant's native exuberance seemed to be coming back to the surface. One signal occasion was a screening of Errol Morris's new film *Gates of Heaven,* which the director Werner Herzog years before had teased Morris that he would never finish. If it ever opened, said Herzog, he'd eat one of the shoes he was wearing at that moment. Now Morris was holding Herzog to his bet.

"I remember distinctly the cooking process," Alice recalls, "and the crazy idea I had—to put it in fat, cook it like confit, because I thought it would soften it up. I cooked it, and I cooked it, and I cooked it, and I cooked it, probably eight hours, and it never happened. That shoe was something formidable. It wasn't just some little Italian loafer. It was a serious shoe. I remember watching him bite into it. He chewed on it for a long time."

Another filmmaker, and one of the Chez Panisse family, Les Blank, had been struggling for some time to make a documentary titled *Garlic Is as Good as Ten Mothers.* He had documented the hellzapoppin' bacchanal of the Chez Panisse Quatorze Juillet dinners of the past three years, and now he had footage of Herzog trying to eat the long-stewed shoe. The film was to be shown at a Les Blank retrospective at the Museum of Modern Art in New York in June, but it still wasn't quite finished, and Les was out of money. Alice proposed a benefit dinner to raise the remaining funds (at $100 a head)—A SPECIAL GARLIC EVENT TO CELEBRATE *ALLIUM SATIVUM,*

FILM, MUSIC, AND THE VERNAL EQUINOX. The menu for March 21, 1979, was, of course, all garlic (except, this time, the dessert) and redolent of the baroque complexities of Jeremiah—executed now, however, by Jean-Pierre.

Galantine of pigeon, duck, and quail,
filled with layers of meats, livers, and garlic mosaics

❦

Whole baked fish, served with a garlic puff pastry
and lobster butter sauce

❦

Spring lamb with three garlic-infused vegetable purées

❦

Roquette salad with goose fat and garlic-rubbed croutons

❦

Poached figs in red wine with garlic-shaped meringues

In July 1979, the menu for the fourth annual garlic festival was head-lined GARLIC FRENZY!!! The dinners featured garlic soup with garlic salad, whole baked garlic, garlic soufflé, deep-fried garlic cheese, garlic crépinettes with garlic potatoes, garlic eggs and garlic sausages and garlic brioche, and, not for the faint of heart, chocolate-covered garlic cloves flavored with rose water.

In the *New York Times,* Mark Blackburn published a piece headlined IT WAS THE FESTIVAL OF THE 'STINKING ROSE,' which read in part,

"Remember LSD?" said Tom Weller. "Garlic is the LSD of the 70s." Mr. Weller, president of St. Hieronymous Press, which prints post-ers designed by his partner, David Goines, was sitting in the garden of Chez Panisse, the French restaurant patronized by the Berkeley elect, waiting for his turn at table.

Several chairs away was Mr. Goines, in a white chef's jacket, recovering from eight hours of peeling garlic for the fourth annual Garlic Festival at Chez Panisse. His posters, the restaurant and the festival are all phenomena of the new Berkeley, which has taken up good living in lieu of revolution. . . .

"The third year it became outrageous," [Alice Waters] said, "and this year I almost didn't do it. People are flying in in Learjets from Los Angeles. It's become absurd. We're booked up three months in advance, and the regular customers can't get in. . . .

Will there be a garlic festival at Chez Panisse next year? "Who knows," she replied.[4]

A similarly dyspeptic reaction to the restaurant's fame and good fortune came from Charles Shere, Lindsey's husband. After *Playboy* magazine had put Chez Panisse on its list of America's twenty-five greatest restaurants, Charles wrote in the *Oakland Tribune,* "It's happened before, and it'll happen again. That sounds complacent, but it's not: it's resigned. . . . In every case the result is a brief upsurge in a particular kind of patron—the one who comes in with a show-me attitude. . . . People really concerned about food values tend not to eat out on *Playboy's* recommendation."

The Chez Panisse culture's oscillation between joy and gloom was by now an inextricable component of its identity. Fame had come, and with it an increase in revenues; then Alice and the staff didn't want to have to live up to the glory. Sometimes, as when she cooked Werner Herzog's shoe, Alice was really happy with Chez Panisse and her place in the world. Sometimes, as when she flew the mesclun in her lap to New York and then started extemporizing to a reporter about moving Chez Panisse to the Napa Valley, she could revel in her idiosyncrasy while also communicating to those who knew her well a deep discomfort with what she and the restaurant had become. Sometimes she presented a big smile to the camera and privately wished she was anywhere else.

Alice's shifting moods were mirrored in those of the whole *famille Panisse.* Year by year the staff had grown smaller and more familial; by 1979, there were fewer than twenty full-time employees. But they were the core, and when things were going well, they were proud to be part of what had become perhaps the most famous restaurant in America, and they worked together in peaceful communion, following the Chez Panisse ethos of fairness, optimism, and excellence. Sometimes, however, in accord with Alice's sudden accesses of bleakness, the restaurant as a whole—for it was by now, it seemed, a single social organism—seemed to lose its *esprit de corps*. Nearly always, Chez Panisse managed to present a calm, contented face to the world. Nearly always, there was something going haywire behind the scenes.

By the time the restaurant's eighth anniversary rolled around in August 1979, Alice's dissatisfaction had become general, and it included Jerry Budrick. Their alienation from each other had grown slowly through time, but Alice had been too shy or too kind or too guilty—perhaps all of those—to break with him entirely. Now, however, she did it. Jerry, of course, had seen it coming.

Why did we break up? Well, I'm an old-fashioned kind of guy, and I believe in honesty and openness, and it turned out she didn't. I always suspected things, because she was off a lot on these trips, and I never knew what she was up to. I just couldn't take the not knowing, and not trusting and not believing.

She was always experimental, and I should have realized that that's how she treated life, with an attitude of "I'll try anything"—try a new restaurant, try a new food, try a new trip, try a new place to go—and that openness would naturally lead to that. I should have realized it when she took up with me. She was living with Tom Luddy. And once she took up with me, it seemed like she became monogamous with me. That's how it seemed.

People, when they meet me and they know I was at Chez Panisse, they ask me, "Well, how was it working for Alice?" And I have to try to explain that I never worked for Alice, I worked *with* Alice. We worked together. We made the plans, we made the schemes, we did all that together, renovations and gardens and wines and all that stuff. It was great, and we had a wonderful time doing it.

· · ·

THROUGHOUT 1979 and the first half of 1980, the creation of the café occupied most of Alice's attention. "I was completely focused on the food. I don't really remember anything about the dining room, because I was just so absorbed in who was going to cook and how we were going to manage to do an à la carte menu. We knew we wanted to have food that was really inexpensive. I wanted to use all our leftovers. That was my theory, that if we didn't use it, we couldn't just throw it out. There were all those expensive cuts of meat downstairs, and that was one way we could save on food costs—use the unused things from the downstairs in the café the next day for lunch."

Alice's friend Cecilia Chiang recommended the architect Lun Chan and a kitchen designer named Bumps Baldauf. Kip Mesirow would contribute his design skills and expert Japanese woodwork to the interior.

The budget for building the café was about $200,000. Thanks to Pat Waters's signature, the corporation had obtained its first bank loan of $50,000. Pat had also borrowed $15,000 personally and lent that to the restaurant. Mary Borelli and Jeremiah Tower, however, each of whom held five hundred shares in Pagnol et Cie, had demanded to be bought out at $50 a share, and there had gone the $50,000. The subsequent sale of those shares brought only half that. Chez Panisse had managed to squirrel away $72,000 from its operating income. That left them $88,000 short.

Alice said, "Don't worry, it's going to be such a hit we'll wipe out that debt in no time." What mattered to her, as ever, were the aesthetics, and they were a dream. Kip's designs for the paneling and lamps melded Japanese design with California Craftsman and a hint of Art Nouveau. Alice hung huge posters for Pagnol's movies on the walls. The kitchen, running narrowly along one wall, was completely open to the dining room. Alice's idea was that the sounds and smells of frying, charcoal grilling, and the new pizza oven would drift throughout the dining rooms.

That oven, however, wasn't at all like the one that had inspired Alice's epiphany in Turin. "Bumps—the kitchen designer—came in," says Alice, and he didn't know anything about Italian pizza ovens, but he knew a German bricklayer. This guy had never even heard of a pizza oven. I was trying to describe what it should be like, trying to remember from that time in Torino. There was kind of a low opening, and a low arched ceiling with the flames licking the top. And he built us basically a German bread oven. Wolfgang Puck came up to see the oven shortly after it was put in, and he said, "Oh, I want one of these for Spago." And he hired the same German bricklayer, and he had the same problems we had.

We tried to adapt it for the next ten years. It used just ten times as much wood as an Italian pizza oven. It cooked a certain kind of pizza, which wasn't really a pizza in the way that an Italian would think about it.

Luckily, we found Michele Perrella. He said he was a pizza maker, and since we had no idea what making pizzas was all about and he knew how to make the oven work, I hired him. He was a shining light from day one.

Finally, we got our friend who did bread ovens out in Point Reyes, and he actually crawled into the oven to investigate. He upped the floor, and he changed some of the dimensions, but he was a bread-oven guy, too, and we had another bread oven. You couldn't get it hot enough. It's a matter of the dimensions, really allowing the fire to go over the top. It's not just a matter of low, it's a matter of the arch in the right proportion. Why it took us so long to get that done, I don't know. It wasn't until we brought an iron insert from Italy and put it in there that the oven really worked.

The Café at Chez Panisse, as it is formally called, opened—"perhaps appropriately," Alice says—on April Fools' Day of 1980.

In the name of informality, Alice didn't want to take reservations, but the café was immediately mobbed, and it wasn't long before people were waiting an hour and more for a table. Crammed into the tiny waiting area, they contributed gratifyingly to the bar income, but too many were getting tipsy or worse before they'd had a bite of food, and some of them, inevitably, would complain vociferously about the unendurable wait they were enduring. The money was rolling in, however, just as Alice had so blithely predicted.

The café menu had a relatively fixed format, but within each category there was constant variation, often even between lunch and dinner. There were always soup, salad, pizza, pasta, usually a poultry dish, usually a meat dish, and as often as possible—according to availability and perfect freshness (not always reliable in those days)—a fish or seafood dish. There had not been room for a pastry installation upstairs, so the half dozen or more desserts offered in the café meant a radical increase in the variety and productivity of Lindsey Shere's pastry department downstairs—which was now fully professional and fully indoors.

Very early on, there were a few café dishes so popular that they were exempted from the norm of daily variation: a salad of just-picked mixed baby lettuces—Alice's passion—with garlic croutons; the calzone that was the specialty of master *pizzaiolo* Michele Perrella, which came to be called simply *la crostata di Perrella;* Lindsey Shere's almond tart; and a cool salad

Alice and Lindsey Shere, with a poster from the Pagnol trilogy behind them

with a warm baked Laura Chenel goat cheese melting gently at the center—the quintessential Chez Panisse Café dish.

A native of Sonoma County, Laura Chenel had studied cheese making under the foremost authority on goat cheese in France, Jean-Claude Le Jaouen, and when she returned to California in 1981, she shyly approached Alice with her first American-made chèvres. She was, in fact, the first American ever to have attempted the French style of goat cheese. Alice loved it.

Alice's idea of warm goat cheese in a salad was apparently unprecedented. "There may have been baked goat cheese in France," she says, "but I don't think anybody had ever combined it with a salad." The salad has proved so popular that it is now seen on a good many bistro menus in France, and it has never been off the menu at the Chez Panisse Café, which buys fifty to a hundred pounds of Laura Chenel's cheese a week. The dish is considered a classic of California cuisine.

· BAKED GOAT CHEESE
WITH GARDEN LETTUCES ·

This is really one of the easiest things in the world, but it can go wrong. I just get one of those logs of goat cheese. It doesn't have to be round, it could be square. You cut slices maybe an inch thick. We marinate those in a dish with some olive oil, pepper, and herbs—bay and thyme. You use pretty fresh goat cheese, not one day old, about a week old—fresh, young, light, not strongly flavored. If it's too strong-flavored, it gets kind of funky when it's cooked. You can just drizzle it with oil—you don't have to cover it, but we do cover it because we make so many at the restaurant. Marinate it in the oil and the herbs anywhere from a couple of hours to a couple of days. I'm not sure how crucial that step is, ultimately, to the flavor. We just got into the habit of doing it.

Then we make bread crumbs out of good bread, French baguette, crustless. We toast it very lightly, just beginning to get golden, and then grind it into bread crumbs. We pack the bread crumbs onto the goat cheese—it adheres because of the olive oil and marinade—and then we bake it at about four hundred, just until it's beginning to soften. You don't want it to be runny, you just want it warm. It's nice to have the cheese at room temperature before you put it in. It's really important that the cheese comes out really golden brown.

Then we make a little salad that goes along with it. That salad can vary according to the time of year and what you have. I rather like it with rocket [sometimes marketed as "wild arugula"]. I love it with figs in the summer, or a few little almonds in the winter. Greens always. Or if there don't happen to be any good greens, it's very nice with just some almonds and figs as a cheese course. I usually toast the almonds unless they're just fresh from the crop in the fall.

And vinaigrette, just very simple. Red wine vinegar and olive oil. Depending on the greens and what time of year it is, if they're a little strong, I might add a little garlic. Or garlic and anchovy. Maybe even a little mustard. If it needs sweetness, you can always put in a little balsamic vinegar. Not lemon juice, because you've already got some tartness with the goat cheese. Some olives would be nice with it. If you were in Nice, you would have Niçoise olives and a mesclun salad. You might do the same.

I don't put the goat cheese on the greens. I put it on the side of the plate, and I put the pile of greens to the side.

Whether or not such a thing as a California cuisine even existed was still being debated (indeed, still is today). In January 1981, in the *International Herald Tribune,* under the headline NEW WAVE CALIFORNIA CUISINE: A MARRIAGE OF MANY AND A MIME OF NONE, Patricia Wells wrote,

The cuisine generates an excitement about food, a sense of experimentation, plus an uncompromising concern for good food and good dining that seems to have been lost in much of America, where fast food, fake French, and fern bar spinach salads are about as haute as many menus get. . . . The new wave California cuisine is perhaps best personified by a little Berkeley restaurant called Chez Panisse.

Later in 1981, the California Culinary Academy convened a panel in San Francisco to consider the existence, or nonexistence, of California cuisine. Julia Child, California-born, chaired the discussion.

Alice, widely regarded as the mother of California cuisine, said, "It has not quite arrived. . . . We are now in the kindergarten stage." She went on to say that California cuisine would not truly exist until more restaurants were willing to deal directly with farmers and artisans. She talked about Sonoma goat cheese, vegetables grown without pesticides, yellow tomatoes, and the fact that Chez Panisse had planted its own gardens.

Julia replied to Alice:

There is not as much of a California cuisine as you chauvinists would have us believe. It is actually such a mixture that definitions cannot be made. Although you mention simplicity, I think menus can be so simple that they become dull. Sometimes I'm glad when I can go back to France, where they really do things with food.

You have an unduly doleful point of view about the way that most people shop for food. Visit any supermarket and you'll see plenty of fresh fruits and vegetables. And if you don't like the looks of what you see displayed at the market, complain to the produce manager. That's what I do, and it always gets results.

Alice's reply, if ever spoken, was not recorded.

"We remained friends in spite of that," says Alice. "I always had a little back and forth with her. She was the most influential culinary leader in America, and I think the whole organic movement could have moved along a lot more quickly if she had taken it up. But I utterly appreciated what she did do. She expressed the joy of cooking. No one else has been able to do that in the way that she did it. Who cares if she was a good cook or not? She had fun, and she shared it with everybody around her table. She brought people to the table. I always liked that part on her TV show when she sat down and ate."

Whatever it was called, and whatever Julia thought of it, what Chez Panisse did was attracting ever wider attention, most of it in the form of breathless praise. Arthur Bloomfield, in *San Francisco Focus* magazine, compared the calzone that emerged from the new pizza oven to "Toscanini conducting the finale of Brahms's Second or Schubert's C Major."[5]

Craig Claiborne, the United States' supreme arbiter of food, wrote in the *New York Times:*

> Where American gastronomy is concerned, there is one commodity that is rarer than locally grown black truffles or homemade foie gras. That is a chef of international repute who was born in the United States. Even rarer is such a celebrated chef who is a woman.
>
> There is, however, one here in Berkeley who could justifiably deserve such renown. Her name may not be a household word from Maine to California, but many culinary experts, both here and abroad, sing her praises without reservation. . . .
>
> Miss Waters makes a cuisine française that is authentically bourgeoise, commanding the basic flavors, which she ferrets out with a passion and astonishing understanding, from good and beautiful products of her native land. . . .
>
> After an altogether joyous lunch with Miss Waters, we insisted on going upstairs for a sample of what had been described by an outstanding East Coast gourmet as the best calzone in the world. . . . Our friend's enthusiasm was not unfounded; the calzone was a triumph of taste and imagination.[6]

What had been for Alice a swirling, ceaseless, sometimes incoherent rush of experiences—crises, inspirations, celebrations, days, weeks, years of

Alice did cook at Chez Panisse from time to time.

time flying by, punctuated by crystalline moments but always so briefly, an impossibly fast-motion film of lovers, waiters, chefs, customers, farmers, and friends blurring into and out of her life—that formless welter seemed now to be assuming a shape, becoming palpably one thing: Alice-Waters-and-Chez-Panisse. Alice, by nature ever attuned to impermanence, came uneasily but also with excitement toward the recognition that she should publish a book that expressed what the entity of Alice-Waters-and-Chez-Panisse was about.

She would model the book on one of her favorites, Richard Olney's *The French Menu Cookbook*. She would title hers *The Chez Panisse Menu Cookbook*. It had to be much more than a cookbook, however. It had to manifest what Chez Panisse was, both on the surface, in terms of ingredients and cooking, and deeper down. It had to express the philosophy and the ethics that were the heart of Chez Panisse, what made it fundamentally different from other restaurants. But the book had to be fun, too, and useful. Organizing it as a collection of menus made it a composition of compositions, like a volume of poetry.

Bob Scheer, Alice's old political mentor, was a friend of Jason Epstein, the distinguished Random House editor, and suggested to him that this could be something worthwhile. "Bob Scheer took me to Chez Panisse for dinner," says Jason. "I was skeptical at first, but bowled over by the meal. Alice joined us for dessert, and I offered her a contract then and there."

"All my friends were brainstorming how I would do this," Alice remembers. "And Linda Guenzel, who was this very obsessive and compulsive customer of the restaurant, as well as a friend, said, 'Well, Alice, you just talk, and what I'll do is record everything you say. Because you say it so well just saying it. And then I'll have it transcribed, and you can pick and choose what you want to put in the book.' So she began doing that, and that's what became the foreword. And I mean, she wrote volumes. But parts of it were written in an adulating way about me. Even though it was supposedly my voice, it was written in a way that I couldn't say it. And after she had transcribed all that, and embellished it, it was extremely painful for me to cut it back. She must have written twenty times as much as what was published as the foreword. It had become her book. She wanted the book! It was very hard for me to find the right tone after that. So I brought Fritz in."

"Alice knew exactly what she wanted to put in the book," says Fritz Streiff. I was just working on the essay, and some of the other text—the material that Linda Guenzel had been amassing.

"Her feelings were hurt when Alice snatched the manuscript away and gave it to me to finish. I remember doing quite a lot of cutting and rewriting, and adding more material. But please understand that I wasn't the writer. It was pretty much Alice's—taken down verbatim, a lot of it."

In a letter dated February 1, 1984, to the San Jose *Mercury-News*, Linda Guenzel (who is now deceased) wrote that her own role had been much greater: "I devoted as many as 15–18 hours per day to work on the cookbook—work which included not only the composition of the text, but the extensive research interviews . . . the glossary, the seasonal calendar, and [much more]."

"I have copies of the first two evolutions of the manuscript," writes Linda's husband, Fred Guenzel, "and the prose in both of them is the same as the printed book."

"After the café opened," says Alice, "we really had a whole new clientele.

We added four hundred people a day! We'd had a staff of about fifteen, and now all of a sudden we had fifty."

The new level of complexity, and the influx of thirty-five people, most of whom had not been inculcated with the Chez Panisse ethos, provided ample opportunity for conflict. Lindsey Shere's sister, Pat Edwards, had come aboard as business manager, and she remembers:

We began to have all sorts of problems with staff, because suddenly you had all these waiters and cooks and busboys, and we had to become a lot more serious about employee relations and following the laws. The busboys would be smoking marijuana between breaks— I could smell it wafting into the office—and the waiters would drink, and they'd be ordering meals for themselves from the cooks. People really didn't take to the idea, after having had such a loose organization, of being controlled in any way. They thought it was their right to do exactly as they pleased.

You would hear Alice and Jerry shouting out in the back at each other. She got to the point where she wouldn't come and ask me to write a check, but she had check-signing privileges, and so she would sneak in on the weekends and take checks. And I was supposed to control her. She didn't like me very much, because I took my job seriously.

There was a time when the law changed, and we had to start reporting the waiters' tips. That was pretty funny. They would claim some exorbitantly small amount. They made huge amounts of money, especially the downstairs waiters, and on top of that they were stealing. We didn't take charge cards at that time, so people were paying cash, and it was going out like water. So I gave them a specified number of guest checks at the beginning of the night, I counted them, and wrote down the serial numbers, and they had to give those back to me. It seems like the logical thing, doesn't it?

Sometimes I wonder why they ever hired me. I was just Lindsey's sister, and an organized person, and not particularly interested in food. I'd much rather grow flowers, actually.

Pat's office was "a tiny little hole in the wall. When they did the plans for the café, they forgot to put an office in. There was a filing cabinet and a desk. It was so small I had to use the handicapped bathroom for filing things. Eventually things got so bad that they rented a big long shed and made a slightly larger office for me in there. Out back. In a shed. Everybody and his dog used that office.

"The staff and I really got along very well. I was sort of like the mother to them. They would come and tell me their troubles and complain about Alice and whatever else was happening." Alice's criticism of the food was often sharp, albeit nearly always accurate. Some of the staff took her brusque manner as a given, knowing that it was about achieving excellence, and not about the person at all. Others, not surprisingly, were hurt or insulted.

Shelley Handler, the first café chef, sought Pat's counsel frequently. One of the cooks working under Shelley, Joyce Goldstein (who would also go on to her own fame), Pat says, was driving Shelley nuts. "Shelley would come into my office, close the door, and sort of say, 'Ahhh, a place of sanity.' Joyce was a very aggressive and very smart and determined woman, so eventually, actually quite soon, Shelley quit, and Joyce took over."

Alice's father had retired from his full-time job, and he and Marge had moved to Berkeley, where Pat now ran a consulting business from their house. The haphazard way in which Chez Panisse conducted its finances had always rankled Pat Waters, and now that he was on the scene, he offered to help see if they could be straightened out. Alice had always been devoted to her father, and she was very happy to welcome him into the business. He collected no salary or fee, and had no official title, but he had Alice's carte blanche to scrutinize whatever he chose, from books to staff management, and he was welcome as well to attend board meetings. There were those on both the board and the staff who were not so happy with Pat Waters's sudden immersion in the restaurant's affairs, but no one dared say so to Alice's face.

Pat asked for a professional appraisal, to be finished by June 30, 1981. To the astonishment of many, it was a remarkably sunny document. "In an interview with Alice Waters," the report said, "we asked about the success of the restaurant and to what she attributed it. Her reply was that she never compromised on ingredients or ideas and that she had a purist approach. She stated that she was not concerned with the cost." Salaries had been raised across the board, and management was "generous with bonuses," but the appraisal pronounced the restaurant financially sound, and set a value on the business of a million and a half dollars. The appraisers even attributed "the revitalization of the neighborhood" to Chez Panisse.

As Chez Panisse turned ten years old in August 1981, the business was prosperous enough for Alice to begin thinking of bigger things, and the great world outside. Alice was thirty-seven years old now, and she was returning to the cultivation of her social conscience. David Goines designed and donated a tenth-birthday poster, which in its first month on sale at the upstairs bar raised $5,000; the money went to an environmental group known as the Abalone Alliance, to help stop Pacific Gas and Electric's proposed construction of a nuclear power plant at Diablo Canyon. The effort failed—the plant was built—but it had reawakened the political passion that had first brought Alice and David together in the wake of the Free Speech Movement.

DISASTER CAME to Chez Panisse with the suddenness of an earthquake. While Jean-Pierre and his wife vacationed in France, Alice had taken over the kitchen. After midnight, in the early morning of Sunday, March 7, 1982, she did the final cleaning after the dinner service. She locked up and went home. In the middle of the night, her phone rang. Chez Panisse was on fire.

My dad was the designated emergency contact. That's why he was the one who called. I came racing down, and I saw the flames coming out of the upstairs windows, and then I knew how serious it was. It was like your child's in there somehow. You couldn't go in. The firemen had completely cordoned everything off. Fire trucks, arcs of water, just a mess. I remember very vividly going in the next day, when they had put out the fire, and the whole downstairs was dripping with water and completely charred. Everything.

We think it started by a live coal being put back into the wood box. Taken out of the fire and put back into the charcoal box again. I was on the grill that night, so who knows. I might have done it myself.

Being in a fire is something. It's a terrible, terrible mess. You can't get the smell out, you can't get the water out. You feel like you're never going to put it back together. We saved a lot of the up-stairs. What we didn't save was any of the downstairs. That had to be rebuilt. Even the floors. We were within ten minutes of losing the building. It was close to getting the main beams, and when those go, the whole place collapses. But they caught it in time.

I really learned something from that fire. It was a big turning point, in that I kind of thought that restaurant was mine, you know? It wasn't mine. It was the people who came to eat there—it was theirs. They were part of it. I hadn't been paying enough attention, I think. I was in a little, narrow, inner-circle Chez Panisse world, thinking we could just do it all on our own. We're going to grow our own, do our own, be our own. But after the fire, I felt like we had to open up the doors and look outside.

This was a sobered, measured, mature Alice Waters. She would never lose her passion, but henceforth it would take considered and intentional form. When she opened up the doors and looked outside, she saw a world of opportunities to put the Chez Panisse philosophy to use.

10.

REBAPTISM
BY FIRE

1982

The blackened, reeking, dripping hull of Chez Panisse on the day after the fire drew crowds of grief-stricken onlookers. But Alice allowed herself no time for grief; there was work to be done. There remained quite a lot of food, wine, and liquor undamaged but legally condemned; it would be distributed to the staff. Alice wanted the whole staff paid during the reconstruction—everybody, down to the dishwashers—but there wasn't enough cash to go around. And she wanted the restaurant back in operation fast. To Alice, there was something strangely energizing about this destruction.

"The morning of the fire, at seven a.m.," Alice's old friend the wine merchant Kermit Lynch recalls, "Alice was at my door in tears. Two days later, she was beaming—dreaming of what she could do now."

"I read *A Pattern Language,* by Christopher Alexander," Alice remembers. In the book, Alexander proposed a radically new way of designing buildings and communities, with their residents as the primary thinkers and actors in their design, arrangement, and construction. "I realized there was so much we could do. That book was my bible. He was a friend of Charles and Lindsey's, and because I admired him so much, we met. And we talked for quite a long time about how to translate my ideas into the reconstruction of the downstairs."

There had been only a narrow single door between the kitchen and the dining room, but the door and the whole wall were gone now. Alice liked it like that. "I had always wanted to be connected, cooking and serving the customer in one room. So when that wall went down in the fire, I just said, 'Let it be.' Sometimes I almost thought I started the fire purposefully."

She asked Kip Mesirow, the master of Japanese woodworking who had been adding his subtle touches to the interior over the years, to conceive a unified design, derived from the style that had served Chez Panisse so well, but now more thorough, more integrated. At Pat Waters's insistence, the restaurant had been well insured, and reconstruction could begin immediately. Support poured in from the friends of Chez Panisse, the staff, and Berkeley at large—clearing out the remains, preparing lunch buffets for the workers, just showing up to pitch in.

The café was less badly damaged than the downstairs, and because it was the restaurant's primary cash generator, the board wanted it back in operation as soon as possible, but Alice wanted improvements, too— restoring the café bar, changing the ventilation, cutting in new windows, building a better waiters' station.

Members of the Cheese Board Collective, the restaurant's longtime friends across Shattuck Avenue, organized a benefit party for March 22, 1982. Chez Panisse would provide whole pigs and lambs to roast, and the Cheese Board staff would serve. Donated items would be solicited for an auction. All the proceeds would go first to the staff, and only then toward building Alice's (and Jerry Budrick's) latest dream, a grand new grill and wood-burning oven in a brick alcove just off the downstairs dining room.

With only ten days to solicit donations, and no advertising except word of mouth, the auction drew seven hundred people. There were many bottles of rare wine—magnums of vintage port, ancient bottles of Château d'Yquem, a Salmanazar (equivalent to eight bottles) of Pommery Champagne. Another lot was a sailing outing for six on San Francisco Bay aboard an eighty-two-foot schooner. Tom Luddy offered a private screening of Marcel Pagnol's *The Baker's Wife,* and Lindsey Shere would bring dessert. Alice, Tom Guernsey, and Jerry Budrick would cook dinner for six at the winning bidder's house. There were dinners at K-Paul's Louisiana Kitchen in New Orleans and Michael's in Santa Monica. There were lingerie, perfume, and a nineteenth-century sword-cane. Twenty thousand dollars was raised for the employees' fund.

The café was back in business on March 23, 1982, just over two weeks after the fire. The restaurant was serving again on April 27, fully remodeled, with a sparkling new kitchen open to the redesigned dining room. The customers could see the kitchen at work, and the cooks could see how people were reacting to the food. The dining room itself retained its golden glow, its redwood shadows, its mirrors and sprays of flowers, but the kitchen, which had always had a homey, cobbled-together look, was now a bright, clear, fully professional space. Its white luminosity and the staff's white shirts were a dazzling presence at the rear of the dining room. "It felt entirely different," Alice states. "To see outside, to see to the front of the restaurant. To see what was going on in the dining room and anticipate that people were coming in and what we had to prepare for. To see the sunset. It was fantastic."

CHEZ PANISSE had become her life, her family, her identity, but Alice was lonely. She began to think about getting older, even to the extent of half joking about a Chez Panisse retirement home in Sonoma County, where the superannuated geezers of the sixties could retire, keep their ideals alive, run a restaurant and maybe a hotel, and, most of all, keep working—together, as a family: "Apartments around a courtyard," she said. "People will gather in the courtyard to work together. Some kind of enterprise in front, facing the street . . . I'm not sure what . . . something useful for the community. And a big garden, of course. And we'll have to be attached to some other institution, with young people. We have to keep that connection. Selection, naturally, will be important. Maybe thirty people . . . I don't know. It has to be just big enough, and just small enough, to allow for—you know—eccentricity."

She was thinking about the present as well. "I was in my late thirties, and I was very aware that I would either have to have a kid or I wouldn't have one. Really aware of that, and I think the tenth birthday of the restaurant and then the fire were the end of a certain chapter. That was a really difficult moment in my life." She had yet to meet a man with whom she could imagine having a child. Her most recent lover was a cook at Chez Panisse, handsome and sexy and smart and focused—and fifteen years younger. (She had hardly ever found a boyfriend outside the restaurant, so total was her inhabitance of it.)

And then, one day that spring, Patricia Curtan and her boyfriend, Stephen Thomas, told Alice that there was someone they wanted her to meet, another Stephen. He was an artist, and he'd been fixing up a loft as his new studio, and he was having a housewarming.

"Patty Curtan said to me, 'I think he'd be really good for you, but I don't know whether you'll be good for him,'" Alice says. "She made lots of suggestions about it, for two or three weeks before this party. It was in May of 1982. I don't remember that I had ever laid eyes on him before. He had come to the restaurant many times before, but I didn't remember him. So he knew all about me, but I didn't know about him. And we met that night, and we never parted."

It seemed to be classic love at first sight. Stephen Singer was, like Alice, small of stature, elegant, stylish, and passionate. Also like Alice, he managed to find clothes that resembled nobody else's. There was an antic quality both in his wardrobe and underlying the intricate intellectual flow of his sentences. He was dark, with dark, intense eyes under thick brown eyebrows. "He had the most gorgeous complexion," Alice remembers. "This lovely red-brown skin.

"We moved in together right away. Not to the house I've got now. I was living in the musician's house—Alan Curtis—this beautiful Mediterranean-feeling house that I just adored, with three fireplaces." Curtis lived in Europe half the year, and his expectation for the other six months was that Alice would move to the basement. The latter half of the arrangement appealed to neither Alice nor Stephen. "So we were there for a bit, and then at Stephen's studio, and then about a year later we bought the house on Monterey Avenue. The one I'm still living in."

Stephen loved wine, loved food, loved travel and luxury. He also was younger. Alice had just turned thirty-eight. Stephen was twenty-seven. He was much more worldly, and wealthy, than an upbringing in Tulsa, Oklahoma, might have suggested. After visiting San Francisco's Chinatown at the age of eight, he decided that San Francisco was where he wanted to live when he grew up. Like Alice, he had taken time off from Cal to travel around Europe, though for Stephen the food was secondary to the art. He had also developed an encyclopedic knowledge of wine.

Alice was uncertain about monogamy, but at the same time she was quite consciously in search of someone who would make a good father. "I had a lot of sort of desperate, difficult relationships right before Stephen. Really just flinging myself around desperately. And they all ended in the same way. They began with this infatuation and this desire, and ended up not being satisfying in any other way. So I decided that desire wasn't at the top of the list, that I really wanted some other kind of relationship. I didn't know what that meant, but I was not going to be dismissive if desire wasn't the driving force of the relationship.

"What is that about?" she asks herself. "Maybe desire is an evolutionary error. Maybe we weren't supposed to live in such a monogamous way, either. Maybe we haven't evolved enough. I feel pretty certain we're not meant to be little twosomes off in a corner. I tell people I'd be happy to have an arranged marriage. If you're going to get married, an arranged marriage has just as much chance of success as finding somebody yourself."

THE CHEZ PANISSE MENU COOKBOOK was published by Random House on August 1, 1982, after two years of intense work by Alice and a

Stephen Singer

whole squadron of collaborators: David Goines had designed the book; Patricia Curtan had helped Alice develop the recipes; Jean-Pierre Moullé had cooked, tasted, and refined the dishes; Carolyn Dille had tested and retested the recipes; Linda Guenzel had transcribed Alice's rambling descriptions and tried to organize them into useful commentary; and Fritz Streiff had come in for the final weeks to polish the prose to a luster. The book was an immediate success, both in sales and in the press (and it has continued to sell in considerable volume through the years). David Goines's dust jacket exactly captured the heterogeneous style of the restaurant's entrance and front windows—part generic California bungalow, part Japanese tea garden, a little Arts and Crafts, a soupçon of Berkeley's own Julia Morgan. The introductory essay, "What I Believe About Cooking," states Alice's philosophy eloquently:

It is a fundamental fact that no cook, however creative and capable, can produce a dish of a quality any higher than that of the raw ingredients. . . .

The unfortunately widespread misconception that cooking that isn't complicated isn't cooking has sometimes proven to be a trap for me. In cooking classes we once gave at the restaurant, I was face-to-face with people's expectations of intricately involved and lengthy recipes. I sometimes felt foolish saying that good cooking meant having the freshest ingredients you could find, and then doing as little as possible to them. . . . I found that it required a tremendous interchange of information and lots of experience in order to convey what it takes to make simple foods succeed. One night, looking at the guests in the dining room as they ate slices from perfect, tiny melons, I began to wonder if perhaps the food had failed to live up to their expectations and that they had, horrifyingly, all come expecting to have filet mignon en croute; instead, all they saw before them was a beautifully faultless piece of melon. Anyone could have chosen a perfect melon, but unfortunately, most people don't take the time or make an effort to choose carefully and understand what that potentially sublime fruit could be.

One paragraph provides not only a guide to Alice's thinking about food but also a kind of character portrait:

When I cook, I usually stand at my kitchen table. I may pull a bunch of thyme from my pocket and lay it on the table; then I wander about the kitchen gathering up all the wonderfully fresh ingredients I can find. I look at each foodstuff carefully, examining it with a critical eye and concentrating in such a way that I begin to make associations. . . . Sometimes I wander through the garden looking for something appealing, absorbing the bouquet of the earth and the scent of the fresh herbs. Sometimes I butterfly my way through cookbooks, quickly flipping the pages and absorbing a myriad of ideas about a particular food or concept.

Jeannette Ferrary, writing in the *San Francisco Chronicle,* recognized in *The Chez Panisse Menu Cookbook* Alice's faith that having the right feelings will give you the results you seek—a very Berkeley, very sixties, very Alice notion: "Even in her most offhanded asides, the author articulates a distinctive California character. This is still frontier country, she implies, free from the constraints of stodgy tradition. Don't repeat eternally the one achievement you have mastered. . . . Never look back, burdening yourself with the memory of the dinner (or whatever it was) that didn't work."[1]

The book's publication set off a series of explosions that still resound through the debate about how much credit, in general, Alice should get. The first text in the book is a page of acknowledgments, opening with these words:

> This book would never have been written but for Linda Guenzel's belief in me and in Chez Panisse. She transcribed my ramblings, organized my thoughts, and overcame my doubts, all with tireless enthusiasm. I cannot thank her enough for the countless hours she has given me so generously. This book is as much hers as mine.

Linda Guenzel said that she had been offered half the royalties but had turned the offer down. What she wanted was her name as co-author on the copyright page and therefore preserved in the Library of Congress. The contract with Random House did not even include her, however, which she may not have known. (The title page credit reads "by Alice Waters" in big type, followed by "In Collaboration with Linda P. Guenzel" in small type, and Alice's name appears alone on the copyright page.)

"Linda was hugely loyal to Alice and to Jeremiah both, and their ideal customer in every way. Linda's feelings were very badly hurt," Fritz Streiff explains. "I thought the work I'd done after Linda had done her part was all okay, all done with Linda's approval. Alice was mortified that she had offended Linda. And they made a deal—a cash payment to Linda—in partial recompense for the slight."

Linda Guenzel was not the only aggrieved party. At the tenth-birthday party of Chez Panisse, a spectacular picnic at the Joseph Phelps Winery in the Napa Valley, in August 1981—a year before the book's publication—Alice and Jeremiah had gone up in a hot-air balloon together. "He had some really nasty things to tell me while we were up in that balloon," Alice recalls. "Jeremiah thought he should have gotten much more credit than the manuscript gave him."

"We had sent Jeremiah the manuscript, and he showed up at the party with it," Fritz remembers. "He had made numerous corrections, and had various cavils, mostly in the section where Alice had reprinted various menus that had been done for special occasions, and she had been cavalier with assigning credit in some cases. And he had suggested corrections. It would be most interesting to look at his notes for that, because I remember going through the manuscript with Alice, and in every case where he wanted something changed, we either removed it entirely so that it didn't matter, or we made the change that he wanted."

In the book, Jeremiah was, in fact, lavishly credited. In a paragraph introducing the section of special menus to which Fritz refers, Alice had written, "Many of these menus were conceived and executed by Jeremiah Tower, who was the chef at the restaurant during its formative years. He developed the idea of regional dinners celebrating the food of provincial France (Brittany, Périgord, Champagne, Burgundy, Alsace, etc.), Morocco, Louisiana, and ultimately, our own region of northern California; his innovative and adventurous menus gave the restaurant its reputation for ambitious experimentation and exploration."

For all that, in *California Dish* Jeremiah refers to Linda Guenzel as "the person who actually wrote it." Also he writes, "I saw that some menus and events that were so obviously mine had been removed"—another way of saying just what Fritz said.

Alice was having personal clashes at the restaurant as well. Jean-Pierre Moullé says, "I was bad. I said I was the chef to a journalist for an article. I said, 'I'm the one who runs the kitchen.' And [Alice] really didn't like that. I was working hard, and I was doing all the work. When you run the kitchen, when you do the ordering, the hiring, and the menu, and run everything, I think you are the chef. And I was stupid enough to tell every-one that Alice was not really cooking."

"Something had to give. He had to go," Alice concluded. It wasn't going to be simple. They would have to buy out Jean-Pierre's contract, and he owned Pagnol stock as well. Nobody in-house was capable of re-placing him, except Alice, who didn't want to. "He was unhappy," she says.

He didn't want my input. I felt like, You're really missing some-thing important not to take my input, because I've been in the kitchen, I've been in the dining room, I know about this. It's a very personal decision I make about who's in that kitchen. It has to do with a lot of other things besides just being a great cook. I'm not even sure I know what they all are. They certainly have to do with a certain kind of diplomacy both in terms of customers and staff. Inspiring the staff, understanding the dynamics of how a kitchen works, trying to communicate with people upstairs as well as down-stairs, not dividing the restaurant in two. Somebody who connects with dishwashers and the foragers and the office as well as the im-mediate staff.

There've been very few people who stayed here very long who didn't have a rapport with me, or if I didn't feel that their cooking was interesting in some way to me personally. I've compromised on other things, but I have never compromised on the cooking piece for very long. There have been a little six months here, a little six months there, when I didn't know what to do except pull my hair out. But even with impossible people—according to the staff—they were cooking well.

Jean-Pierre was (and remains) married to Denise Lurton, of the fa-mous Bordeaux family—they own or operate some twenty châteaux—and both of them were homesick. Jean-Pierre began to look forward to some good simple labor in the wine cellars, to working on the house he still owned and restoring its old barn. He and Alice agreed that he would stay at Chez Panisse through September 1982, and—so he thought at the time—then leave and never return.

"THEN PAUL CAME," says Alice with a gesture of gratefully outstretched hands, as though receiving manna from above. This was another fine example of the classic Chez Panisse pattern: Just at the right moment, the right person seems to appear.

"I grew up on Chez Panisse," Paul Bertolli recalls. "When I came to study at Cal, Chez Panisse had just opened. I remember going in and smelling the smell. It smelled like my grandmother's kitchen."

Paul's maternal grandmother presided over his family's kitchen in San Rafael, not far north of San Francisco. She was Italian-born, from the foothills of the Alps north of Venice, and she loved to cook. Eventually, his other grandmother, from near Milan, came to live nearby, in El Cerrito. "Two different traditions, really," he observes, "two different accents, dialects, two styles of cooking. It was great."

He loved food, but music—lute, guitar, and most of all piano—seemed to be his destiny. He won awards at the San Francisco Conservatory of Music when he was still in high school. He graduated from Cal in 1977 with a double major in composition and piano. But in his postgraduate study under a master teacher in New York, he grew disillusioned about his prospects as a concert pianist. "There were these Taiwanese girls who were half my size and half my age who could play circles around me," Paul remembers.

I decided, Okay, I'm going to take my last six thousand dollars and go to Europe.

I settled in Treviso, and I got a job in a restaurant that specialized in mushrooms. I fell in love with Italy. I thought, This is the greatest place to eat or drink or look at food or be at a table. I was twenty-three years old, and I felt like I had discovered the world.

Later I lived on a farm near Panzano. I began to learn about discovering what's there already, in nature. I really got the idea that these people eat this way because they live here and nowhere else.

When he returned to California, Paul decided to try for a job at Chez Panisse, and persuaded Alice to come to lunch. "At the time, Patricia Curtan was cooking, with Mark Miller, Jean-Pierre Moullé, and Alice. They all came to lunch. The asparagus soup I cooked in an aluminum pan, and it turned brown. I undercooked these little cannellini beans. I had this salmon that was poached, and decorated—sort of the wrong direction for Chez Panisse."

"He cooked this salmon out in his backyard," Alice remembers. "He covered it with nasturtium blossoms, and I just thought, Oh, my goodness, this is just too-too."

In 1981, Paul got married and went back to Italy. "I worked in three restaurants in and around Florence, and then I worked as a private chef for Sir Harold Acton in his Villa La Pietra. It was a great job. He didn't know what to do with me; I wasn't really a servant. He had a butler who would dress him and bring his cherries and tea in the morning. I would show up at ten o'clock in his study, and he would tell me who was coming to dinner.

"I fed not only Sir Harold and his guests, but his staff, which was huge. There were something like fifteen gardeners. He had two women who did nothing but iron all day, and he had a woman who worked full-time taking care of his glass collection."

With his skills sharpened and his urbanity elevated, Paul returned to Berkeley in the late summer of 1982. Suzy Nelson, who had been a waitress at Chez Panisse and was a longtime friend of Alice's, was giving a luncheon party based on a sequence of fancy wines, and she wanted food good enough and simple enough to highlight the wines. She hired Paul Bertolli. Alice was among the guests.

"That meal really turned my head around," says Alice. "Paul made *vitello tonnato,* and he cooked lamb over fig branches. He pushed that smoke into the dining room, perfuming everything. I'll never forget that.

Jacques Pépin, Alice, and Paul Bertolli

The lamb was sensational. And he did this prune semifreddo with nocino, a green-walnut liqueur, which I had never tasted. *Mmm!* He got me."

"This time"—Paul laughs—"*she* called *me!*"

Alice says that the earthiness and clarity of flavor in Paul's food were "a breath of fresh air for me. I loved that he had such an instinctual way of cooking. It was a beautiful thing to cross the border into Italy, into the land of olive oil and garlic and anchovies and a whole other palate. Plus I was about to have a kid, and he made me feel secure."

It may be worth noting that Alice doesn't mention Stephen here. Despite her pregnancy, they were still not married. But with a child on the way, she knew that her involvement in Chez Panisse was bound to lessen, and Paul's easy assumption of authority was a considerable comfort.

Whatever amount of authority Alice loaded onto Paul Bertolli, he never bowed under the weight. "Smiling off my reluctance," he would write some years later, "she believed in me sooner than I did."[2]

· PAUL BERTOLLI'S TRIPE AND PASTA ·

Paul made a tripe pasta that was the best. The best. I've had tripe lots of ways, but his cooking of tripe absolutely rivals anything I've ever tasted. Paul did it, obviously, Italian style, Florentine style. He made a *mirepoix*—carrots and celery and onions—along with garlic and olive oil, and he cooked the tripe with that for a long time in chicken stock, with tomatoes and pancetta, till it was really tender. With parsley, bay, and thyme, probably. And a little cayenne. The tripe was in strips, and he made egg pasta that matched it exactly. He finished it with fresh chopped parsley, Parmesan, and a bit of butter. It was so good.

"At first," Paul remembers,

I had to send all my menus over to Alice for review. She'd come in and taste and criticize. Sometimes she wouldn't say anything, and you would just have to know how to read her. The frustrating part was that there was a last-minuteness to a lot of her decision making. People call her a visionary. I think she has reactions more than visions. She can see best in a moment of crisis. When everything was about to happen, and something wasn't right, she had no qualms about saying, "We've got to do something about this." Well, she could have done something about it three hours ago, too, if she had applied herself, but there is something about this live moment when she has a reaction and things have to change.

"It is important to remember that you are preparing food, not culinary artwork," Paul would write in *Chez Panisse Cooking*, published in 1988. "Cooking is a commonsense practice, not alchemy. Listening and watching closely while you cook will reveal a richly shaded language understood by all the senses—the degrees of a simmer, the aroma of a roast telling you it is done, the stages of elasticity of kneaded dough, the earthy scent of a vegetable just pulled from the ground—it is everything to mind these details."

In his insistence that the cook's primary—and most noble—goal is to prepare food, not art, and that cooking is not alchemy, Paul exactly captures the difference between the French and the Italian approaches to food—the difference, too, between Jeremiah and himself. In the three principal chefs of the first twenty years of Chez Panisse—Tower, Moullé, Bertolli—can be read the history of Alice's own gastronomic fascinations.

Until the arrival of Stephen Singer and Paul Bertolli, Alice's focus had been largely on the moment, on pleasure for its own sake, on aesthetic refinement and sensual satisfaction. Now she was thinking about the earth, about responsibility, about the future. She had begun to recognize that pleasure had a moral dimension. And as has always been the case, she internalized her concerns so thoroughly that they were immediately personal: She was asking herself what she, herself, should do.

Some of Alice's detractors accuse her of ignoring a moral conflict inherent in Chez Panisse. To achieve the level of excellence that it does, it has to charge high prices. Aren't those high prices—entailing as they do the exclusion of the poor and, in fact, much of the middle class, too—a betrayal of the counterculture's idealism?

"That's like saying that a really simple-tasting soup can't be as divine as blinis with caviar," Alice replies. "The excellence, the perfection of it, can be there. It's about a way of doing work. It's about a way of focusing. Having fine-tuned senses so you can make really right decisions. Anybody can do it."

"It's interesting, isn't it?" says Charles Shere. "There's always been a sort of tension between the peasant and the gentility in Alice's makeup. She loves grilling over an open fire in the backyard, but she prefers it if the backyard is behind a manor house. But she is basically a democrat. She's a person who sees everybody as being intrinsically on the same footing and of equal merit and worth, and she sees her mission as facilitating the intermingling of these equally footed people."

"My sense of the ethics and politics of food was coming to the surface.

I mean, those values were instilled in me during the Free Speech Movement, and my early travels in France. But it didn't really start to come together till the early eighties," Alice says. "It had to do with becoming friends with the farmers and understanding deeply that the food at the restaurant was as good as it was because the produce and the ingredients were as good as they were. The farmers were the people who really got it, about the ethics of food."

Alice had left some of her democratic idealism behind with the defeat of Robert Scheer in 1966. Because she was so drawn to beauty, and to excellence, she could never have identified with the radical egalitarianism of the sixties far left. But she was seeing now that the purity of her devotion to excellence could inspire large numbers of people. Her deepening understanding of the relationship between healthy land and a healthy society would provide the platform from which she could speak. And the child growing in her body was an irrevocable investment in the future.

"It all started with Fanny," she says.

11.

A WORLD
FOR FANNY

1983–1984

P regnancy. Oh, my," Alice sighs.

It was amazing and mysterious, but I never got sick at all. In fact, I went to China when I was four months pregnant, and I ate everything. The trouble was that Fanny came early. Everything was fine until I went to New York to cook at my friend Anne Isaak's wedding in the heat of the summer. July 1983. They had this big party out in Sag Harbor, and I thought I could help grill. But apparently, Fanny didn't like that, because when I got back to New York, I just felt like, Oh, my God, something has changed. Something is really different inside. I went to the doctor when I got home, and she said, "You have to go to bed and stay there, because the baby is going to come too soon." She was supposed to be born at the end of September, and she was born the fifteenth of August, 1983. She was okay, she was just little. I had a cesarean birth. It was quite a trauma. But Fanny was great. The difficult thing was that she got colic two weeks later. I didn't know what that was about, but she couldn't sleep more than an hour at a time for three months. It took Stephen and me a couple of weeks to realize that we were the nurses in the emergency room, really—that we could never have a normal life as long as this child was unhappy. So he never went to work, and I never went to work. For three months.

Colic is an imperfection in the digestive system. Some little glitch, so every time the food comes to that point, it's very, very painful. They arch their back, and they become just inconsolable. We came to understand that the only way to make her happy was sort of sensory overload. We would turn on the shower in the bathroom, and I'd put her into her little Snugli, and I'd turn on the vacuum, and I'd sing to her all at the same time, and then she would go to sleep finally. All these things simultaneously. Which of course drove us over the edge, too. Every friend we knew came and helped take care of Fanny when she was crying. And she was crying for three months. And then she stopped, magically. And became the wonderful kid that she is. It took me a while to catch my breath, but I never went back to work in the same way. I couldn't.

Paul was cooking, and I was going to the restaurant a couple of nights a week, and Stephen would go to work a couple of days when I didn't go in to the restaurant. He had just started up a wine shop in San Francisco, called Singer and Foy. That's when Bob Carrau came into my life. He was Stephen's best friend, and he took care of Fanny while Stephen cooked dinner for them all and I went to work. He basically lived with us for fifteen years. I mean not really living there, but almost. He went on our vacations with us. He became Fanny's uncle/other father. He was always looking out to see how people were feeling. He's still that way.

"Stephen and I were friends at Berkeley," Bob Carrau remembers.

He was in two of my classes one quarter—a film class and an aesthetics class—and he talked so much that I kept thinking, This guy is either one of the smartest people I've ever met, or he's the biggest asshole I've ever met, and as Stephen said later, jokingly, "And I turned out to be both." I didn't really connect with Alice, because she and Stephen had this romance, and they kind of went off into her world. I saw Stephen every now and then. Then I remember seeing Alice when Stephen had an art opening. She wanted to do the food at his studio party, and I said I'd go help. That was my first experience with what she's like when she's all wound up in cooking things, and I was just a guy from the suburbs, not a very sophisticated person, so it was a whole new experience. I was like, Wow, what's going on here? I mean, whoa!

Stephen moved into Alice's house, and I went over there for dinner one night. It was just the three of us, and it was very uncomfortable for me at first, because Stephen and I, when we used to hang out, it was more like—you know, guys, smoking pot and drinking and goofing around. And now he had this woman friend who was very refined, in her own weird way, she's sophisticated, and she's a little older, and she has all this experience of traveling and knowing all these famous people, and she's almost European, and I was, especially back then, just kind of "Uh, hi."

She started shaving white truffles on something we were eating, like a pasta or something, and she was so excited, she was treating it like it was something precious, you know, and I remember thinking, This is an interesting smell. I had no idea what truffles even were. But I did like them.

Alice and I connected much more once Fanny was born. Stephen always wanted company being the father when Alice was working, and I was someone he could call, and I would just come over and hang out. It was always fun, because there was always good wine, good jokes, and he could cook too.

I get sad thinking back on that time, recognizing the naïveté of all of us, and all the stuff that was under the surface that we were all probably trying to express, but at the same time it was a very fun time for us. We traveled a lot together, and Alice and I could go someplace on our own, or Stephen and I could go someplace, or they could. I always related to Fanny as this clever and interesting person—not really as a child so much. She was as much a pleasure to be with as Alice was, or Stephen, so it was never like this issue of, Oh, I have to babysit.

And then I met Sue Murphy.

Sue was a professional actress and comedienne, and had to travel frequently, but having become Bob Carrau's lover, whenever she came back home to Berkeley she was now ipso facto a member of Fanny's team of caretakers.

I'm a gay person, but back then, I was kind of going all over the place. I had really strong feelings for Sue, and I said to her, "Listen, I don't really understand this totally, but if you're up for exploring this, I'd like to."

I liked being part of that family, and I think Stephen and Alice and Sue all liked it, too, and we actually grew into this kind of interesting foursome. In retrospect, I think I was facilitating what was going on between Alice and Stephen, but it was mostly a real pleasure for me.

Alice and her friends Patty Curtan and Sharon Jones remodeled Alice's garage into what Bob Carrau recalls as "an ad hoc day-care center for their kids." The mothers, and sometimes the fathers, as well as Bob and Sue, were all caretakers. It was a very busy place, and a great place to be a kid.

About this time a debate began among Alice's friends, which continues today, over whether she is too busy, overcommitted, in danger of burning out—a recapitulation of Tom Luddy's worry in the early days of the restaurant. Throughout the years of her friends' concern, however, Alice has virtually never slowed down.

She often seems so frantic, her mind on so many tracks, that she can't finish a sentence. Asked simply how she is, Alice cannot just say, "Fine," and be done with it. She stammers, hesitates, leaves half a sentence hanging, starts again, trails off—by which point her interlocutor tends to charge ahead with the conversation. The impression is of a brain about to boil over, or implode. Corby Kummer, a senior editor and food columnist at *The Atlantic,* is a longtime friend, and he says,

> Once, I had this idea of her as this fragile flower, always on the verge of bursting into tears. It took me a while to see her will of steel. In the early to mid-eighties there was a perception that she was always one step away from a breakdown, throwing up her hands and leaving the restaurant. People don't think about that now so much. She's more confident and straightforward now, while always keeping the seductive girlishness that is so much a part of her.

"After I had Fanny, I did change," Alice says. "I guess I mostly changed in relationship to the restaurant, although I'm sure Stephen would see it in a different way. Having a kid, always my mind was divided. Always my life was divided. Being a mother divided me from the restaurant. I tried to do everything and obviously failed on all fronts. Deeply. But I knew from the very beginning that Stephen and I couldn't bring up this kid by ourselves. I don't know what we would have done without Bob Carrau and Sue Murphy. It was great for them—they loved being part of the family—and it was great for us, because we loved having them there for us as family. That continued from '83 until '97. Then, when it all came apart, it was very hard. Very painful."

ALICE WAS HORRIFIED at the prospect of Fanny's growing up "without understanding what food meant to the survival of the planet." Most of the food on the market was tainted in some way by pesticides, or hormones, or antibiotics, or cruelty to animals, or bad farming practices, or poor treatment of farm workers. Finding genuinely untainted food—for the restaurant or for her family—was a continual struggle. Fortunately, she had a team of like-minded others as concerned as she was—friends and family close to home, and a growing grassroots movement on a national scale. In addition to improving the business practices of the restaurant, Alice's father had

Stephen, Fanny, and Alice

taken an interest in finding farmers who didn't use pesticides or other harmful chemicals. Pat Waters drove hundreds of miles through northern California in search of them, and found a number, though not enough to supply Chez Panisse on a regular basis with everything it needed.

"In 1983, we hired my friend Sibella Kraus—she was a line cook at the restaurant at the time," adds Alice. "She would go out and just comb the hills looking for farmers who would grow these particular varieties that I wanted."

Sibella remembers:

Alice had the fantasy that you'd have this total system where you were using up everything on the farm, and you'd have this ideal ecological and economic situation. Well, it didn't work. If a pack of aphids came, there went the salad.

We did have some wonderful suppliers, but getting the stuff to the restaurant was an incredible hassle. We would get Laura Chenel's cheese sent to the bus station. I'd call and say, "Okay, so-and-so, pick your corn now, the bus is coming in an hour." Alex Waag, Nathalie Waag's son, used to drive the van and fetch things from the bus. I had a car stained with blackberries. There was the joy of discovery, but most of the time I had no idea what I was doing. I would pick apricots that were sublime, but when I got them to the restaurant that evening, they were good for ice cream, if that.

Then I left Chez Panisse, and I went to study agricultural economics at U.C., and I started meeting farmers who were passionate about what they were growing. I'd meet people who were growing eight kinds of heirloom Japanese eggplant. These were products nobody had ever seen or heard of.

I went to Alice and a couple of other restaurateurs and said, "Hey, I'm meeting these farmers, and don't you think you would want me to try to hook you up?" So that summer, 1983, we set up the Farm Restaurant Project, to bring local farmers and chefs together. We produced a weekly distribution of produce available by direct order—that is, straight from the farmer to the restaurant. Nobody had ever done that. And that grew into an annual celebration called the Tasting of Summer Produce. A hundred people gathered to taste and compare the whole array of summer produce that had been donated by the growers, and the chefs prepared a wonderful meal. For the first time, the farmers and the chefs were talking to one another about their particular needs. It opened up a whole world.

It was a well-kept secret that Alice had actually been married once upon a time, very briefly—it was something of a marriage of convenience, to help a young French filmmaker named Jean-Pierre Gorin get into the United States. In 1978, Jean-Pierre Gorin had been able to return the favor by introducing Alice to a remarkable farm near La Jolla, California, where the Japanese-American Chino family was producing some of the most delicious fruits and vegetables Alice had ever tasted, in stupendous variety. The items available on one single day, as reported by Mark Singer (Stephen's brother) in *The New Yorker* of November 30, 1992, included:

beets (yellow, golden, red, white with red stripes), carrots (white, orange, yellow, golden, red, long-and-tapered, thumb size, in-between),
turnips (white, golden, red, black, white-and-purple, round, long),
radishes (white, red, red-and-white, purple, pink, daikon, red-fleshed
Chinese, green-fleshed Chinese), celeriac, fennel, escarole, white endive, red endive, white cauliflower, Romanesque cauliflower (pale
green with a stegosauroid architecture), mibuna, mizuna, bok choy,
choi sum, cilantro, French thyme, winter savory, lemon balm, rapini,
garlic chives, nasturtiums, basil (lemon, cinnamon, Thai, French, piccolo fino), Vietnamese coriander, Chinese spinach, Chinese long
beans, French green beans as slender as candlewicks, purple cabbage,
green cabbage, flat black cabbage, two dozen varieties of lettuce, a
plastic tray of mixed lettuce hearts—and that's not all.

And that was in January.

For the produce of the Chino Ranch, Alice gladly broke her rule about
using only local supply; this produce was just too good to pass up. Arrangements were made for a weekly delivery by jet. A Chez Panisse representative would meet the plane at the Oakland airport, pack the boxes into a
waiting van, and race up the freeway to Berkeley. (For the less perishable
items, there were also occasional deliveries by car.)

Sibella Kraus and Catherine Brandel, the restaurant's first official forager,
found a number of unique, often eccentric farms. Foremost among them
were Green Gulch farm, in Marin County (a venture of the San Francisco
Zen Center) and Warren Weber's Star Route Farm in Bolinas. Warren was
a perfect addition to the Chez Panisse community—a Shakespeare scholar
with a doctorate from Cal, and one of the first growers to pursue all-organic
farming. He had started Star Route with five acres in 1974 ("with a horse-
drawn plow and a lot of long-haired ambition," he says), and had never
veered from his dedication to grow organic produce that also tasted great.

Sibella says, "Alice's philosophy, and mine, was always to seduce and
educate. 'Taste this peach. Now that the juice is dripping down your chin,
let me tell you about the farmland where that comes from, and how endangered it is, and what you can do about it.'" Sibella explains,

The label for a box of Warren Weber's mesclun,
designed by Patricia Curtan

When you're around Alice, you understand the sensibility of "This bean might do for dinner today, but I know there's a better bean out there. Get me a better bean."

I remember distinctly a morning when someone had given me a hint about this farmers' market out in Stockton. The market was under a freeway. There were all these Southeast Asians, everyone sort of in Indo-Chinese costume. Chickens in cages. It was another world. I brought back things I had never seen. I remember bringing back a cardoon, and Paul Bertolli says, "Oh! cardoons! yes! Song of my heart, a cardoon!"

ALICE'S DIVIDED ATTENTION had its effects on the restaurant and on her personal life. Stephen was not getting the attention he felt he was due, and Alice was not feeling as committed to Stephen as she would have liked to feel. There was little overt conflict, seldom a raised voice, but a quiet dissonance was making itself felt.

At Chez Panisse, the front of the house seemed to be plagued by personnel problems, and once again there were mounting complaints about the service. A 1983 memo to the staff set out "five causes for immediate dismissal." The list paints a nice picture of the monkeyshines behind the scenes:

1. Stealing from the restaurant or employees
2. Being drunk on the job
3. Fighting on the premises
4. Throwing food on the premises
5. Smoking marijuana on the premises during hours
   of operation

It may be inferred from this that Alice's own behavior was by this time a great deal more disciplined than that which she once had tolerated and taken part in back in the early days of Chez Panisse. Her moral maturation had given her an enhanced appreciation of discipline, as well as a recognition that some kinds of what some people called fun could be truly destructive. She had seen it up close in two men she had been very close to—Jeremiah Tower and Jerry Budrick.

At the same time, in the back of the house, Paul Bertolli's kitchen was becoming a quiet, studious, professional workplace. "It was a new game when I got there," he says. "It was a real transition point in the restaurant, when it began to be run more like a business and less like an incestuous family. I don't think I was necessarily responsible for that. But there was new blood. A new generation of cooks started to come in who hadn't been part of the whole flower-people movement and how that mutated into the cocaine and nitrous oxide and all that excess."

"Some people will give you the impression that the place was in perpetual turmoil," says Alice. "In fact, by the eighties, everything was pretty stable, thanks to Tom Guernsey. Maybe one week we'd have some turmoil, but mostly it was pretty smooth. Paul Bertolli was also a stabilizing force. So was the birth of Fanny. The few who had big problems, or who've been disaffected, seem like big figures in the story, because that's where people's attention is drawn. There have been hundreds of people who've worked at Chez Panisse—many of them for years on end—who've learned, and been changed, all in a very quiet way."

AS FAR AS Alice was concerned, her father could do no wrong, and what Alice felt strongly about, the board nearly always went along with. In April 1983, Chez Panisse began paying a monthly stipend of $1,000 to Pat Waters's consultancy company, Organizational Dynamics. Chez Panisse needed all the help it could get. With the opening of the café, the publicity from the fire, and the publication of *The Chez Panisse Menu Cookbook*, cash flow was way up, but there still wasn't a penny of profit.

As long as there was enough money to pay the staff well and buy the best ingredients and put out the best food they could, Alice still didn't care about profit. Paul Bertolli and she were of one mind about that. "Alice and I had a real rapport," says Paul,

inasmuch as Alice had ideas but not necessarily the way to get there technically. She would say, "Make this taste good." I remember this particular dish we were working on, a pasta with sweetbreads and green beans. She said, "Can you make this taste right?" and I did that. The problem with the way people were cooking pasta at Chez Panisse was that it was sort of a California sauté approach. Italians build flavor from the bottom up. You have to spend some time building that flavor. What I did that time was take some veal on the side and make a little *fond* [caramelized bits that stick to a pan in a sauté] in the pan, and I crisped the sweetbreads. I did a deglazing of the *fond* and used *mirepoix* in that, and used some of the braising liquid from the sweetbreads. I browned the sweetbreads, so I got another *fond* and then poured that over the first one, so I got this sort of double-consommé process. That's how you build flavor. And then I worked all the fresh ingredients in at the end, and a little splash of cream, and that worked pretty well.

Alice had some amazing flights of fancy. I remember I was on a Meals on Wheels thing with her in New York City, and she'd seen some James Beard cookbook—a book from the fifties, I think, on entertaining. He had these enormous ice cubes, like five-foot ice cubes, with vegetables floating around in them. Frozen in there. I don't know how. I remember arriving in New York at four thirty in the morning and taking a ride up to a very tough section of the Bronx where there was this giant ice cube factory. And there I was with boxes of beautiful Chino vegetables and wire and weights, trying to get these vegetables down into the ice blocks as they froze. It was just ridiculous. They kept floating up to the top, there wasn't enough weight, but Alice really wanted this to happen. I thought, This is nuts, this is really nuts, do we really have to do this? But somehow I did it. It didn't look very good, and it didn't really work, but we did it. A lot of stuff like that happened.

Alice compares Chez Panisse in the 1970s to "an unruly child, just like a kid from age one to ten—difficult to take care of. And we weren't very good parents. Everything was touch-and-go." In the 1980s, however, she says, "We were trying for a transition to a more stable time. Trying to become a real professional restaurant. Our traditions were developing. We were established, but still always pushing forward."

"We moved toward making everything from scratch," says Paul Bertolli. "I developed an understanding of a menu as a form like writing a sonnet. I came into conflict with the board of directors, who always wanted to have a garden salad on the menu. That was sacrosanct. 'We have a five-course menu, and the fourth course is always garden salad.' But if I'm getting dull on garden salad, that's going to communicate to the customer. Well, a member of the board came to me one day and said, 'You can't touch that garden salad. We've all decided. Just live with it.' So I lived with it. But it started to feel formulaic to me. That's the problem, obviously, with any form that you repeat—redundancies. To keep the thing alive, you've got to turn it upside down, turn it all around, and I wanted to do that."

Alice's freedom from hands-on involvement in Chez Panisse was not uninterrupted. When Joyce Goldstein, the café chef, left in late 1983 to start her own restaurant, Square One, in San Francisco, there was once again no one in-house who Alice thought could handle the job. The café had problems—bad staff morale, confusion about reservations, continuing theft by some of the employees, disagreements about the menu, space conflicts with the downstairs kitchen (where much of the café prep was supposed to take place in the morning but often ran over into the downstairs restaurant's allotted time).

Alice's solution was to hire not one but two chefs. "My idea," she says, "was that each of them would work three days on, Monday-Tuesday-Wednesday and Thursday-Friday-Saturday. They would have complete responsibility for the time they were there. The other three days they might come in for a meeting, but mostly they'd be free to go out and forage or think up new ideas, or just be with their families. There would be cooperation, and friendly competition, and exchange of ideas."

The first "co-chef" Alice brought aboard was David Tanis. David had been part of the old after-hours crowd and had worked at restaurants all around the Bay Area, including a couple of brief stints at Chez Panisse itself. He had just the right kind of background. Even as a little kid he had loved food. He had gone to Deep Springs College, a converted cattle ranch in the desert near Bishop, California, where all twenty students not only studied the usual college courses but also ran the ranch. They cooked, carried mail, fixed fences, milked cows, cleaned stables, fed chickens, made cheese, slaughtered animals. Serious European chefs would come sometimes and cook for months; there were also distinguished professors from elsewhere in California who would rotate through a term or two. After that, David recalls, "I began faking my way into restaurant jobs. I'm not sure how much talent I really had, except to reproduce what I saw the good cooks doing—monkey see, monkey do."

The second co-chef Alice hired was Claire O'Sullivan. For reasons that remain unclear, there was instant friction between Claire and David. There ensued what David recalls as "ten days of constant drama. Then Alice had her father fire me. I was devastated." That was classic Alice: She faces an emotionally fraught task, and somebody else executes it.

Claire's friction was not with David alone, apparently, for she resigned the next day. In twenty-four hours the Chez Panisse Café had gone from having two chefs to none.

It took Alice about a minute to decide to call David and beg him to return—to be café *chef*, not co-.

"Alice was not going to just turn me loose, however," David recalls. "She wrote all the menus for the first six months. She tasted everything, over and over. She criticized everything I did. There were days when I would just cry like a child. Alice was always fiddling with the food up to the last second. We were constantly reprinting the menu. It was 'Oh, let's change everything right now, I've had a better idea.'" And then she would disappear, rushing home to be with Fanny.

UNDER PAT WATERS'S fiscal discipline—and despite continuing problems with employees making off with wine, desserts, and nearly anything else not bolted down—Chez Panisse was finally making money. They weren't making much, but it was enough for Christmas bonuses, a couple of new cars, and satisfied auditors. Paul Bertolli and Alice Waters were each making $42,000 in salary, plus stock and bonuses. Alice had, in addition, a considerable income from book royalties, and then, in June 1984 came the second cookbook, *Chez Panisse Pasta, Pizza & Calzone*, this time carefully attributed on the cover to three authors—Alice, Patricia Curtan, and Martine Labro.

By 1984, Chez Panisse had become what Alice wanted, and more. With Paul Bertolli firmly at the helm, Alice was free to want more, to expand her horizons, to dream again. She never lost touch with old friends, however. Late-night phone calls out of the blue, invitations to pitch in on a dinner party at her house, a birthday meal with a beautifully printed menu card designed by David Goines or Patricia Curtan—she held on fiercely to friends and family. "Alice is a very loyal person," says Barbara

Fanny and Alice, with Jim Maser
in the background

Carlitz. "She doesn't leave people behind. She continues to gather people around, but not at the expense of old acquaintances or old friends. She's very sure of herself philosophically, and not so sure of herself in terms of human relationships. She has absolute conviction, mixed with timidity, which is a beguiling style. I think that's what has made her the natural P.R. magnet that she seems to be."

In the spring of 1984, Alice helped her sister Laura Waters Maser, and Laura's husband, Jim, establish the tiny but instantly successful Café Fanny, serving breakfast, snacks, and lunch. Café Fanny was only a few blocks from Chez Panisse, cheek by jowl with the wine shop of Alice's longtime friend Kermit Lynch. Kermit went way back with Jim Maser, too, having been lead singer in Jim's rock band, the Roaches. Many of the customers ate their Café Fanny takeout lounging on their cars in Kermit's parking lot, and it was perhaps the closest thing yet to Alice's original vision of a hangout.

"And Fanny was growing up right there in the restaurant," Alice says happily. "She was part of it. Everybody there was her friend. They were wonderful babysitters. They liked to cook for her. They had the same set of values. And then she had Bob Carrau and Sue, who took her out into nature and did things for her that I couldn't do. She was a happy child, a really happy child. And she loved the food at Chez Panisse, including some things you wouldn't really think a little kid could even stomach, much less love. Anchovies!"

· ANCHOÏADE ·

The way we did it was sort of à la Austin de Croze [co-author with Curnonsky of *Le Trésor Gastronomique de la France,* published in 1933]—with dried figs, almonds, garlic, olive oil, and anchovies.

Always salt-packed anchovies. That's all we ever use. I soak them awhile, and then I fillet them quickly, and let them sit in water again to get some of the salt out. Then you make a paste with those and the other things with your mortar and pestle.

The best way to cook it is over fresh, green pine needles. You get a really wonderful, special aroma. We almost burned down the restaurant a couple of times, however. We put the pine branches right in the wood-burning oven, and they were too dry and caught fire. We didn't do that many times.

So you just grill some toast, and spread the paste, uncooked, on the warm toast. I think our latest version is to grill the bread and then spread the paste on the hot bread without cooking it. I always have to ask all the cooks about how they cook this, because we have advanced since the medieval days of the restaurant.

12.

ALICE
TAKES FLIGHT

1985–1986

The middle 1980s brought to Chez Panisse a maturing that characteristically mirrored Alice's own. In the spring of 1985, Alice's father proposed that Chez Panisse be completely computerized: the purchasing, the checks, the accounting, the financial analysis, reservations, everything. Alice, who hated virtually anything high-tech, was horrified, but she submitted, for it was by her own choice that her father, without a title, a staff position, or a seat on the board, had effectively taken charge of the business of Chez Panisse.

One manifestation of Alice's technophobia was that the restaurant still didn't take credit cards. With the café packed near bursting every night and the price of dinner downstairs rising rapidly—from $25 in 1980 to $40 in 1984 (a 60 percent increase)—there was a lot of cash flowing into Chez Panisse. And this cash flow was really cash, which can disappear without a trace if the malefactor is half clever.

No cash flowed through the kitchen. The worst a cook could do was to swipe a bottle or two of wine or a truffle, maybe gobble a furtive slice of tart in the walk-in refrigerator. The back of the house, therefore, was a world apart from the front, and since the arrival of Paul Bertolli in the restaurant and David Tanis in the café, the better angels of the restaurant's nature had been thriving in the kitchens both downstairs and up. A memo from David to his staff expresses the Chez Panisse ethos during this period at its best:

> We are all at different stages of development. Some of us are career cooks, and some of us are cooking our way through college: some of us are cooks because we haven't quite figured out what we really want to do—some because we finally have! Any of these can be good reasons for cooking at Chez Panisse . . . if [your] cooking is approached with passion, with an eye toward beauty, with care; if efficiency is important, if improvement and shared knowledge are important; if cooking in a "normal" restaurant would not be enough. . . .
>
> Learn to cut an onion beautifully, to reduce a sauce to just the right consistency, to grill a piece of bread perfectly. Know when the pasta is "relaxed," when to stoke the fire. Make your plates lovely and simple. Rub your salad leaves lightly and let them fall from your hands naturally. . . .
>
> If your technique is faulty, it may be because your appreciation of the medium is not refined. Conversely, if you are having trouble with a visual aesthetic, it might be because you haven't mastered a certain technique. Please avail yourself of the many resources here. Talk food, read, get involved. Cook the staff meal; cook at home. . . .

This is not how most chefs think. The refinement, the intellectuality, and the philosophical bent of David Tanis were the kinds of qualities that moved Alice most deeply. His memo makes clear why it is so hard for anyone who has ever cooked at Chez Panisse to cook anywhere else, and why it is so hard for Chez Panisse to bring aboard anyone trained elsewhere. Chez Panisse sends not only apostles into the world; it also sometimes sends out alumni who try to be explorers, who venture into the larger restaurant world and then flee back to the home that Chez Panisse has become for them. As a rule, Chez Panisse welcomes their return, even when their departures may have been awkward or worse. They return, of course, with new experience and often valuable ideas. In this way Chez Panisse fertilizes the wider world of restaurants and is fertilized in its turn.

As easy as it can be for an alumnus to return, it can be equally difficult for a newcomer to penetrate the Chez Panisse culture. A cook with however brilliant a résumé from somewhere else may be turned aside with little more than a glance and a few polite words from Alice. You've got to "get it" to work at Chez Panisse. And "getting it" is a very elusive quality: The "it" is the whole thing—the ethic, a commitment to being your best, the sense of style, the palate, the nose, the intellect, the instinct, the personal manners, the ability to sense intuitively what Alice is all about, even when she cannot put it into words.

By the mid-1980s, Chez Panisse was doing very well (in every aspect except the bottom line). *Newsweek* hailed the restaurant's food as "a revolution in American cooking."[1] *Vogue* described dining at Chez Panisse as "one of this country's most sensuously satisfying, highly personal eating experiences."[2] In *House & Garden,* Jason Epstein (Alice's editor at Random House) wrote, "She penetrates to the essence—the soul, you might say—of a quail or an oyster or even of a sack of flour or a bottle of oil."[3] The *San Francisco Chronicle*'s restaurant critic wrote, "I've never found the food at Panisse as consistently good as it is now."[4] Marian Burros wrote in the *New York Times,* "More than any other single figure, Miss Waters has been instrumental in developing the exciting and imaginative style that has been labeled New American Cuisine."[5]

Chez Panisse and Alice Waters were still (and are still) not to everyone's liking. In his *Private Guide,* Robert Finigan thought Paul Bertolli's cooking came nowhere near Jeremiah Tower's (it should be noted that Jeremiah had become a friend of his). Finigan demoted the restaurant from four stars to two and stopped going there. *California* magazine called Chez Panisse "fussy and self-conscious," with "all the verve of a requiem."[6] In *The Nation,* David Sundelson wrote, "The triumph of Chez Panisse represents a new privatism, a sad turn inward, away from public issues and commitments."[7]

Alice had become known as the mother of the New American Cooking, or California cuisine, as it came to be called. Was she the personification of this new movement because she grabbed credit from others? Was it because she always went running to the nearest camera or reporter's notebook?

The answer is not simple. Certainly she liked the attention, the admiration, the fame. What is determinative, however, is not so much Alice herself as contemporary culture, which demands that every story have a hero. If you're a writer, you'll find it very hard to sell an article about an idea unless that idea is embodied in a hero (or a villain). People don't want abstractions; they want flesh-and-blood heroes. In Alice, so soft-spoken, so passionate, yet also so flustered and inarticulate sometimes, people had found a hero who was also unmistakably, unheroically human.

"Total strangers," wrote *California Living* magazine in April 1985, "call her Alice."

Alice was not instinctively comfortable in the spotlight. "I remember flying to New York one time," says Charles Shere. "Lindsey and I were sitting three or four rows behind Alice, and somehow, the way the seats were, I could see through the spaces between the seats to Alice. I just happened to see her pick up the in-flight magazine. She opened it up, saw a full-page picture of herself, closed the magazine, and put it back in its pocket. And she was closing it in a real hurry lest one of the people next to her should see it. It was a very funny moment. She was embarrassed." But she also knew that she had a role to play that no one in her right mind would have spurned.

"It is the fact," says Barbara Carlitz, "that a large number of dedicated people have let it be Alice's show, and have not piped up and said, 'Wait a minute, Alice owns two percent of the restaurant at this point,' or something, or, 'But wait a minute, Alice had three partners,' 'Wait a minute, there's a board that really ran it,' 'Wait a minute, there's a manager,' 'Wait, there's a chef.' No one has ever done this, with the possible exception of Jeremiah. I presume it's partly for two reasons. One, she's so damn good at it, and the myth is probably more enchanting than the reality to people. And two, I have to presume that people genuinely respect Alice enough to let her have that."

There is also to be considered "the Matthew effect," which was first described by Robert K. Merton.[8] In a series of interviews with Nobel laureates,

Merton found, "They repeatedly observe that eminent scientists get disproportionately great credit for their contributions to science while relatively
unknown scientists tend to get disproportionately little credit for comparable contributions." Merton gave the effect its name based on chapter 25,
verse 29, of the Gospel According to Saint Matthew: "For unto every one
that hath shall be given, and he shall have abundance: but from him that
hath not shall be taken away even that which he hath."

In July 1984, Jeremiah Tower opened his dream restaurant, Stars. In its
chic and jazzy premises in the heart of San Francisco's Civic Center—home
to City Hall, the library, the opera, the ballet, the symphony—Stars was in
the perfect position to cultivate the rich, powerful, and publicity-seeking.
The food was exciting, the atmosphere electric, and Jeremiah triumphant.
On the wall he hung a framed letter from Alice, written in happier times,
praising him profusely. Displaying that letter, he told the *Chronicle,* was "a
little bit of malicious vengeance. People can see in her own handwriting just
who is whose disciple."[9] He seems not to have known how self-degrading a
gesture hanging that letter on the wall at Stars was.

In a piece in the *New York Times* by Marian Burros on September 26,
1984, Alice's words on Jeremiah show a vividly contrasting character:

"He had a bold way of doing things," she said of Mr. Tower, who is
now co-owner of the Santa Fe Bar and Grill in Berkeley and owner
of the two-month-old Stars. "He was not hesitant," Miss Waters
said. "His cooking is more elaborate than mine, more flamboyant
and richer. I'm more garlic and olive oil—he's more cream and butter. But initially I was fascinated by his combinations, things I
wouldn't have thought of."

There's perhaps a subtle little knife twist in that "initially," but the
otherwise gracious tone is that of a smiling winner.

Alice had mastered her self-representation to the media—with the media's helpful assistance—but she had yet to master Chez Panisse. An aver-

age of twenty main courses were going missing every night. An exchange of memos among the staff sought to identify the strengths and weaknesses of Chez Panisse at the moment. Paul Bertolli thought David Tanis worked too slowly and "wasn't a leader." David Tanis's riposte was, "Our food must not be compromised." Fritz Streiff, always a thoughtful analyst of Chez Panisse, thought the restaurant "needed a radical change, to attract people lost due to loss of novelty, lack of local reviews, lack of variety."

For the fiscal year ending June 30, 1984, total sales had been a robust $2.7 million. Twenty-three thousand dinners had been served downstairs, more than a hundred thousand meals in the café. And Chez Panisse had finally shown a profit. Two percent.

Any other business would have considered that barely scraping by, but at Chez Panisse it was cause for jubilation. Pat Waters got his computer system—$46,000 worth. The restaurant lent Jerry Budrick $12,000 to buy a car. Alice's salary was raised to $52,000 per annum plus 10 percent of net income. Paul Bertolli got a similar raise, and a three-year contract. Pagnol et Cie insured the life of Alice Waters for one million dollars.

In the restaurant downstairs—under Tom Guernsey's sole leadership, now that Alice had largely given up acting as hostess—the front of the house began to run nearly as smoothly as the kitchen. "Bill Staggs and Tom were the most perfect waiters," says Alice. "They were like ballet dancers together. Everything just *worked.*" Thanks to Pat Edwards's hawkeyed vigilance and Pat Waters's computer system, the finances had begun to make some sense. Alice's father claimed that the new system was saving Chez Panisse $10,000 a month. The service had regained its style of polite familiarity, hospitality, generosity, and casual expertise. The waiters were taking home a lot of money, legitimately gained. Was all this good news just another of the restaurant's habitual fluctuations, or was Chez Panisse growing up?

What was clear was that Alice was letting go a little. By late spring of 1985, she was sometimes coming in only once a week, to help set up the downstairs dining room and act as hostess for the evening. There were also times when she would whirl through to taste the day's fare—often every item on both menus—and offer her customary detailed and merciless advice. But the rest of her time belonged to her daughter, and perhaps, a

Charles and Lindsey Shere

bit, to her relationship with Stephen, and to a grand new project that foreshadowed grander ones to come.

Alice was proposing to turn the restaurant of the Oakland Museum of California into a living exhibition of her philosophy. Food would be as fundamental a part of the museum's mission as the art it showed and the history and science it taught. The landscaping would be transformed into a "teaching garden," where children and other museum visitors would learn how crops were grown and turned into food. Then, in the museum dining room, they could eat what they had just learned about. With Fanny turning twenty-one months old, Alice was particularly interested in children's food. She foresaw the museum snack bar "selling sack lunches for children. They could eat lunch on benches in the garden. I wanted a demonstration bakery, where people could watch tortillas being patted out by hand." When asked how much it might cost to get the project off the ground and whether she expected it to turn a profit, Alice answered, "There's always money for good ideas."

That same spring, Pat Waters found a person who he believed could run Chez Panisse like a real business. Two percent was not Alice's father's idea of decent profit. Moreover, an effective manager would give Alice all the more freedom to spread her wings. The board authorized $15,000 for a six-month trial of Richard Mazzera as general manager.

Barb Carlitz had long been a member of the Chez Panisse board, as well as a virtual member of the Waters family; her recollection of the advent of Richard Mazzera is this: "Pat Waters served as pseudomanager for a while, and he decided we really did need to have somebody. Richard Mazzera was very young, very ambitious, attractive, probably in his mid-twenties. Pat, I think, considered him in some ways the son he'd never had. He considered him certainly a protégé. Some people in the restaurant hated Richard, and some liked Richard. Everyone was very suspicious, after all these anarchic years of nobody with a title of manager."

Pat Edwards, who thought *she* was the manager, was incensed. As she fumed, her sister's attention was inevitably elsewhere: Lindsey Shere was about to publish *Chez Panisse Desserts,* with a very large first print run of sixty thousand copies. Patricia Curtan had designed the book, and the painter Wayne Thiebaud—famous for his lush depictions of pastry—had illustrated it.

Lindsey's retelling of one of her favorite recipes demonstrates the subtlety essential to making simple food extraordinary.

· LINDSEY'S FRUIT GALETTE ·

Peaches, nectarines, and plums are great for this. It's easily translated to apples and pears, too. One of the great things about a galette is you can make it any size you want. If you want something for two people, you can make a little one. You start with a *pâte brisée,* of whatever size you need for what you're making. The one I use, for six to eight servings, is a cup of flour, six tablespoons of butter, a quarter teaspoon of salt, and a quarter cup of cold water. You just put it together like pie crust, very quickly. I usually chill it then for a little while to let the flour relax a bit.

I roll it out really thin, as thin as possible, into a big circle. I usually bake it on a pizza pan, but it could be on a flat cookie sheet. If you've got a pizza stone, putting the pan on that would be an ideal way to bake it, because you want to get heat to the bottom of it very quickly.

So you roll out a big circle and lay it on the pan. Then I usually make a mixture of equal parts of sugar and flour. For this size I'd use about two tablespoons of each and spread that over the bottom of the galette, out to about two inches from the edge. It's there to sit under the fruit and thicken the juices. Sometimes I add macaroon crumbs, or even a thin layer of almond paste.

If I were using peaches or plums or nectarines or pluots [a plum-apricot hybrid], I would use about a quart of sliced fruit. You can either arrange the fruit in a fancy design on the dough or just scrumble it around. Peaches I peel usually, but not plums or nectarines.

Now this is the part where you have to make a judgment. I sprinkle the top with sugar—more if it's something like plums, and less if it's something like peaches. You can sprinkle it reasonably heavily, because those things become much more tart when you cook them. If you want to test it, what you should do is cook a bit of the fruit in a tiny little pot, and sugar it and see how much you need. I can't give you any measurement. It's just something you have to try.

When you've sprinkled the fruit with sugar, fold the edges of the dough up over the fruit. You can pleat them in or gather them in, depending on how good a seamstress you are. Then I brush those folded-over edges of the dough with water, pretty heavily, and then I sprinkle just the edges really heavily with sugar, so there's a thorough coating on it.

It goes into the oven to bake at four hundred degrees for forty-five or fifty minutes. You should rotate it in the oven, and watch to make sure that the caramel on the crust is not burning. The thing you want to be sure of is that the fruit is thoroughly cooked, and that it's boiling in the center of the galette, because that will cook the flour on the bottom.

When it's done, immediately slide it onto a rack to cool, so that the bottom doesn't get soggy. In the first five minutes or so, while the juices are still bubbling, I use a pastry brush to pick up those juices and glaze any of the fruit that looks dry. After that, the juices disappear into the flour, so you've got to be quick. And that's it.

WHATEVER SUBSURFACE friction there was between them, Alice and Stephen seemed determined to overcome it, if only for Fanny's sake. On September 23, 1985, with two-year-old Fanny as flower girl, Alice Waters married Stephen Singer in a simple ceremony in New York's Central Park.

Why there? "Part of it," Stephen explains, "was that it sounded exciting, interesting, unconventional, and part of it was that if we had gotten married in Berkeley, the social obligations would have been huge. We went to New York as a way to not have to invite anybody. It was just our immediate family, so there were about, oh, sixteen, eighteen, twenty people at the wedding."

"It was in the herb garden," says Alice. "It was quite beautiful. By a pond in the herb garden."

"She had all the Pagnol fantasies going on at the same time," recalls Alice's sister Ellen. "She named her daughter Fanny. When Alice and Stephen got married, she wore a dress that could have been a double for the dress that Fanny wore in the wedding in *César.*"

On their return from a three-week honeymoon in Tuscany (with Fanny along), Stephen went back to work at Singer and Foy, and Alice found familiar troubles at Chez Panisse. Jerry Budrick was drinking on the job again, complaining about his salary, and having trouble at home, too. Alice

Alice and Stephen's wedding

and the board agreed that when Jerry started acting badly in the restaurant, there needed to be some way to get him off the floor, though they didn't say precisely who was to do it, or how. Any other business probably would have fired him, but this was Chez Panisse, and Jerry was family.

Alice defended Jerry as long as she could, but the board was adamant. His drinking while working was not to be tolerated. Still, they were remarkably compassionate. In the fall of 1985, Jerry was given a sabbatical of six weeks, with full pay. He began work on a new business, developing a spring water source in the Sierra Nevada foothills. To pursue that, he decided to take the full year of 1986 off, though he remained a member of the board of directors of Pagnol et Cie. In 1987, Jerry Budrick and Chez Panisse parted ways for good. He continued to own 14 percent of the restaurant for the next five years, however, and continued to serve on the board through the same period.

"Alice is very tough," says Greil Marcus. "She wouldn't be where she was if she weren't. But these board decisions sometimes took a very long time, because Alice had to be convinced that we had to be cruel about it, and that's not her way. And sometimes it gave her cover for getting rid of people. She could either convince herself that it wasn't she who was doing it—which would be true, it would be the board—or it could be communicated through other people: This isn't Alice getting rid of you, this is us. It took a long time to get Jerry Budrick out, to isolate him, to push him into his own venture, the water business that he was trying to start. But ultimately you slam the door, and there is no route back."

With the restaurant full every night, great reviews still pouring in, herself newly married, in the autumn and winter of 1985–1986 Alice was full of optimism. She hired Stephen, first as a consultant, to restructure the wine list, and then to take control of the whole wine operation (which was still losing five hundred bottles a month). She put her shares in Chez Panisse into joint tenancy with Stephen. She persuaded North Point Press to publish a special edition of Marcel Pagnol's memoirs to commemorate the restaurant's approaching fifteenth birthday, and wrote a foreword for it herself. Despite her mistrust of technology and any sort of large corporation, she acceded to her father's insistence that Chez Panisse begin accepting credit cards.

Never had Alice seemed so certain about everything. When her sister Ellen Pisor was planning a first trip to France, she called Alice. "I wanted to really experience some of these wonderful things that she'd been talking about for years, and I said, 'Where should we go?' And she said to me in her own declarative style that there wasn't anything worth going to in southern France anymore. It was all built up. The Parisians had come down and taken over all the windmills. It was overrun by tourists. It was ruined, ruined! I got off the phone, and I thought, Oh, my God, it's ruined, and I've never been there. I have nothing to compare it to, so will I think it's ruined? I was very discouraged. Then Alice said, 'Let me think about it.' About two days later, she called me at midnight—she always forgot whether I was three hours behind her or ahead of her—and she said, 'Okay, I've got a place for you. Nathalie Waag's. It's great. She's got a little house outside of Bonnieux, and she serves meals, and she'll take you to the markets, and blah, blah, blah. I'll send you some stuff on it.' And you know, it really was quite wonderful."

Chez Panisse was beginning to have fun again. One anonymous jokester created a bogus menu identical in style to the real one, and then he interleaved copies of the fake among the real:

Tuesday
Parrot leg tartare, beaks & guano
Bird-face soup with pesto
Grilled glazed parrot breasts with yellow and red
  feathers, sautéed parakeet feet
Garden salad
Feuilleté of flight feathers, back claws and budgie
  droppings

Wednesday
Mixed grill: Amazon parrots, macaws, cockatiel &
  conure with Chino Ranch peppers, pesto & grilled
  cat paws
Pasta with sun-dried conure beaks, herbs & perch
  gunk
Roast tenderloin of macaw breast with garlic sauce,
  warm guava & papaya
Garden salad
Warm guano & avocado gratin

. . . and so on, down to the pièce de résistance:

Saturday
Double yellow head & green bean salad
Risotto with cuttlebone & shredded cage paper
Young canaries grilled & roasted with red wine sauce
Provençal stuffed birdy assholes & grilled vegetables
Warm guano tart with lavender-honey ice cream

"Why parrots?" asks Alice. "I have no idea. Whoever it was slipped these in with all the other menus, so you never knew who was going to get one. They just put them in there, printed exactly the way that our other menus were printed. So at first we didn't find it. It was very cleverly done. We just laughed hysterically. I don't know how long it went on. I know I shouldn't have let it."

On the fifteenth birthday of Chez Panisse, August 28, 1986, the North Point Press's limited edition of Marcel Pagnol's memoirs, *My Father's Glory and My Mother's Castle,* went on sale at the bar. In the foreword, Alice expressed with particular clarity the Pagnolian dream that sustained her: "an ideal reality where life and work were inseparable and the daily pace left you time for the afternoon anisette or the restorative game of pétanque, and where eating together nourished the spirit as well as the body—since the food was raised, harvested, hunted, fished, and gathered by people sustaining and sustained by each other and by the earth itself." She ended the little essay with a recipe very much in the spirit both of Pagnol and of Chez Panisse:

· GRILLED QUAIL WITH WILD HERBS
AND OLIVE TOASTS ·

Marinate the quail with olive oil, a little sweet wine from Provence, fresh thyme, rosemary, and sage for several hours. Salt and pepper the quail. Grill them over fairly hot wood embers about forty-five minutes on the skin side, until nicely browned. Turn over and cook a few more minutes. While the quail sit, toast thin slices of bread over the coals and spread them with a paste of olives crushed with garlic and made smooth with olive oil. Serve with a salad of bitter greens and a bottle of Bandol.

13.

DEATH
AND LIFE

1986–1987

I n 1986, it had been scarcely four years since the United States Centers for Disease Control had coined the term *acquired immune deficiency syndrome,* but AIDS had already torn its merciless way through gay communities across the country, nowhere with greater ferocity than in the San Francisco Bay Area. The disease was not a killer only of homosexual men, although they were by far its most numerous and most prominent victims. And Tom Guernsey had it.

"Despair doesn't begin to describe what we felt," says Alice. "I had never been so devastated, brokenhearted, there's no word strong enough. My dearest, sweetest, irreplaceable Tom. He was so afraid, and so courageous. He was going to keep working."

As the birth of Fanny had awoken Alice to the future, the coming death of Tom Guernsey awoke her to its fragility.

I felt I had to do something now. There was nothing we could do to save Tom, but the illness was so ghastly, such torture, it tore people's lives apart. People with AIDS were living alone, and dying alone.

Mutual affection à la famille Panisse: *David Tanis,*
Tom Guernsey, and Alice

And there were suddenly so many. Vince Calcagno, the owner of
Zuni Café in San Francisco (this was before Judy Rodgers became
partner), had lost five friends in one month, and he was organizing a
big benefit to raise money to help take care of people with AIDS. Tom
and I had to be involved. It was going to be called Aid and Comfort.

April 1987 brought two changes with long-term consequences for Chez
Panisse and Alice. She decided to give the two-chef idea another try, asking Catherine Brandel to be co-chef with David Tanis in the café. She also
hired Gerald Rosenfield to replace Catherine as the restaurant's forager.

"Ah, Jerry Rosenfield," sighs Alice, sadly. "He was a great writer, and
very important to me personally. I'd met him during the Scheer campaign.
He was a moral force. An M.D., a psychiatrist, but he hadn't practiced in
a long time. After Bob Scheer's campaign, we lost contact, and years later
he just appeared one day, with a bucket of mussels."

Richard Seibert, a longtime pizza chef in the café, remembers, "Doctor Jerry had been out at Bolinas harvesting mussels, and thought they were the most delicious ones he had ever had. So he put a few dozen of them into a Folger's coffee can, snuck up, dropped them in front of Alice's back door, rang the doorbell, and ran."

Alice recalls, "He was destitute, living on the streets, just barely making it. He'd had big depressions, and that had made him a whole different person. So I bought the mussels, and then he brought more, and then he brought more."

Jerry's first task as forager was to find meat supplies as good, and as pure, as the produce the restaurant was getting from Green Gulch, Warren Weber, and the Chinos. He threw himself into the job. He wrote rhapsodic reports on his travels, the farms he found, and the people. Typical was this one, of October 20, 1987:

> Tonight's lambs were raised by Lori Gibbs of Acampo, in San Joaquin County. These are registered Southdown sheep, and Lori's show animals have won prizes at country fairs, and one of her year-ling ewes was champion at the California State Fair. Lori is twelve years old, and this is her 4-H Club project.
>
> [He goes on to describe the feed, the absence of medication, the heritage of the Southdown variety of sheep.] Perhaps it has some-thing to do with their ancient lineage, but I have noticed, looking over the animals at the fairs, that the Southdown is characterized by a personableness and self-containment not seen in most other breeds of sheep.

"Every time Jerry brought something," says Alice,

> he noticed something about the restaurant that needed to be attended to. The way the staff was treated, or how they greeted people coming in, or how I presented myself out in the world. He was always thinking about the people who weren't being considered. He would remind me how people were feeling about working at the restaurant, and how I needed to not forget the people who were my real friends, and not get

carried away with the fame of the restaurant. He would stay and talk with the dishwashers late at night, and he'd tell me that I needed to pay them more, and pay them more attention.

He wrote me long letters about all these things. Handwritten, three pages. Who were the honest and worthy people to buy food from, who was trying to take advantage of us. Treatises on garbage— he got me out there standing in the garbage Dumpster one time, made me clean it out myself. And boy, we changed our system right after that. Ever since then I've been obsessed with compost.

"When I first started there," Richard Seibert recalls, "part of Jerry's job was maintaining the outside grounds. He was responsible for recycling all the wine bottles and for keeping the garbage cans scrubbed out. I found a note in my paycheck, I forget exactly when, that said [he reads]:

As summertime draws near, it behooves us to minimize the miasma emanating from our Dumpsters. Therefore, we earnestly request that any sacks containing organic matter with sufficient moisture to leak (which would smell if not refrigerated) be tied with string. For your convenience, ready-cut lengths of string may be found by the dishwashers' dumbwaiter and upstairs under the counter by the rear waiters' station.

"That pretty much sums up Jerry," continues Seibert. "He was very crazy. When he was sane, he was incredibly bright.

"As *famille Panisse,* we'd all take care of each other if we got sick. So a committee was organized, and groups of people would take turns with Doctor Jerry to help reintegrate him back into the world."

"Jerry was my conscience," Alice says. "He was very important in my life. But ultimately he was having these horrible outbursts in front of the restaurant, and we'd have to call the police to take him away. He was sinking, going way down. Having fits of anxiety and terrible anger. Psychotic episodes. He knew it himself. He knew he had to be restrained. He was a peaceful person, physically, but a raging in-your-face yeller. Over anything. Maybe somebody had left the remains of their lunch on a table out back. The littlest things. And I was a public figure, and he wanted me to make the world right. I wasn't doing it right, or as fast as he wanted me to do it. I think he would be proud of me now, but . . ." Her voice trails off.

With Jerry Rosenfield spiraling into madness and Tom Guernsey growing sicker, the imminence of pain and death inspired in Alice what, in an essay some years later, she termed "a deepened appreciation for the joy and life in food."[1] A salad, a carrot, a plum, at its best, perhaps mere hours from its plucking, was in a sense still alive, and gave life not only to the body but to the mind of its eater. A fish too long out of water confessed its deadness in its sunken eyes, its graying skin, the doughy slackening of its meat. A fish fresh from the sea glistened with aliveness, its eyes moist and full, its muscles firm, its scales still sparkling. The life in food, Alice believed, wasn't just a metaphor. "We have always seen the meal as a center of the human experience," reads the restaurant's official pronouncement on sustainability. "At the table we are nourished and gladdened, put in touch with the source of life. . . . It is central to both the deepest and the most joyous of human activities: generosity, companionship, nourishment, growth."[2]

Alan Tangren, who had been at the restaurant for years, became the next forager, and it was in that capacity that he grew into something of a Chez Panisse institution. He had grown up living part-time on a farm in the California Sierra Nevada, with a grandmother who was a great cook. Alan himself cooked all through college and graduate school, eventually emerging as a professor of meteorology. But he couldn't keep away from the stove. He began cooking for the famed gourmet Darrell Corti in Sacramento: "He would have dinner parties at his house, and after every course he would come into the kitchen with his critique of how the meal was going. He was a great teacher. I thought by then that I was ready to cook at Chez Panisse. But Alice didn't."

He persisted nevertheless, and was soon doing lowly tasks in the café under chef Joyce Goldstein. Joyce had introduced more regularity and less variation in the café menu.

"It was very codified," says Alan.

Joyce made all the decisions. I think Alice was sort of distracted at that time, with Fanny and traveling. We had actual recipe books. Joyce's recipes. There was less experimentation. It was still seasonal to a certain degree, but you knew that every Friday we would have the wild rice and beef tenderloin salad.

Then when David Tanis came to the café, I started doing all kinds of things. I was the café chef on Mondays, and then the rest of the week I worked either in the prep kitchen or on the line or whatever needed to be done. Chez Panisse has always cultivated that sort of pinch-hitter quality. It's Alice's way of letting people find their own place. She talks about tossing the cards in the air. In my case, it's meant I've been able to do lots of different things. It's why I've stayed here so long.

Joyce Goldstein demurs. "There were no written recipes for the café; whoever was in charge of the menu and the kitchen created the food. (Eventually I put together a binder with recipe outlines and descriptions that I typed at home and brought in.) My weekly menu plan had to be approved by Alice before it went into effect. If she did not want something on the menu, it went. I would give the menu to her to read the week before. So if we occasionally ran a filet and wild rice salad, she approved it. And the customers loved it. We got rave reviews and endless repeat business."

"Alan did that job for ten years, and he was always marvelous," says Alice. "He loves to surprise people. You know, 'You think you know what a blackberry tastes like, but taste this one.' And *pow*! He has such an amazing palate for fruit that when Lindsey retired, he was the obvious choice for pastry chef."

"It really was a leap of faith on Alice's part," says Alan. "She just said, 'Oh, give it a try.' And it took me a year to learn everything. I was totally dependent on Lindsey's recipes, and the pastry sous-chef, Mary Canales, who knew much more than I did. And of course Alice was always reaching for the next thing, wanting to do something differently."

(Alan Tangren would leave Chez Panisse in 2006, after twenty-five years in which, in Alice's words, "he just always knew the right thing to do." He is now raising flowers on his family's old farm in the Sierra.)

Chez Panisse by now had relationships with a number of excellent farmers, but the restaurant remained dependent on their choices of crops, and their harvesting schedules. Alice wanted to work with a farm that would grow what she wanted, and when. Her father undertook the task of interviewing more than a hundred farmers, all within a hundred miles of Chez Panisse. With the help of agriculture experts at the University of California at Davis, he whittled the list down to eighteen, and then to four. Toward the end of 1985, when Pat and Alice Waters interviewed the finalists, the winner was indisputable.

Nobody could ever have dreamed up Bob Cannard, or his farm in Sonoma County. His crops were choked with weeds. Some of the weeds came in wild—rye, filaree, mallow—but some he planted himself—barley, vetch, triticale. It looked like total disorder: a tomato plant here, a pepper there, three cabbages, a cluster of carrots. When Alice walked Bob's fields, the ground was as springy as a mattress, so rich was it in organic matter. Bob would clutch a fistful of topsoil and shove it under her nose. "It's delicious!" he would proclaim, and pop some in his mouth. He talked nonstop. He would pluck a fruit or vegetable, carve off a piece, and, grinning, command, "Taste that." It would be, reliably, the best turnip, radish, apricot, carrot, or avocado Alice had ever tasted. "Happy plants!" he'd exclaim. Sometimes he sang to them.

And he loved to talk about them. "You can read the whole plant," he said. "It's right there before you, and if you pay attention to the nature of the bark and the quality of the leaves and the growth habits and all of the observable and smellable and tastable characteristics, you can see the past history of a plant. In its new growth, you can see its present. If it had a bad past and has a bad present, why, then, it's going to be pretty difficult for it to have a good future, but a sick plant is one of your greatest teachers. The most important yield, as far as I'm concerned, is that I have been able to become a true cultivator of nature. I can go out into almost any circumstance and grow almost anything. With health. With health."

Bob Cannard

When Bob bought the land, in 1976, it was in miserable shape, the soil compacted to hardpan, the creek dead dry.

I picked this place specifically because it's somewhat isolated. I wanted to be out of the eye of general humanity, and not having people tell me that I'm doing everything incorrectly. I wanted to do everything incorrectly. I wanted to figure out how to do it correctly by doing it incorrectly, because it's obvious that the conventional agricultural dictates are incorrect, because our soils are in decline, our crop quality and food quality are in decline.

The place had had forty thousand turkeys on it for forty years, and the soils were heavily eroded and toxified by turkey manure and pretty well poisoned off with herbicides. If I'd wanted to make money, I could have selected a very fine soil, and I could do things wrong and never know it, and I could do things right and never know it. But I wanted a soil that I would know by observing if I did something appropriate and if I did something incorrect.

Under Bob Cannard's care, the creek began to run year-round, thronged with turtles, salamanders, and the tiny smolts of steelhead trout. The farm comprises only thirty cultivated acres (a hundred and fifty more acres, not cultivated, serve as watershed), on which Bob produces some two hundred varieties of fruits and vegetables. Leading a visitor on a tour, he says,

Well, let's see, here we've got my olive trees, about six hundred of those, just getting started, really. Got about a hundred gallons of oil this year. Here are persimmons, plums, apples, favas, figs, lemon verbena—you know how Alice loves that lemon verbena tea—broccoli rabe, leeks, beets. Over here we've got our raspberries, and artichokes, chervil, rocket, various lettuces. Chez Panisse trucks all their organic waste up here, you know, and I put it to work. Table grapes. I don't know how many varieties of them. Every vine's a different one. I'm starting a little cow herd, a British breed called Dexter. They're good for beef and milk both. Chez Panisse is my only customer, except I do still go to the farmers' market over in Sonoma town, Tuesday evenings and Friday mornings.

My setup with Alice has changed a bit lately, because Alice wants to support lots of farmers, though we do have, in my perception, kind of a marriage relationship. I've been monogamous, but my partner hasn't been. But I can't be too critical. She's got other social support reasons. Right now, they're using a lot of my stuff because it's winter and a lot of the sunny-day farmers go away, but come summertime, when all the easy-to-grow, nice-tasting things like tomatoes come in, well, they get lots of stuff from lots of other people.

All this is wildlife habitat. Nothing's fenced except the cows. The deer don't bother me. I let them have what they want. Only real problem right now is the ground squirrels. Here's apricot, more plums, endive, escarole. If your plants are healthy, they'll coexist with the bugs. They turn out to be better food, too. There's a completeness about these plants that they share with the people who eat them.

A good farmer's got to know how to assess plant health. You see those dead leaves rotting? That's not a problem. That plant's feeding itself for the future. Some bugs help you, too. The cucumber beetle visits the zucchini flower—never poops in it, either—and then at night, when the flower closes, the bug protects it.

"Finding Bob Cannard was a thrill," Alice says. "I have always had an excitement about meeting people who were growing beautiful fruits and vegetables, all different varieties, and picking them at the right moment and bringing them to us. I can't think of anything that really excites me more."

· GOOD THINGS FROM CANNARD FARM ·

When we started work with Bob was when we began to grill scallions and leeks, because he sent us so many little tiny ones. You just put some olive oil and a little water on them, and some salt on the grill—a pretty hot grill—and you move them around for just a couple of minutes. Serve them in a little pile with, oh, prosciutto, or chop them up and put them in a frittata.

Bob used to bring us down cherries on the branch, and we'd just put the branches on the table.

He has sensational carrots. He claims they're ten times as healthy as anyone else's carrots. It has to do with the way that he nourishes his soil. Carrots are really his specialty. He made us all believers in carrots. And carrot juice.

For little kids who come to the restaurant, we make a salad that we call a dipping salad, where we take a little wedge of lettuce, like a little heart of romaine, and we'll do carrot curls from Bob's carrots, and serve that with a little bowl of vinaigrette. The kids dip and eat, which is a great thing to see.

Bob's carrots have certainly transformed our carrot soup, which is one of the classic Chez Panisse soups. It doesn't get much simpler than this. But when you can get carrots as good as Bob Cannard's, it's just sublime. When I've got really perfect carrots like that, I don't use stock, just water.

I start by cooking some onions in butter or oil with a little bit of thyme for about fifteen minutes, until they're soft and sweet. You want enough butter or oil to really coat the onions. Then I add the carrots. They should be sliced all the same thickness so you don't have some overdone and some underdone. I add a little salt, and I taste.

Then I add water and just simmer till the carrots are tender. Not falling apart, but fully cooked. Always tasting to be sure. You've got to get the salt just right. Then I put it through the food mill. You could use a blender or a food processor, but I think the food mill gives it a nicer texture. The medium holes.

At the end, you can float a little butter or herbs or lemon juice on top, but you should be very careful that the garnish doesn't overpower that lovely, delicate flavor of carrot. I wouldn't use cream. We're not cream people when it comes to vegetables.

On a Sunday in October 1986, at the Stags' Leap Winery in the Napa Valley, the entire staff of Chez Panisse met for a retreat. The day began with the distribution of a questionnaire, a swim in the estate's lake, and a lunch of organic hot dogs and hamburgers. Then came the meeting. Grievances were aired; classes for the staff were planned in such subjects as butchery, knife sharpening, pastry, and wine tasting; representatives from each department were chosen for staff meetings. Fritz Streiff led a toast with his poem "Written in Honor of Richard Olney":

Food neither good to look at nor to eat,
Deracinated diet, dull in the extreme,
Carcinogenic, tasteless, incomplete,
Dehumanizing: this is the cuisine

We might be eating still had we not read
Elizabeth David and begun to think
About the better ways we could be fed.

  Our lives were changed forever. Food & drink
Became for most of us our raison d'être.
We cannot thank or praise enough. We only
Can lift our glasses to our two great maîtres,
To Mrs. David & to Richard Olney:
We toast you with the most profound emotion.
Rhyme can't contain our homage and devotion.

Alice talked passionately about the goals of Chez Panisse. "Our primary motive is not profit," she said. "Our number one goal is to educate
ourselves and the public. . . . Why do so many people eat at Chez Panisse?
Obviously for the delicious, real food; but they also want to feel like part
of an extended family. That is another goal of the restaurant: to try to operate like a family." She laid heaviest stress on what was becoming her
most cherished ideal: "our responsibility to the rest of the world."

Alice had always been generous toward members of the *famille Panisse*
who needed a sabbatical, some psychotherapy, investment in a start-up
such as Steve Sullivan's Acme Bakery, a loan for whatever reason. She also
gave to public causes that touched her heart—the famine in Ethiopia,
political refugees from El Salvador, local hunger programs, a synagogue's
Hanukkah bazaar. But she had begun to realize that supporting good causes
wasn't enough. Chez Panisse, in its very identity, stood *against* things, too—
most notably, industrial agriculture and the ever-declining quality of
what Americans put in their mouths.

"Those of us who work with food," she wrote in "The Farm-Restaurant
Connection,"[3] "suffer from an image of being involved in an elite, frivo-
lous pastime that has little relation to anything important or meaningful.
But in fact we are in a position to cause people to make important connections between what they are eating and a host of crucial environmental,
social, and health issues."

hez Panisse and its extended family and like-minded people elsewhere ere a very small force to stand up against the juggernaut of industrial agri- culture. The situation was bad when Chez Panisse opened, in 1971, but it was radically worse fifteen years later.

Genetically modified corn had made possible the production of high- fructose corn syrup at vastly lower cost than any other sugar, and that corn syrup was now appearing not only in desserts but in an astonishing range of food products. Consumers often didn't perceive the added sugar, but they came to prefer the products that contained it. It was, in effect, addictive. And it drove people still further away from the somewhat bitter-tasting foods—broccoli, Brussels sprouts, leafy greens—that were the most nu- tritious. Fast-food companies, and soon other restaurants, discovered that portion sizes could be increased at low cost, and that larger portions were preferred by many consumers. The corporations were offering to school districts special deals that would reduce their food costs substantially; cafeterias that actually cooked and served real food, therefore, were being replaced by vending machines and microwaved, portion-controlled meals- ready-to-eat. High schools rarely required their students to stay on cam- pus at lunchtime anymore, so it hardly mattered if they served nutritious food, because McDonald's and its kind were very often conveniently sit- uated nearby. "These guys find where the exits are on the freeways before they've been built," says Alice, "and they buy the land next to the school!"

"High-fructose corn syrup," wrote the *New York Times,* "can hinder the body's ability to process sugar, and can promote faster fat growth than sweeteners derived from cane sugar. . . . Since the advent of the syrup, consumption of all sweeteners has soared; the average American's intake has increased about 35 percent. . . . A study in the *American Journal of Clinical Nutrition* showed that the rise of type 2 diabetes since 1980 had closely paralleled the increased use of sweeteners, particularly corn syrup."[4]

Americans were getting fatter fast. Fast food—high in calories, low in utrition—was the fastest-growing segment of the food economy. It was seductive. "Food shouldn't be fast," Alice insisted. "And it be cheap."

There was profound moral reasoning behind Alice's adamance. The fast-food industry was part of a larger agro-industrial complex that was causing harm on a scale few Americans understood. "Factory farms," with thousands of acres producing only one crop, sustained by vast inputs of petrochemicals, were becoming the rule—and destroying their soil's natural productivity, destroying wildlife habitat, poisoning the water, wiping out thousands of family farms.

The processed food that occupied more and more supermarket space was much more profitable than mere fresh raw ingredients, and the agribusiness companies' marketing campaigns were persuading the public to buy more and more of these "convenience foods"—far less nutritious than simple fresh food, and far more expensive.

The little family farm, with a few head of livestock, some chickens, small plots of this-and-that crop, was the kind of farm Alice loved. Each was home not only to a human family but also to nesting birds, weasels, badgers, rabbits, quail, squirrels, sunfish, deer. (And many of these free-loaders were food themselves for the farm family, for free.) But such a farm was no longer competitive in the marketplace.

On agribusiness's strategic map, Chez Panisse and the few other food enterprises that acted more on the basis of conscience than on that of profit were nothing more than flyspecks. How could Alice Waters and her one little restaurant hope even to slow the agro-industrial juggernaut?

"Well, somebody had to do it," she says.

She knew that only as a public figure—one of greater stature than she yet was—could she hope to be effective. If it meant cultivating reporters and critics, if it meant membership in the mercilessly scrutinized, surreal world of global celebrity, and recruiting her fellow celebrities to the cause, she was going to have to do it. That was how you reached people in numbers sufficient to make a difference. Her increasingly public role, of course, decreased the time she could devote to her private life. She felt obligated to Stephen, grateful to Stephen, guilty about Stephen, but of the decreasing private time she had, she devoted most to Fanny.

Alice's path toward celebrity was abundantly potholed. In the *Oakland Tribune*'s gossipy "East Bay Ear" section on February 10, 1987, a little squib marked the end of Alice's great dream for the Oakland Museum, with its teaching garden, its revolutionized dining room, its organic sack lunches for kids:

> The French magazine *Cuisine et Vins de France* recently asked its readers to name the 10 best chefs in the world. And guess who made the top 10? Alice Waters! The Chez Panisse owner is not just the only Californian on the list, she's the only American. But is she good enough for the Oakland Museum? Naaah!

She had set forth an elaborate and passionate proposal, and had garnered a good deal of verbal support, but in the end the museum rejected the project in toto. "My interpretation of what happened," Alice explains, "was that there were factions within the museum all vying for the same pot of money. We were going through a group outside of the museum that was willing to finance the whole thing. But the fund-raising arm of the museum wanted to have a lot of influence on how the project was run, and the fact that we could bring so much money to it was a cause for jealousy within. The people on the staff never could see that this was something that would benefit everybody."

One of the aims of the museum project had been to reach children, to teach them the inextricably bound deliciousness and social values of good food. "It was disgraceful, the way children were being fed at school. Public and private. Still is," Alice says. Chez Panisse taught those lessons well, but a dinner at Chez Panisse, or for that matter lunch at the café, was not an experience remotely possible for the majority of the people of Berkeley, much less those from poverty-wracked Oakland. Within scant miles of Chez Panisse, "Children were going hungry! I had to do something."

So much for the museum. A new and much grander vision had come to her: an American Les Halles (the central market of Paris, now demolished), a great market in downtown Oakland, only a few miles from Chez Panisse. The produce would be local, seasonal, mostly organic, and of the highest quality, but because the farmers would be selling directly to the public, with no middlemen, produce prices could be lower than in the supermarkets.

Alice found a great location for the market—the seventy-year-old remains of Swan's, a fresh-food market that had thrived from the 1920s to the early 1940s, and then been driven out of business by the postwar exodus of the middle class from downtown Oakland. The new market would be a place where not just food and money were exchanged, but ideas, too. Sibella Kraus had provided a stirring example with her Tasting of Summer Produce, which had made it possible for the first time for farmers to sell their produce directly to restaurants and the public. The food at the Tastings was much fresher than anything from a wholesaler's warehouse, and the farmer collected all the profit. At the new market, the network of Bay Area farmers and cooks that had formed around Chez Panisse and Sibella's projects would be able to talk to one another face-to-face, sharing ideas and galvanizing their sense of common purpose.

There would be no single proprietor. Small local merchants, farmers, fishermen, dairymen, and ranchers would own shares in the market. Steve Sullivan had agreed to build a branch of his Acme Bakery. "I loved the thought of the smell of baking bread drifting through the marketplace," Alice says. The Monterey Market of Berkeley, the Bay Area's best greengrocer, had agreed to join in, as did the longtime fish supplier of Chez Panisse, Monterey Fish. Then, in one fell stroke, the financing collapsed, and the developer pulled out.

"I put all my best effort into making [the market] go, but thank God it fell through when it did," Alice says now. "I say 'thank God' because I was actually relieved. The construction costs were turning out to be so insanely high that there was no way it could have been affordable for the people I wanted to shop there."

She was soon involved with smaller but more effective means of getting good food to poor people. Share Our Strength was an organization of restaurants that distributed their leftovers and unused supplies to the hungry. Alice supported the local Daily Bread Project, with a similar mission. She supported the Food First Institute for Food and Development Policy, a think tank studying the root causes of worldwide hunger.

"It was very distressing, realizing that poor people were buying these highly processed industrial foods. They were much more expensive than good organic produce! We had beautiful farmers' markets coming in all over the Bay Area, all over the country, in fact, but most of them were in affluent areas selling to affluent people."

Over the next several years, Alice was involved in a number of experiments aimed at bringing less-affluent buyers into the world of farmers' markets and organic produce. Some were modest successes, but most were unable to surmount the social barrier that made poor people feel uncomfortable in the farmers' market milieu—the expensive foreign cars in the parking lots, the expensive clothing on the shoppers, the embarrassment for people who spoke poor or no English.

Yet Alice was learning that small gestures could set large examples. She was thinking long-term. Each attempt, even when it failed, brought new believers to the cause. Legislators could be lobbied, bigger sponsors sought, more communities involved. "You had to start somewhere," she says today, "and show that it could work. What we're missing—what so many people are missing—is an education of the senses. Poor people in this country, for the most part, eat badly because they are victims of an intense campaign to keep them eating industrial processed food. We've got to start countering that."

Reaching children was important not only because they might be changed for the rest of their lives, but also because the schools bought food in such immense quantities that if they changed their purchasing patterns, the effects on the landscape and the small-farm economy would be tremendous. "One lunch at a medium-size school uses two hundred and fifty pounds of potatoes. Multiply that by the number of school days and then by the number of schools in the district, and then by the number of districts in the state. Think of the organic farmers that could sustain! Think how much cleaner the air and the water and the earth would be! It could change the world."

Alice now saw clearly what was to be the mission of the rest of her life. It was all of a piece: from her father's garden to Montessori through the birth and growth and flowering of the Chez Panisse ethos, and ultimately, to the philosophy and practice of sustainability—ecological, agricultural, and social. Like Alice's own journey, it all began with gardens and children.

ON JUNE 8, 1987, a thousand people paid $250 apiece to enter the red-and-white fantasia that the Japanese designer Eiko Ishioka had created for Aid and Comfort at San Francisco's Fort Mason. Alice recalls,

> Eiko created this space that was just magical. It had a little bridge that you went over to come inside. The whole ceiling was covered with these gorgeous, billowing white parachutes. She wanted to suggest going into the body.
>
> Eiko didn't speak English very well at that time, but this is somebody who is a perfectionist. She wanted it all done right. And she was in Japan. So I had this really excruciating but enormously inspiring experience of trying to take her ideas and produce them. She wanted everybody working there to wear a red cotton apron, and she wanted them dyed exactly the right color of red. When they turned out to have ties on them that were made out of nylon, and the dye didn't take right, she said, "Get new ties and re-dye them." Which I did. I'd asked the dyer to do it as a favor in the first place, and then I had to tell them to do it again. I was using up every favor I had.

This was Alice's first experience with the big time outside the restaurant world, and she was at first daunted by the complexity of bringing it all together, but she also learned two important lessons.

> One of the important moments for me was when the fire inspectors came in the day before the event and said, "No candles in the stream." There were supposed to be candles floating in the water in this black tunnel. Eiko was uncompromising about this. "Alice, you get those candles." I spent all day and half the night trying to find out who could give us the dispensation. Finally, I found him. Some

top guy in the fire department. I had somebody, some politician, call him up in the middle of the night. He called back and gave me dispensation. And that's when I knew that you need to know the person at the top.

The other big thing I came to understand was that when you work with a group of people who all have experience and are professionals about what they do, you can collaborate and make something greater than the sum of its parts. You can let go. You don't have to have control over every part. You can trust it.

Chez Panisse, Zuni Café, and a dozen of the Bay Area's other best restaurants served a fourteen-course meal, prepared in four separate kitchens on-site. "The dinner," said the *San Francisco Chronicle*, "was sensational—not merely by banquet standards but by the standards you normally would apply at a great restaurant."[5]

Linda Ronstadt sang "Desperado." The Kronos String Quartet played Jimi Hendrix's "Purple Haze." Bobby McFerrin sang all the songs from *The Wizard of Oz* in ten minutes. Shirley MacLaine, notorious for her belief in reincarnation, said, "May I say that this is the best dinner I've had in four thousand years?" Joel Grey, Carlos Santana, Herbie Hancock, and Boz Scaggs performed. Michael Smuin of the San Francisco Ballet choreographed a pas de deux from *Romeo and Juliet*, accompanied by the full ballet orchestra. The show was broadcast by San Francisco's public television station, KQED. There were five hundred limited-edition portfolios of prints, each page printed by a different artist, with contributions from Richard Diebenkorn, Wayne Thiebaud, M. F. K. Fisher, and Diana Kennedy, on sale for $175 each.

Bill Graham, the famed impresario of the Fillmore auditoriums in San Francisco and New York, had produced the entire event for free. Tom Luddy had coordinated the production for free. Everyone who served, cooked, waited tables, built the sets, raised the funds, performed, and cleaned up—including Alice and a number of other members of the *famille Panisse*—worked for free. Over half a million dollars went straight to local AIDS charities.

"That was a disappointment, actually," Alice recalls. "We thought we were going to raise a million. We should have charged more."

For the finale, Chanticleer, San Francisco's highly regarded all-male chorus, sang "Lean on Me," as the hundreds of volunteers poured onto the stage to join them. The audience stood and sang along, many in tears.

14.

SUSTAINABILITY

1987–1991

Alice had always demanded the best of everything, and through the late 1980s, her criteria for what was best were growing more precise. She had never compromised on the quality of the food she bought for the restaurant and for her family, but now she wanted the way it was grown, harvested, handled, and shipped to be virtuous too—that is, to be good for the earth and its creatures, and good, if possible, for society.

In August 1987, Fanny turned four years old. Her preschool classmates envied her school lunches, and sometimes she succeeded in acquiring from the other children some choice forbidden item or another, but for the most part Fanny preferred what her mom provided.

Jerry Rosenfield had a new burst of energy in 1987, and his madness seemed to be under better control. As a forager, he had seen the wide disparities between good farms and bad ones, and he still had a strong intellectual influence on Alice. She now insisted that meat for Chez Panisse come from livestock that was treated humanely. She started reading the poems and essays of Wendell Berry, whose strict standards far surpassed

· FANNY'S SCHOOL LUNCH ·

One of the salads Fanny loved was my Greek salad. I put a few romaine leaves in there just for some body, and other greens in the salad, whatever was good from the garden in my backyard. In summer I'd add slivers of colored peppers and whatever little tomatoes were around, gold or red or green. Even if I made salad for her several days in a row, I changed the colors or how I was cutting the greens and the vegetables. Often I added some olives. I usually used those Greek Kalamata olives. I got some feta cheese, and I would season it with chopped-up fresh oregano and pepper, and I would crumble it on the salad. Oh, and cucumbers. Sometimes you can do little wedges of those small Mediterranean cucumbers. I used the Armenian sometimes—they're kind of lime green, a great color. There were the little Japanese ones, depending on the time of the year and who had the organic ones at the farmers' market. That was the salad that I did many, many variations on. Usually, I would make garlic toast to go with it, and then have a little separate container with the vinaigrette in it. For dessert, usually a piece of fruit.

I would try to surprise her every day with something different. She always loved salads and loved vinaigrette. As she got older, sometimes I would put in things from the night before, some chicken breast or something, as part of the salad. She always had some sort of leafy greens and herbs.

Alice's: He still plowed his Kentucky farm with horses. She discovered Wes Jackson and his Land Institute in Salina, Kansas, which was looking for ways to reform agriculture systemically, with the aim of recovering the ancestral health of all the natural systems that sustain the growing of food.

At the same time, Alice was examining the life of Chez Panisse on the small scale. The beef they were getting was okay, the lamb was excellent, the pork was variable, but the chickens never came close to the rich, dense, muscular complexity of the famous *poulet de Bresse*. She began her search with letters like this, to Pat Bridges and Bart Ehman of Pine Ridge Ranch, the restaurant's primary chicken supplier:

> *Dear Pat and Bart,*
>   *I am writing to let you know that we are engaged in a search to find, or to help develop, a chicken that has the qualities of old-fashioned chickens that some of us remember from our childhood and others have eaten in rural areas of Europe. . . . Two backyard growers in Sonoma County are planning to raise a small batch each of Buff Orpingtons and Plymouth Rocks. They will range on green pasture with up to 20 square feet per bird to the age of four or five months. . . .*

A new and highly accomplished cook, Christopher Lee, joined the staff in 1988, and soon was out foraging on his own. Chris's reports, like Jerry Rosenfield's, were exhaustively detailed. It's hard to know how useful some of this was for a restaurant, but it makes delightful reading:

> Enid and Frank Dal Porto raise crossbreed Suffolk sheep. . . . At its 1500′ elevation, the ranch is typical foothill woodland: undulating hillside and pastureland, wooded in spots with various oaks, California bay and lilac, gooseberry, and yerba santa. An intermittent stream, Big Indian Creek, runs through the land. The stream is usually dry by the 1st of July, though it ran strong and swift with mountain snowmelt the afternoon I visited the ranch. . . . From the Dal Porto hilltop home, the creeping housing developments of the Sacramento area can be seen to the northwest. . . .
>   Frank mentioned several times the dependence upon nature which the farmer is subject to. . . . In the spring, when the water flows freely, the grasses are green and in some spots lush and thick. But soon, without runoff from rain or snowmelt, the pastures will dry. This will immediately affect the animals by reducing their feed, but will also subject them to injury by the dried, curlicued seedpods of

the filaree plant, a species of *Erodium,* which become entangled in the wool of the face and make their way under the skin.

The ranch seemed a placid, even idyllic spot, with the sun shining down, the stream flowing through, the sheep grazing, and Frank Sr. cutting his newly grown asparagus stalks for his evening supper. . . . It made one feel satisfied with life, its bounty, and that bounty's seemingly easy availability, we observers being blind to the hours and years of cultivation necessary to produce all this. . . .

The report was accompanied by photographs of Frank Jr., of someone bottle-feeding an orphan lamb, and of the green seedpods, the dried seedpods, and the skin-piercing corkscrew of the unsheathed seed of *Erodium cicutarium.*

Only at Chez Panisse. Only Alice would pay money—considerable amounts of it—to bind her restaurant to its suppliers in so lavish and poetic a fashion: Christopher Lee's and Jerry Rosenfield's foraging did discover some valuable new food sources, certainly, but they carried their tasks out as much like artists as like restaurant buyers, and the relationships they developed between Chez Panisse and the farmers went far beyond the commercial. They were weaving together an extended family.

Where Christopher's reports were leisurely and mellifluous, Jerry Rosenfield's were densely packed with research, not without their own lyric flair, and, perhaps, a bit manic. Ed and Gerry Jastrem were raising the Barred Plymouth Rocks and Buff Orpington chickens in which Alice had expressed interest. Dr. Jerry wrote:

By the time we—Chris Lee and I—encountered them they were nearly full-grown pullets, enclosed in a large yard built around three American elm trees. Vigorous and active birds, they were foraging in their yard which, though cleaned of green growth, still contained enough attraction to keep the birds pecking at it. . . . The Barred Rocks, proud of carriage, particularly exuded a sheen of handsome good health and vigor. . . .

At our behest, taking our cue from the fact that the renowned

Bresse chicken is fattened on corn and milk during its final weeks, the Jastrems have added a portion of dried milk and rice to the pullets' feed, the rice, also a high-starch grain, substituting for the corn. Although American poultry growers have never been enthusiastic about rice, even where it is grown, it was the Chinese who developed the big birds, the Cochins or "Shanghais," which were the sensation of the memorable Boston Poultry Show of 1849. . . .

"The memorable Boston Poultry Show of 1849"! Only at Chez Panisse.

IN ADDITION to Alice's work for sustainable farming and social justice, there was social injustice that needed to be confronted at Chez Panisse. "For eighteen years," she wrote to her board of directors, "we have been struggling with the inequities and distortions of the traditional tipping system. At our restaurant the quality of the food and the skill and taste of the cooks are at least as central to our success as the quality of the service. Unfortunately, traditional tipping has created great disparities in earning between the serving staff and the cooking and support staff."

What was more, there was believed to be tax cheating among the waiters, who got the great majority of their income in cash. In the back of the house, income was fully documented and fully taxed. Alice's father believed that a fixed service charge could be accurately tracked through the computer system and equitably distributed to the whole staff, front and back of the house alike. Alice agreed. Her hope was that Chez Panisse, as in its earliest days, would again feel like one team.

In April 1988, frustrated by the lack of progress toward equity and order, Pat Edwards resigned. Alice's father was running Chez Panisse behind the scenes, and Richard Mazzera had the official authority of his title as general manager, while Pat was left to her own devices, with little to do—one of several methods Chez Panisse has developed over the years for sending messages that Alice doesn't want spoken aloud. "Alice was quite happy, actually, when I quit," Pat recalls. "She hugged me and said, 'Yes, it's time for you to go.'"

In 1989, after a year of highly charged internal debate, Chez Panisse adopted the system nearly universal in France and in many other European countries—a simple 15 percent service charge, to be distributed fairly to the whole staff. They even used the French descriptor *service compris*.

The waiters protested, but Alice's determination was iron. At first, the waiters made the system decidedly misleading: The service charge was shown clearly on the check itself, but the waiters would also leave the gratuity line and the total both blank on the credit card slip. Diners who had had some wine, or who may have tended in any case to dash off tip and signature without close examination of the bill, could easily be tipping 30 or 35 percent. In time, however, it was made a rule that whenever a customer left a tip significantly exceeding the service charge, the waiter was to point out the error. If some customers still wanted to leave big tips, that was fine, but at least they would be doing so consciously.

The grumbling eventually died down. The service charge rose to 17 percent. The system is still in place, the charge is now 18 percent, and the staff of Chez Panisse, front and back of the house alike, do very nicely. "It's another form of sustainability," says Alice. "If the restaurant's going to sustain itself, and do things right, everybody here has to be doing things right, including the business itself. That means we provide good medical insurance, and time off, and retirement savings plans, and understanding of people's difficulties. In return, we expect what we almost always get. People stay. They like working here. It's a good place to work."

As Alice had learned at Aid and Comfort, getting the very best people and expecting their best worked a good deal better than constant critical oversight. The next major cookbook, *Chez Panisse Cooking*, published in October 1988, comprised more than four hundred pages of precisely, sometimes elaborately detailed recipes for the earthy, robust, and uncomplicated food that was now the Chez Panisse standard. It was Paul Bertolli's book more than Alice's, a fact reflected in the byline "By Paul Bertolli [in large type] with Alice Waters [in small type]."

Fatigue: Tom Luddy and Alice

M. F. K. Fisher praised Paul's "artful use of information about how to cook." Richard Olney called the book "a celebration of purity. The food is imaginative but never complicated; it is"—despite Paul's own modest deprecation of the term—"art."

COMMITTED NOW TO WORKING on very large-scale problems, still making all the major decisions at Chez Panisse, maintaining what was becoming a more and more difficult marriage, raising Fanny, traveling, giving talks, Alice was starting to lose touch with something simple and basic inside herself. She had fallen into the situation that characterizes a great many people of very high accomplishment—so busy, so completely absorbed in their work, so resistant to any image of themselves except that of the supreme accomplisher, that they unconsciously sacrifice self-awareness, self-doubt, and the vivifying power of tranquil reflection. Many people who have known Alice through the years still have no idea what Alice's inner life is like. That is probably because nearly all her life has been lived on the outside, in plain view.

"I lived in a haze, almost," she says. "I would respond to things very spontaneously. I never thought about how I was feeling. I never had a sense of my physical body. It was almost like you're in a half sleep. Like you're being led. Driven. I wasn't in charge of my life. It was just unfolding before me. There were so many things coming at me, and I was responding, and I was moving, and I had things in my mind, and I made things happen, but I felt like what I was doing wasn't deliberate. It wasn't considered. I didn't have any awareness of myself. Everything always seemed fate."

And fate did strike its blows. In September 1989, a burglar broke into Charles and Lindsey Shere's house in Berkeley and stole Lindsey's purse. It would have been a crime of no great moment were it not for the fact that the purse held Lindsey's precious recipe book—eighteen years' worth of painstakingly perfected work stuffed into a three-ring binder. She had no backup copy. Lindsey had intended to publish a second volume of Chez Panisse desserts, but that was no longer feasible.

The *New York Times,* the *Wall Street Journal,* and dozens of other newspapers covered the story. Lindsey offered a no-questions-asked reward of $500, and the local sanitation crew let Charles rifle through their morning's harvest, but the recipes were never seen again.

In June 1990, Tom Guernsey died. "He was cremated," remembers Robert Messick, one of Tom's best friends and now head of the restaurant's reservations department. "We took his ashes to Tassajara"—a Zen meditation retreat in Big Sur—"and we scattered the ashes in a creek. Tim [Piland, Tom Guernsey's partner] said, 'Now this begins Tom's journey to the ocean.'

"The Monday after he died, a bunch of us gathered at Trader Vic's and had mai tais. Tom loved that old Trader Vic's in Emeryville, and he and a lot of other people from the restaurant used to go there a lot. We continue to do that, about ten or fifteen people, on his birthday, every year. Alice always comes if she's in town."

"Tom had brought a certain very California sense of aristocracy with him," Greil Marcus says. "He wasn't from California, but he carried himself in an unpretentiously princely way. He radiated confidence, and he was the mainstay of the restaurant. He could and did do everything, whether it meant fixing a toilet, dealing with a staff crisis, dealing with a food provider, bringing bonhomie to the dining room, radiating a sense of warmth and an eagerness to make any dinner a special occasion. The restaurant suffered horribly when he died, because we had lost this person whom everybody trusted, everybody relied on, and who trusted himself, who believed that he really could solve all these problems, and that the restaurant was his home."

At about the same time, although Jerry Rosenfield was still on the payroll as forager, his mental health was in decline again. He was throwing tantrums in the restaurant, yelling at people on the sidewalk, browbeating Alice mercilessly. Finally, Alice admitted that he had to go. Two weeks later, Jerry was in jail. On his release, he was ordered to report to the Berkeley Mental Health Clinic, but he came and screamed on the sidewalk in front of the restaurant, then charged inside and told the customers that the kitchen was trying to poison them. Only the threat of a permanent restraining order finally persuaded Jerry Rosenfield to stop harassing Chez Panisse.

"I tried so hard to help him," Alice recalls, on the verge of tears. "A lot of people here really loved him."

Jerry eventually moved to the small remote town of Albion, California, in Mendocino County. Bruce Anderson, owner and editor of the *Anderson Valley Advertiser*, remembers him as "very smart, very friendly, a very gentle soul." Jerry Rosenfield lived quietly in Albion until his suicide in the early 2000s (sources differ regarding the precise date).

SOMETHING WAS SLIPPING AWAY, some elusive, precious spirit. Alice didn't know what was wrong. Some kind of bipolar dynamic was at work again in the collective psyche of Chez Panisse. Whenever things were going tremendously well, it seemed, something terrible would happen and the good mood would crash. "I started thinking, Maybe we should just close the restaurant," Alice remembers. "Quit while we were ahead."

On the nineteenth birthday of Chez Panisse, August 28, 1990, Alice held a meeting with the board and the chefs for the purpose of candidly bringing to light all the strengths and weaknesses of the restaurant. Barbara Carlitz, as board secretary, recorded these cryptic notes:

Topic: What is good, what is bad at the restaurant, and what changes do we wish to enact?

What is good:
Great cooking staff
Many multitalented diverse people on staff
Wide clientele both upstairs and down; lots of regulars
Nineteen years of tradition and reputation
Best restaurant in comparison to others
Sense of family
Wonderful sources of foodstuffs
Two different spaces, one lively, one intimate—
Price not yet a deterrent
Own our own building
Most people find it an inspiring place to work

What is not so good:
The "family" has too many children
Failure to satisfy our own sense of mission
Lack of harmony between upstairs and downstairs
Lack of discipline and focus
Poor service because of lax management
Shaken confidence
Failure to foster independence in key staff
Too many bosses with no one in charge
Victimized by own reputation
Lack of spirit in downstairs dining room
Failure to utilize all of the facility
Dictated by clientele; not doing what we really want

Not responsive to changing taste in foods

Not responsive to changes in the Bay Area

Not making enough money

After-lunch topic: What scenarios are possible for change?

Consolidating into one restaurant

Cheaper set menu family-style downstairs

Café downstairs

Open seven days

Become a cooking and waiting school in conjunction with farm

Become an Indian restaurant, Chez Punjab?

Sell produce and prepared foods downstairs

Move to the country

Close at age twenty

Most of the "what is good" items, while true enough, were either the old clichés of Chez Panisse or of little real significance. The "not so good" things, taken together, were a collection of truly grave faults, especially that painful "no one in charge."

The "scenarios for change" were either trivial or fanciful, except for the last: "Close at age twenty." The meeting ended with no conclusions.

Alice was preoccupied with her different causes now, with being a devoted, attentive mother to Fanny, and with finding her way half-blindly through a fog of marital dissatisfaction. Stephen was physically present at home, but psychologically, most of the time, he seemed both to Alice and to himself far away. Both of them longed for a resolution, but neither made a move. They both seemed in some way paralyzed. And Alice's "half sleep" encompassed even Chez Panisse.

AID AND COMFORT II was set for September 22, 1990, at the outdoor Greek Theater on the Cal campus. September is almost always dead dry in the Bay Area, but just as the composer John Adams raised his baton to conduct the Berkeley Symphony and open the event, rain began to fall in heavy, lashing curtains. Alice had worked for months to plan and prepare a sit-down dinner for five hundred people at $500 a head; box lunches for six thousand; performances by Laurie Anderson, Bobby Short, the Kronos Quartet, Herbie Hancock, Bobby McFerrin, and Philip Glass.

"Bobby McFerrin and Laurie Anderson improvised this nonstop performance to keep everybody there in the pouring rain. And probably five thousand people stayed. Nobody else performed, but it didn't matter. It turned into a genuine happening—a kind of free-for-all, in the most beautiful way."

Robert Messick recalls, "It rained so hard, but it was all right, because somehow it made us think of Tom Guernsey. His ashes went into the ocean, and water from the ocean goes up into the air. I've always felt that it was Tom coming down on us in the rain after it had been recycled from river to ocean to clouds."

PERHAPS IT WAS Tom Guernsey's absence that was bedeviling Chez Panisse. Alice said the company needed to impose some discipline, but the fall of 1990 was an epic of indiscipline. The books were a mess: Richard Mazzera reported that since the advent of *service compris,* there had been an overall shortfall of $150,000 in the café alone. Despite complaints about the soaring cost of Carrie Wright's flowers, Alice insisted that Pagnol et Cie pay Carrie $1,300 for her medical insurance and $3,000 for a four-week vacation. Alice had spent $23,000 of the restaurant's money on Aid and Comfort II, not counting the considerable labor and food donated by Chez Panisse. In response, the board ordered a moratorium on charitable contributions for the remainder of the year—a ruling that Alice violated repeatedly, with, among other donations, a gift of $10,000 to local food programs. An early freeze wiped out 90 percent of Bob Cannard's crops; he owed Pagnol et Cie $10,000 and couldn't pay.

This was not sustainable. If it kept up, Chez Panisse was on its way to oblivion.

Nevertheless, with little to go on but faith, Alice decreed that Chez

Panisse would survive. Not only that, the twentieth-birthday celebration in August 1991was going to be the biggest party she had ever thrown.

What had happened? In 1990, she had bottomed out, not quite knowing why. And in 1991, still not knowing, she bounced back. It was classic Chez Panisse, and classic Alice Waters: Ignore the odds; never say die; in every crisis, an opportunity.

15.

STAR POWER

1991–1994

The twentieth-birthday party, in August 1991, took the form of a gigantic farmers' market up and down both sides of the restaurant's whole long block of Shattuck Avenue, in honor of the farmers and other suppliers of Chez Panisse. "We had little booths for every sort of food," Alice says. "Inexpensive, so anybody could come—everything from fresh fruit to corn on the cob. Paul made spit-roasted pork sandwiches and manned his own booth. Originally, I thought we might have thirty or forty booths, and get, oh, a couple or three thousand people. We had fourteen thousand."

There was a grand dinner afterward at the Jewish community center for all the growers and purveyors, prepared and served by the staff of the restaurant. The whole celebration cost some hundred thousand dollars, yet Chez Panisse managed, miraculously, to break even.

That evening in the restaurant, which was open for business as usual, the menu served downstairs added one new course—the soup—and this time also listed the salad as a separate course, but it was otherwise a replica of the first meal Chez Panisse ever served:

Pâté en croûte

❦

Fish consommé with tomatoes, leeks, garlic, and parsley

❦

Roast duck with olives

❦

Garden salad

❦

Warm plum tart

There were two big differences. First, this dinner was rather more pro-fessionally and calmly produced. Second, the price of dinner on opening night in 1971 had been $3.95. Adjusted for inflation, that was thirteen 1991 dollars. The price of the twentieth-birthday dinner was precisely five times as much: $65.00.

Two weeks later, five Berkeley residents signed the following letter to the *San Francisco Chronicle:*

Editor: The recent display of self-indulgent consumption on Shat-tuck Avenue in Berkeley is testament to this city's gutless pseudo-progressive agenda. . . . Amazingly, there was not a coherent, observable statement in this "progressive" microcosm to the effect of our deteriorating environment's role in sustaining and support-ing these foods! While our environment goes to hell, Lamborghini Leftists pig out on its fringe benefits. . . . This city is becoming a parody of itself and its purported ideals.

Lamborghini leftists! Was that to be Alice's constituency? Well, yes and no. The fact is that any non-profit-making movement must live on gifts. If the movement is to be large, so must the gifts be. Chez Panisse, with its high ideals and high prices, was well fitted to the task of attracting the most desirable sort of potential donors: rich people with fully function-ing consciences. The movement for sustainability and conservation required funding, certainly, and therefore wealthy benefactors, but it also required people in large numbers, and they didn't have to be wealthy. Few if any of the fourteen thousand folks eating organic peaches and pulled pork at the birthday party had arrived there in Lamborghinis.

The word *foodie* had made its debut in 1982,[1] by which time there were already millions of foodies, many uncomfortable with terming themselves *gourmets*. By 1991, there were millions more. Not many of them seemed concerned with the ethical aspects of food, but they were nevertheless Alice's natural audience. She was in increasing demand as a public speaker, an interviewee, a celebrity chef for a benefit dinner. In 1992, the James Beard Foundation Awards—the food world's equivalent of the Oscars—named Chez Panisse the Restaurant of the Year and Alice Waters Chef of the Year. Increasingly, when Alice went to a food-related event, she was mobbed. Among foodies, only two people were such icons as to be known by their first names alone: Julia and Alice. "And I hate that word *foodie*," adds Alice.

As Alice grew more and more widely known, some old friends began to pull away, lamenting that she had no time for them anymore, all she wanted to do was hobnob with the rich and famous. Others argued that she was unchanged, as loyal and generous as ever. New friends did multiply, and some of them were in fact rich and/or famous. Alice grew weary of the traveling, and she was in agony in front of a crowd or a camera, but when she was called on, she nearly always accepted. As Tom Luddy had done twenty years before, her closest friends were begging her to say no once in a while, to slow down, relax a little—but when Alice spoke, she could feel the electricity of her audience's excitement, and she knew that meant that they were starting to understand how much meaning food had. She was a teacher again.

She studied public speaking and camera presence. There were more and more demands on her time—more than anyone could possibly commit to. She still clung to the idea of herself as a person of the restaurant, who cooked, who tasted, who organized, who heard the complaints and soothed the misunderstood geniuses of her staff. Jean-Pierre Moullé was back again, working under Paul Bertolli downstairs; Alice did not know how long she would be able to hang on to Paul, who was getting restless, and she worried about what would happen when, as was probably in-evitable, Jean-Pierre would wish to be chef and so titled. David Tanis re-turned from a six-month sabbatical in September 1991 and told her that rather than resume his post as co-chef in the café he was moving to Santa Fe, and Alice was back at the stoves again until she found a replacement in Peggy Smith.

And still the invitations came, and still she said yes. Alice Waters—sometimes alone, or so it felt—was teaching the world what virtuous agri-culture meant for the earth and posterity, and why there was healing magic in the simple gathering of family and friends around a table.

Such was Alice's vision; her own reality differed from it. In 1991, she and Stephen had been together for nine years; Fanny was eight; and both Alice and Stephen believed deeply in maintaining a real family for Fanny. When they traveled, they always brought her along. Bob Carrau often joined them, and Sue Murphy sometimes, too. They picnicked together, went to the movies, attended Fanny's school events together. But the nameless enmity between Alice and Stephen continued to fester.

Fanny spent more and more of her time at Chez Panisse. "What struck me," Fritz Streiff recalls, "was how seamlessly Alice made Fanny part of all of her life. Fanny was in and out of the restaurant all the time, and I think it's fair to say there was some bemusement amongst the staff, a little bit, because everything had to stop for Fanny."

As long as Alice was at the restaurant or at home, the illusion of fam-ily normality could be maintained. But she was ever more often away, as her public obligations multiplied. She was a star. The eleven-year differ-ence in their ages, Stephen now says, "only became an issue in that as I grew into my sense of adult self, the needs that that presented were not so much in conflict with where Alice was in her own aging curve as much as where she was in her public agenda. And that public agenda wasn't really part of where Alice was in her aging—it's where the curve or the tra-jectory was in her life."

In a further effort toward togetherness, Alice and Stephen worked on fixing up the bungalow on Monterey Avenue, and converted the old "ad hoc day-care center" into a freestanding studio for Stephen. With the new studio, he resumed his artwork. He continued to be the wine buyer for the restaurant, but he had also decided to open a restaurant of his own. In partnership with the former Chez Panisse cook Jonathan Waxman, he opened Table 29 in the Napa Valley—a good forty miles from Berkeley.

Alex Witchel, in the New York Times of April 17, 2002, described Table 29 as "a short-lived disaster," but it did get Stephen away from Alice, which, more and more, is where he wanted to be.

For Alice, the gap between reality and what she imagined—whether France or family—was not as wide as for most other people. Whatever she imagined, she believed she could bring into being. Chez Panisse was the proof of that.

While her vision of her family life proved stubbornly resistant to actualization, Alice found comfort in revisiting her vision (or myth) of Chez Panisse in a new book project with Bob Carrau. It would be the story of the restaurant from Fanny's point of view. Published in 1992, *Fanny at Chez Panisse* evokes the mythical Chez Panisse, where "The inside of my mom's mouth knows how everything at Chez Panisse is supposed to taste," and "I don't know why they write menus ahead of time, because they always end up changing everything at the last minute," and "I can never tell who actually runs Chez Panisse." The fictional Fanny also says:

> My favorite day at Chez Panisse is Bastille Day. Bastille Day is like the Fourth of July in France, only it's on the fourteenth of July. There's a big party every year and everybody gets real French and kisses each other, and since Bastille Day happens at the same time of year that all the new garlic comes in, there's always a big, special garlic dinner that night. Everything they serve has garlic in it: garlic soup, garlic butter, garlic mayonnaise, garlic pizza, garlic oil, and one time they even had chocolate-covered garlic cloves. I'm not kidding. At the Bastille Day dinner there's music and laughing and everybody sits at long tables and talks to each other. The Head Garlic Lover wears a big hat that looks just like a big head of garlic—all billowy and white. . . . My mom likes Bastille Day a lot because it makes

her feel like she's in those old French movies she likes so much. Everyone gets together to eat and drink and laugh and talk and cry and sing and dance just like Fanny and Panisse and their friends did.

"I always wanted to communicate with kids about food," says Alice. "I loved those books about Eloise at The Plaza, and I thought a way to communicate with kids and with their parents would be to write a book that appealed to both. I had this idea for a while, but it wasn't until Bob Carrau volunteered to help write it that anything happened. He said, 'You write it, Alice, and I'll help you.' Well, he wrote it, and I helped him.

"Years later, my friend Joy Carlin and I had been talking about making some sort of film for children, and she said, 'I have a crazy idea. I want to make *Fanny at Chez Panisse* into a musical.'

"She'd already been working on it, with this musician named Joe Landon, who had been the playwright-in-residence at the American Conservatory Theater. And they came over, and Joe sang this little song, 'Arugula, arugula, arugula!'

Suki HILL - Bastille Day 2003

Le Quatorze Juillet

"I couldn't imagine that it would come to something, but it did."

There were songs called "Make Me a Pizza" and "A Little Emergency" and "Dessert." The character of Fanny had been somewhat changed— she was a teenager now—and the script, at Alice's behest, was more political than the book had been. Alice insisted that the show include her message that "if you make the right choices about food, it changes the quality of your life and changes the world around you." This was classic Alice, too—so *serious*—and hardly an enhancement of the show's value as entertainment.

"And, well," she says, "it certainly wasn't the huge roaring success that Joy had imagined. Later there was a full-scale production that ran for six weeks, but it started off as a workshop at this little studio in San Francisco. Jill Eikenberry played me. I thought it would just be great if she came over to the restaurant and played me all the time. I could leave."

It was a joke with an unfunny subtext. Alice wanted someone to play her role. So she could leave. She was caught up now in being ALICE WATERS, imprisoned in her public role. She knew she couldn't quit, of course; the cause was too important. "One thing that everyone loves about Alice but also drives everyone crazy," Bob Carrau says, "is how she's always into the struggle. It can be annoying to some people, because they just don't want to think of this stuff all the time. There's a kind of sad beauty in it all— her fixation on injustice and her relentlessness about it. I'm sure it also allows her to stay out of her interior, too. So there's that side to it—her fixation on social justice as a way to ignore personal fears."

The gap between the world imagined in *Fanny at Chez Panisse* and that of the actual restaurant was also stubbornly resistant to closing. "In 1992, September, I believe," Greil Marcus recalls, "Alice asked me to talk with Paul Bertolli, who was having a hard time with the fact that he was a great chef, he was doing innovative things, he had his own ideas, he had his own point of view, but he was feeling unfulfilled. One day he said that he was terribly frustrated with the fact that Alice got all the publicity, and that his contributions weren't recognized in the world at large. And what I told him was, 'You're right, you aren't getting the recognition that you deserve. Your contribution isn't appreciated by the public, by food writers, by feature writers, by television crews. And it never will be. There is no way that a shy, retiring man, regardless of his talents, can stand up to an infinitely charming, vivacious, articulate, eloquent woman. It will never happen.' And he quit two days later, which had not been my intention. I had no desire to get rid of Paul. Not at all. I was just telling the truth."

Confronted again with the Jean-Pierre conundrum, Alice decided to make him her co-chef, at least for the moment, knowing it couldn't last. Jean-Pierre surprised her, however. He distinguished himself, and by the spring of 1993, Alice felt free to leave the kitchen in his hands.

In 1993, Chez Panisse was probably the best it had ever been: The food was superb, almost consistently; the service was clicking; the spirit was joyful again.

In April, Lindsey Shere won the James Beard Foundation Award for Pastry Chef of the Year. Michael Bauer, of the *San Francisco Chronicle,* gave Chez Panisse his highest rating, four stars.

If there's one restaurant that has become a cathedral of gastronomy in the United States, it's Chez Panisse in Berkeley. It is the birthplace of the "California Cuisine" movement, and just about every chef in the country has been inspired by Alice Waters. Its reputation is so exalted that it would be next to impossible for it to meet the myriad expectations we all have of it. But in many ways, Chez Panisse still does.[2]

Late on the evening of August 12, 1993, the junk-food-loving president of the United States phoned Chez Panisse from *Air Force One,* hungry. Alice was in San Francisco, but a phone call brought her back across the Bay Bridge at high speed. An hour later, Bill Clinton and company descended on Chez Panisse. Trying not to notice the forty Secret Service agents swarming through the restaurant, Alice did her best to set a scene of gracious hospitality, spreading before the president a late-night snack of golden nugget tomatoes, fettuccine with corn and crabmeat, a salad of green beans and chanterelles, pizza without cheese (it was not allowed on his diet), house-cured prosciutto, and, for dessert—the course she knew Clinton loved best—blackberry ice cream, blackberry shortcake, rasp-

Lulu Peyraud and Jean-Pierre Moullé

berries, strawberries, Gravenstein apples, and a lemon custard with wild strawberries. Alice wouldn't let him pay. The *Chronicle*'s coverage noted:

> Waters, who turned down an invitation to cook at Ronald Reagan's inaugural in 1982 (saying she didn't know where Washington was), took the opportunity to buttonhole the president about San Francisco's Garden Project, where prisoners grow specialty crops for sale to restaurants like hers—and how important it is to be "connected" to what we eat and grow.[3]

The *Chicago Tribune* picked up another part of the conversation.

> While Clinton ate, she says, she discussed her worries about assuring that future generations will have a wide variety of good foods. The president, in turn, told her there had been some talk of starting a vegetable garden at the White House.[4]

Clinton was almost certainly just turning on his customary charm, but to Alice Waters that was an opening wide enough to drive a tractor through. A garden at the White House!

This just happened to be a time when Alice was freshly charged with fervor. It had been only a few weeks since she had attended a meeting in Hawaii that gave birth to the first group ever to try to turn chefs into active environmentalists, the Chefs Collaborative. At that time, chefs didn't set themselves up as leaders, or philosophers, or moral paragons. Some of them considered themselves artists, but their medium was food—they didn't try to reshape society. The creation of the Chefs Collaborative meant that Alice's ideals were gaining a foothold in the real world.

Chefs have real power to influence food consumption patterns. About two-thirds of all the fish bought in the United States, for example, goes to restaurants.[5] If restaurants began to buy fish only from sustainable fisheries, the oceans would soon be very much improved. In February 2006, for example, the Compass Group, the world's largest food service company, announced that it would henceforth purvey only sustainably harvested fish and seafood;[6] that single decision is saving at least a million pounds per year that would have been harvested from unsustainable fisheries and fish farms.[7]

Presidents and chefs can have powerful effects, but Alice's thoughts always came back to children. Adults had to be persuaded; children simply learned. For years, every day when she drove home from work, she would pass the Martin Luther King, Jr. Middle School. "I thought it was abandoned, because it looked so run-down. Graffiti on the windows, burned-out grass."

Curious, she went in one day. She discovered that most of the students bought their lunch at a snack bar inside the school, which didn't even cook the food. Its "kitchen" was a microwave oven. Its menu comprised reheated pizzas and hamburgers, potato chips, and soft drinks. Alice expressed her distress to the principal and invited him to lunch at Chez Panisse.

"I think he wanted me to plant a garden and beautify the school. In fact, I didn't know what I had in mind. I just walked around the school, and then it just hit me. I thought, There are a lot of schools with gardens, and they teach a lot of little things around food. Not so many, but some. But what's really important, I was thinking, is the whole cycle from the garden, back into the garden. As an old Montessori teacher, I believed in the education of the senses. And what better way could we educate the senses than through a school lunch program that was designed to teach kids about sustainability?

"I talked to the principal; I talked to the school board; I talked to anybody who might make a difference. I'd tell them, 'Think. We need to know where our food comes from. We need to know how to take care of the land. We need to know how to feed ourselves, and we need to know how to communicate with each other. Because we all live here together.'

"Three-quarters of the kids in this country don't have one meal a week with their family. That's a breakdown in our whole culture. How do we pass on our information, our values, to our children? Around the table!"

The project would take years to develop, but in Alice's imagination it took shape quickly. She would create a garden at Martin Luther King, where the children, about a thousand of them, in the sixth, seventh, and eighth grades, could learn to plant, cultivate, harvest, cook, and serve food that they themselves grew. Each activity could be tied to something in the curriculum. "For instance, they're studying Egypt. They might be making Egyptian bread and listening to Egyptian music and gathering and cooking together." Moreover, the program could serve as a shaper of young citizens: The kids would learn table manners, cooperation, mutual consideration, and a love of beauty.

It's important to encourage all the other values that are beyond nourishment and sustainability and the basic things. Beauty. When you set a table, you know, take time to do that—teaching the pleasure of work—that's probably one of the most important lessons. It's also about diversity. It's about replenishing. It's about concentration. It's about sensuality. It's about purity. It's about love. It's about compassion. It's about sharing. How many things? All those, just in the experience of eating, if you decide you're going to eat in a very specific way. It changes your life, and it changes the world around you.

This is the first generation of kids who haven't been asked to come to the table. And we're seeing the results. They're out there not knowing where they are. They're wandering around, disconnected. Shockingly so. And when they're not being sensually nourished, nothing's coming in except the McDonald's information. Fast food not only comes with poisons inside the food and destruction of the environment, but with the values that are part of it. It says food isn't important. It's cheap, you can eat it fast, and you don't have to eat with your kids. Food is for entertainment, and it should be all the same. It's okay to drink Coke and eat hamburgers every day of the year. Things that aren't advertised lose value. Only things that are advertised are really what's important.

In such a world, Alice could hardly close Chez Panisse. It was her public platform, her private bedrock, her true home. And to nearly any person of stature or fame or influence—a person, that is, through whom the philosophy might be promulgated—an invitation to dinner at Chez Panisse as the personal guest of Alice Waters was a powerful inducement.

She always had plenty to say. "You begin with food," she would say, "because it's the essence of life. If you're seduced by something that's beautiful and nourishing, you want that experience again. You're looking for that, and you realize that it's growing right over there, and you want to take care of that thing right over there. I look at the median strips in the highway, and I want to plant them. And I wonder, Why are the roads so wide? You could have an acre of fava beans there."

Alice has always been an extraordinarily persuasive person. It is as natural a part of her as her hands, her girlish voice, or her blue eyes—all of which come into play in the exercise of her charm. She likes to touch people. She will rest her hands on your arm, draw you close, hold your attention. Her voice, which can turn curtly dismissive or cynically harsh when it needs to, rarely needs to; much of the time it is so soft that you have to lean in to catch what she is saying.

"Alice," says Greil Marcus, "is the person who says, 'Of course it's possible,' when everybody else is saying it's impossible. She'll simply smile and, without any agitation at all, say, 'It can be done, it will be done, it's going to happen, you'll see.' She really does believe that she can change the world, she can change individual people one by one, she can improve people's lives. This isn't just rhetoric that she trots out whenever she is given an award."

More than anything else she had ever wanted to do, the kids' garden at Martin Luther King would bring Alice's beliefs to life. A Montessori garden. She would call it the Edible Schoolyard.

Alice Waters was going to be fifty years old on April 28, 1994. She had achieved everything a restaurateur could ever hope for. This, then—the promulgation of her philosophy, especially to children—would give shape and meaning to her fifties.

ON MAY 31, 1994, Stephen Singer had a terrible accident. "I was riding near our house. I'm a very active bicyclist," he recalls. "I think what might have happened is a misplaced sewer grate left a gap that my tire went into at the bottom of a hill. I don't remember. I woke up in the hospital. It was a serious accident. Part of the reason I have a mustache is that I'm covering up scars. My lip was cut in two in a couple of places, and my nose was basically lifted off my face and put back on."

Sue Murphy remembers, "I believe Jim [Maser] brought Stephen back from the hospital. I remember distinctly sitting on that couch when Stephen walked in the door and I saw his face. I was going, Oh, Christ, because they didn't dress it, it had to be all open, and he had ripped his face off. He literally ripped his face off. He tore his lip up, all the way up here, up his nose. So they had sewn that back on, and it was just—he was deformed-looking. And he'd knocked out his front teeth. If he hadn't had that helmet on, he would have been dead. He didn't break the orbits of his eye, so they didn't bandage that up, and his eye was just open and leaking."

"Alice was in New York," says Bob Carrau. "I called her, and she did say, 'Should I come back or not?' I said, 'Alice, I really think you should.'"

"We explained it," Sue Murphy recalls, "but maybe we weren't as clear as we might have been. It was the type of thing where you get on the phone and go, 'He's okay, he's all right,' because you don't want to make her think he's going to die. Granted, if I was Alice, I probably would have gotten the first plane home. But I also defend her, because she had two people who were family who were saying, 'We're here.'"

"I didn't understand how serious it was," Alice says. "I had no idea. They should have said to me, 'You need to get on a plane right now.' They were trying to protect me."

"Sue and I both remember a moment between Stephen and Fanny that was quite tender, before Alice got home," says Bob. "It was pretty shocking to look at him, but Fanny kind of stepped up to the plate and was gentle, caring, and nurselike instead of freaked out."

Alice came home not the next day but the one after. "I remember picking Alice up at the airport," Sue recalls. "I remember her walking back from the gates, and I was thinking how tiny she was in her little black outfit, little black hat, motoring along at a thousand miles an hour down the corridor of the airport. And I remember very clearly, when we got in the car, before I started the car, looking at her and saying, 'You need to be prepared for what Stephen looks like.'"

"He was so concerned about what he looked like," Bob says. "The day Alice was coming home, I helped him get in the shower, helping him bathe. He wanted to get dressed, and he wanted to look all right. I can understand being freaked out about not wanting to scare people, but he really felt that it was his image on some level that was most important to Alice, and I thought, Not only is it a telling thing about their relationship and Alice, it's also a telling thing about how he feels about himself. What does it mean that in your most intimate relationship, what you're most worried about is your appearance?"

"I used to have a notion that I needed to be pretty self-reliant," Stephen says, "because if I ever really needed Alice, I wasn't sure if she would be able to even see that I needed her, let alone be up to the task, and I know that she thinks that she wanted to help me."

Stephen was in pain for months. Surgery followed surgery. Plastic surgery. Restorative dentistry. He was badly disfigured, and the healing was slow. "I really needed her to be there," Stephen recalls, "but she couldn't be there. I don't want to dwell on this very much, but there was a change in my thinking about what my needs were. I wouldn't say that our life went straight downhill from that moment, but some information was definitely introduced into our experience together that made me realize I wasn't getting what I needed."

"It was a horrible accident," says Alice. "And I think Stephen was never aware of what kind of post-trauma shock he had. We tried therapy. Just little bits and pieces. I had some curiosity about it, but I never really followed through."

Alice's principal response to the deterioration of her marriage was to take refuge where she knew she was loved. She occupied her public persona with greater comfort. Many of her admirers were more than admirers—they loved her. She had dozens of friends who loved her. And there was always *la famille Panisse*.

Alice was spending a lot of time in the restaurant again, planning menus, tasting, advising Jean-Pierre, fine-tuning. At home, she continued to function as Fanny's doting mother, as household manager, as hostess to friends who would all pitch in together on long, boisterous dinners in the kitchen or in the garden. Alice wanted Fanny's life to feel as normal as possible, despite the domestic tension. "We had lots of friends over," Alice says. "We ate at home at least a couple of times a week, and we brought Fanny to eat with us at the restaurant, too."

Drawing on one of her heroes—Lulu Peyraud—more and more often, Alice was cooking directly over a wood fire. Clearly there was a sort of solace in it, a mental teleportation to Lulu's older, more elemental world. One of Fanny's favorite things was what Alice just called "the egg," cooked in a heavy, long-handled iron spoon that Alice's friend the blacksmith Angelo Garro had forged for her.

· THE EGG ·

You make a little fire. A little fire. Two logs parallel and not too far apart, and then when that gets going, you lay a log or two over the top, and when that log across the top gets going, it's like a little salamander [broiler]. And then you need a spoon, an iron spoon that is not too cupped, more of a flat spoon, although you could do it in a cupped one, like a ladle. But it's better to do it in a flatter spoon. With a long handle. I've been going around to fireplace shops finding old utensils. I suppose you could use a stainless steel kitchen spoon, one that you don't mind destroying by putting in the fire that way. But it has to be a spoon that has enough density that it's not going to burn the bottom of the egg before the top of it puffs up and gets cooked.

You want the freshest possible egg, like it just came out from under the chicken, and you crack it in the bowl and add some salt, a little pepper. Sometimes I add a little hot pepper, a little Middle Eastern pepper that Paula Wolfert gives me. Marash, it's called.

So I put a little bit of olive oil in the spoon. Sometimes I put it on the fire to warm up a bit. And sometimes I don't. Then I pour the egg in the spoon, very carefully. If your spoon and the olive oil are already nice and hot, the egg begins to set right away, and so you're not so likely to have the egg spill off before you get it into the fire. You put it under right away, with the bottom right on the coals, and the burning log above. It all puffs up when you do that, and it browns a little, too. It's like putting it into a pizza oven. You're getting a really hot floor and a hot top, too. You keep it there for a minute or two, and then you have another spoon right handy, and a piece of warm toasted bread that's been rubbed with garlic and a little oil. You take the second spoon and loosen the edges and just slide it onto the bread.

Fanny and I like to eat it with a little salad of some sort. Sometimes we'll have some tomatoes in the summer. I love a little watercress salad. This morning I made the egg for a friend and served it with a parsley salad with a little bit of basil. I usually eat it with a fork and knife because it should be runny in the center.

Stephen remained in place, a good father to Fanny, living in the bosom of his family, but he and Alice were no longer occupying the same world.

16.

INTO THE GREAT
WORLD

1995–2001

The Edible Schoolyard was not a new idea. Back when the University of California at Berkeley had a college of agriculture, a professor named Ernest B. Babcock had written a brochure titled "Suggestions for Garden Work in California Schools." Published in 1909, it looked back at school gardens of the century before—the Philadelphia Vacant Lots Cultivation Association, the First Children's School Farm in New York City, the Whittier Garden at the Hampton Institute in Hampton, Virginia.

In Ventura, California, in 1907, a teacher named Zilda B. Rogers had written, "The children will gladly leave their play to work in 'our garden.' . . . Since commencing the garden work the children have become better companions and friends. They have learned to respect other people's property and to feel that there is a right way of doing everything."

There was a right way of doing everything—a very Montessori, very Alice notion. "The school garden," wrote Babcock, "has come to stay." He was wrong. By the late twentieth century, the school garden was essentially extinct in the United States.

At the Martin Luther King Middle School, Alice had seen an opportunity for a magnificent rebirth of the idea. MLK had a campus of seventeen acres, most of it covered in asphalt. In its place, she wrote, would grow a "comprehensive solution to both the neglect and the underutilization of the physical plant and its surroundings . . . experience-based learning that illustrates the pleasure of meaningful work, personal responsibility, the need for nutritious, sustainably raised, and sensually stimulating food, and the important socializing effect of the ritual of the table."

Alice had learned from the grand successes of the Aid and Comfort and twentieth-birthday events that it was just as easy to think big as to think small. In her initial proposal for the Edible Schoolyard, she wrote:

> The core of the intended learning experience for the students is an understanding of the cycle of relationships that exists amongst all of our actions. The tangerine peel that gets tossed into the compost pile becomes a feast for the organisms that will turn it into humus, which enriches the soil to help produce the fruit and vegetables that the students will harvest, prepare, serve, and eat. The health and well-being which they derive from the garden is recycled back into their attitudes, relationships, and viewpoints. Thus the discarded peel becomes the vehicle which provides tomorrow's city planners, software engineers, artists, and master gardeners their first adult understanding of the organic concept of interconnectedness.

She recruited an army of volunteers—gardeners, contractors, artisans, bakers, general volunteer labor. She recruited curriculum developers. The Berkeley Horticultural Nursery offered to donate plants and to teach the kids to plant and cultivate them. The family foundation of a friend of Alice's gave $15,000 in start-up funds.

Alice saw the Edible Schoolyard as a local pilot project that could, in time, function as a global paradigm. Thinking big, she wanted the president of the United States to know about it. She had recently seen Bill Clinton again, at a fund-raising dinner that she and Chez Panisse catered in San Francisco. On December 9, 1995, Alice wrote a long letter to the president and the vice president, with a copy to the first lady.

Dear Mr. President and Mr. Vice President:

Our project, the Edible Schoolyard, plans to create and sustain an organic garden and landscape that is wholly integrated into the school's curriculum and lunch program. . . . Help us nourish our children by bringing them back around the table, where we can pass on our most humane values. Help us create a demand for sustainable agriculture, for it is at the core of sustaining everyone's life. Talk about it; promote it as part of the school curriculum; encourage the spread of farmers' markets; and demonstrate it with organic gardens on the grounds of the White House and the Vice Presidential Mansion. . . .

It was Hillary Clinton who replied first, on January 15, 1996:

Dear Ms. Waters:

I appreciate your writing and agree wholeheartedly with your views about the family meal. In my new book [It Takes a Village] *. . . I talk about the importance of this time-honored ritual and our efforts, no matter how busy we are, to dine together at least once a day. . . . We have established a roof garden here at the White House where we grow a variety of vegetables and herbs. . . .*

Sincerely yours,

Hillary Rodham Clinton

On February 1, 1996, the president wrote to Alice:

Dear Alice:

Thank you so much for your kind and interesting letter. I appreciate your words of encouragement, and I am delighted to learn of the Edible Schoolyard project.

*I agree that in facing the challenges of tomorrow, we must continue
to recognize America's deepest values and obligations—from helping our
youth prepare for the future and restoring hope in troubled neighbor-
hoods, to revitalizing the bonds of family and the spirit of community.
We must work together to make this country a place where opportunity
and responsibility go hand in hand.*

You have my best wishes.

Sincerely,

Bill Clinton

Al Gore wrote that he and Tipper had an herb-and-vegetable garden
and a greenhouse, and that they tried to eat together as a family as often
as possible.

A roof garden and a cloud of hot air about "facing the challenges of
tomorrow" were not what Alice had in mind. "I wanted a big, prominent
demonstration garden in full sight of the public." But she did now have
the ear of the president of the United States, his wife, and the vice president. And the president was calling her Alice.

In July 1996, Alice catered another private fund-raising dinner for Bill
Clinton, with thirty of his top contributors paying $25,000 apiece for
a Chez Panisse meal at a private residence. "I went through six cases of
peaches," says Alice, to find the thirty-one perfect enough for the occasion.

But this was only one of three dinners that Clinton had to go to that
night, and he skipped dessert. Alice did manage to put a peach in the
president's hand as he was leaving, and was later told that he had eaten it
on his way down in the elevator.

She told Marian Burros of the *New York Times,* "[Clinton] talks about
community all the time, but you can't just demand that of people. The
way you have that happen is when you eat and care about their nourishment around the table, and the bigger table is the community. He should
be planting a kitchen garden on the White House lawn."[1]

Burros also reported some telling details from her visit to Alice's home.
Alice, as ever, was helplessly candid:

"I know I'm on overload when I can't sleep at night, and my stomach hurts, and I can't stop for a second to have a conversation with Stephen, and Fanny is frustrated, and the people at the restaurant say they can't get a straight answer."

Her husband, Stephen Singer, an importer of Italian olive oil and the restaurant's wine buyer, complains that she doesn't know how to set priorities. "I'm asking myself to let unimportant things go," she said. "I'm really too critical." (At that, she got up from the chair and cleaned a spot off the kitchen wall.)

The Edible Schoolyard was coming together with amazing ease and rapidity. The new kitchen was in place, and sixth-grade classes were already cooking in it twice a month. The acres of asphalt were being removed. An Aztec dance group had come for a cover-crop-planting ceremony: Bell beans, fenugreek, crimson clover, oats, and two species of vetch were now enriching the depauperate soil. The outdoor pizza oven was under construction.

The more Alice thought about the subject, the less she was willing to give up on the Clintons. On December 17, 1996, she wrote again.

> *Dear Mr. President,*
>
> *The prospect of your second terms fills me with hope—hope that you'll seize this opportunity. . . . I continue to believe that the very best way to bring people together is by changing the role food plays in our national life. There is a growing consensus that many of our social and political problems have arisen because we are alienated from meaningful participation in the everyday act of feeding ourselves. . . .*
>
> *A program like the Edible Schoolyard ought to be in every school in the country. . . .*
>
> *Respectfully yours,*
> *Alice Waters*

On February 24, 1997, the president replied:

Dear Alice:

... The Edible Schoolyard project ... complements the steps my Administration has taken to improve the nutritional health of our nation's children through the Department of Agriculture's Team Nutrition initiative. ... I'm proud to say that edible gardens are part of the curricula now being used in over 16,000 Team Nutrition schools. ...

Sincerely,

Bill Clinton

Team Nutrition schools, indeed! Alice knew that the federal government's influence on school lunches was almost entirely negative; surplus cheese and other industrially prepared foods of the lowest quality were what school lunch programs got. "I think Clinton wanted to do something about it," she says, "but he didn't want to put any money behind it. The government did a lot of talking, and passing out of leaflets about how we have to pay attention, but the serious stuff was unfunded."

WHILE ALICE DREAMED of Edible Schoolyards multiplying around the globe, Chez Panisse ticked along in its usual way—wracked by occasional storms of employee dissatisfaction; still barely profitable, if at all; producing delicious meals week after week—and from time to time Alice had to tear her eyes away from distant horizons to focus on matters at hand. In 1996, she restored the two-chef system in the downstairs restaurant, promoting Christopher Lee, who had been a Chez Panisse cook and forager for eight years, to be co-chef with Jean-Pierre Moullé. Jean-Pierre was disappointed, but he made the best of it.

In the summer of 1996, Alice's assistant, Gayle Pirie, left to open a restaurant of her own, Foreign Cinema, in San Francisco. By this time Alice had much too much to do to function without an assistant. A friend recommended a young woman named Cristina Salas-Porras as a replacement, and once again one of the classic Chez Panisse patterns manifested itself: Just the right person had appeared at just the right time.

Cristina had grown up in El Paso, in a life of considerable privilege. She was the youngest of six children in a matriarchal, culturally Mexican family that owned a chain of movie theaters in the United States. Her mother served on the board of the Federal Reserve. Cristina spent her junior year in high school in Japan, and went on to a major in East Asian studies at Middlebury College and postgraduate work at Keio University, one of Japan's most prestigious institutions.

She also loved food. She had loved her grandmother's Mexican cooking, she loved to cook on the family cook's night off, and she loved the elegant, spare food of Japan. She had had a job looking after VIPs for the Hotel Park Hyatt in Tokyo—a place where VIPs are taken very seriously—and that had enabled her, she says, to taste "food that even the Japanese didn't have access to." When she returned to America, she didn't know exactly what she was going to do, but it had to have something to do with food. She and a brother-in-law began experimenting with olive oils, and their "O" brand of blended oils won an award at a major fancy-food show as the best new product in the United States. But when Alice called, Cristina saw an opportunity for "something I really, really wanted—an opportunity to be in a mentoring situation with someone I respected and who knew more than I did."

With her almost-black hair pulled sleekly back, her large, dark, frank eyes, and her pale olive skin, Cristina had the mien and the bearing of a Spanish noblewoman, though without the austerity: That wide, easy smile was pure American. Her manners were perfect, her gaze direct, her answers concise, her intelligence obvious. This was far more than Alice needed in an assistant, but she sensed in Cristina a kinship and sympathy that she needed more than administrative acumen.

"I just loved her manner," says Alice. "I loved her spirit, her beauty, her international focus—speaking Japanese fluently, and Spanish. And she was somebody who had worked in the hotel business and knew about hospitality. She was the youngest in her family and always was there helping her older sisters and brothers, and had such a close relationship to that extended family. She loved older people and loved little kids, and she just completely, completely won my heart."

Cristina Salas-Porras

Also in 1996, Alice published *Chez Panisse Vegetables.* It was a remarkably encyclopedic cookbook, not just a compendium of recipes. Each vegetable got its own introductory essay exploring its essential nature, its behavior under different cooking methods, its prime season, and its history.

For the twenty-fifth birthday of Chez Panisse, in August 1996, "I didn't want to have a big huge party like the twentieth," she observes, "so we had a week of parties, and every day we had them for a different kind of group of people." The first, on August 23, was for Alice's fellow restaurateurs and chefs. The next was for the Chez Panisse "family tree"—friends, lovers, ex-staff, and family. Sunday was for growers and suppliers; the Los Angeles chef Wolfgang Puck drove the Chino family up from southern California for their first-ever meal at Chez Panisse. Monday was for Alice's artist and film-community friends. Tuesday was for wine people, and Wednesday, August 28, 1996, the actual anniversary, was for "old and dear friends" from the early days of Chez Panisse.

"Every night was so full of celebration, it was like having six huge New Year's Eves," Alice says. "I nearly died. I was worn out. It was right at the time when Stephen and I were having huge problems. So I was in a state, and I think this series of parties kind of pushed us over."

Stephen was planning to open a tapas bar, to be called—dipping as his wife had done into Pagnol's Marseille trilogy—Bar César. It would be situated directly next door to Chez Panisse. To Alice's friends, that uncomfortable proximity seemed both dependent and defiant. Alice herself simply kept her distance, and her own counsel.

"I used to spend hours with Stephen in those days," Bob Carrau remembers. "He was so angry at her. We used to ride bikes together, and the whole time would be about, 'Alice better let me open Bar César or I'm going to leave her.' I just thought, He keeps saying he wants to be out of Alice's shadow, but he keeps standing in it. I kept saying, 'Stephen, why don't you open a place across town?' What really was going on is he wanted her approval, and she wasn't giving it."

It took another year for Alice and Stephen's problems to come fully to the surface. One day in the summer of 1997, Stephen told Alice that he had fallen in love with someone else, a friend of hers. Alice was devastated.

"It wasn't a mutual decision," Alice says. "He said he still loved me, equally, but he had to tell me. It was very hard. Very painful.

"Walking and talking with friends is a kind of therapy for me. It was really important for me then. Fortunately I had a kid, and fortunately I had a family at Chez Panisse. Fortunately I had some money. I don't know how people manage. I was really lucky. I called all my friends. I was crying for help from everybody. Anybody."

Sharon Jones was one of Alice's oldest friends, one of the restaurant's first waitresses, a veteran of opening night. In the mornings, she and Alice walked together, often for miles. "Having her marriage fall apart was the biggest unexpected thing that had ever happened to Alice," says Sharon. "It took her a long time to process it, but I'm really proud of the way she came through it. Two or three years after my marriage broke up, when I was complaining about not having another relationship that was meaningful enough, I can remember her telling me, 'I don't know why you can't just go out and find somebody. There are lots of people around here.' She was very glib about it. And I thought, You don't know what you're talking about. It's not so easy, Alice. Then when her marriage broke up, her ability to empathize with people grew enormously.

"Alice has something that the world, I think, associates more with males, which is that you can fix it. I mean, she's such an improviser and such a problem solver. But there are some things that you can't fix, and this was the first thing that she could not fix."

"She didn't go out with anybody for a long time," says Bob Carrau. "I think she felt totally old. There was a whole period when she kept repainting her bedroom and moving furniture around, and going like, It doesn't feel right. I kept saying, 'Alice, the reason it doesn't feel right, it's never going to feel right, it's not anything to do with what furniture is in here and what paint is on the walls, it's because your husband left you!' And I'd come the next week and there would be Chinese boxes all over the place, and then the next week she was thinking of moving her bedroom into the living room, and then moving the house. She didn't even want to cook for a while. She would go to the restaurant and do things, but you'd go over to her house and she'd either get stuff from Chez Panisse and serve it, or we'd walk in the kitchen and she would go, 'You guys make dinner,' which to me was great because it meant she was relaxed enough to just bail. But you know, ever since then, she hasn't really been involved with anybody. I think she's so wonderful and she could be, but she keeps herself really wrapped up in business, and she's really manic, and so it's hard for her."

Stephen and Alice agreed that they would divorce, though they continued to live under the same roof well into the summer of 1997, when Fanny turned fourteen. The fact that they managed to live together under such circumstances shows how deeply committed they felt to keeping at least the appearance of family, for Fanny's sake. They held off telling her till the last possible moment.

Fanny Singer recalls, "It was a shock. I must have sensed their discord, but for some reason I have very few memories building up to the moment they told me they were splitting up. Then it took me a while before I could really communicate with my dad. Anyhow, I never lived full-time with him after that. I stayed mostly with my mom at our house, which is still, to this day, very much my true home. My life was tied up in that place. And my life is still very tied up in hers."

"Things were very difficult for Stephen and me before then," Alice says, "but I thought we would be married forever. I knew he was unhappy. I knew he wanted me to change my life, and I know he felt like I made all the decisions about everything, but I don't know, I just thought somehow we could work it out. I was really, really unhappy. It was excruciating."

Another loss closely followed the loss of her husband. On October 14, 1997, Lindsey Shere retired as pastry chef. Lindsey had been the proto-type of all that was gentlest and most straightforward in the Chez Panisse way. "I was just so sad," Alice says. "She was a real partner, and a mentor, and had a beautiful way with people." Charles would continue to sit on the board of directors of Chez Panisse, and Lindsey would continue to attend board meetings, so she was not lost altogether, but, Alice says, "I knew it would never be the same."

Alice's closest friends, among them Bob Carrau, Sharon Jones, Sue Murphy, Fritz Streiff, and her new friend Davia Nelson (a movie casting director whom she had met through Tom Luddy), all felt an almost parental responsibility for Alice. "Alice is one of the strongest people I have ever met," says Davia, "but she also needs people to help her, in the same way that she helps others to distill things. So many things are com-ing at her simultaneously. Alice is the opposite of a loner. There is a fragility and a vulnerability about her, but she is always part of a group. If Alice walks around the track—something she's been doing a lot of—she always walks with a friend, and that friendship is strengthened, because she is a woman of ritual, of movement, of connection."

Over her first year, Cristina Salas-Porras had grown from Alice's assis-tant to Alice's confidante and adviser. Cristina recalls that time:

At first it was just scheduling and press and stuff like that. Alice susses you out as you go along. I came here during probably the hardest time in Alice's life. I didn't know her. I was a stranger to her, and yet I had to be privy to all of this terrible private stuff. It was very stressful. Alice was very unfocused and unhappy. The first two years were very hard.

It was hard to focus Alice on all the different components of the office. There were no systems, there was no filing system, there was nothing, and so I pretty much got to build it from the ground up—creating a way of doing things in the office and giving some structure to the way Alice was working. But in the beginning I had to check every single thing with her, and it was hard to get her attention and hard to move things forward. She was doing too much. What became easier is that over time, as I gained her trust, she just let me make those decisions and she didn't even know they were being made. And sometimes I made decisions that she wasn't comfortable with, but she said, "That's the position I've put myself in, so let's move forward."

Alice had been doing some public appearances, but not nearly as many as she began to do. Over the course of the next few years, things really changed, for a combination of reasons: Alice was able to redirect her energy in some ways away from the restaurant. She was starting to realize that she wanted to take food out of the food context and take it more into the social and cultural context. So we started being a little bit more strategic about what kinds of things she would do outside of the restaurant. And maybe that meant doing a show on the Food Network that she would have never considered doing before, but we did it because it reached a bigger audience or a different audience, and we weren't always preaching to the converted. We started being more selective about the things she would do and wouldn't do, which was hard for Alice. We had to convince her sometimes that we had to start reaching beyond our group of followers.

"I needed Cristina so much that year [1997]," says Alice, "and she was wonderful. She also became a great friend to Fanny, and she still is. Cristina has been very important to Fanny."

With so much pain in her recent past, Alice was seeing herself in the future now, climbing a very high hill step by step. She knew that if she could reach the top, she would be in a position to see her ideas take hold on a very large scale. There would be obstacles, there would be setbacks, but Alice knew now that she was succeeding, and that success fed on success.

THE EDIBLE SCHOOLYARD was a magnificent success. Alice created the Chez Panisse Foundation to assure its funding and, in time, to fund like-minded ventures wherever they might be possible.

At the Martin Luther King Middle School, the asphalt had all been removed, and the gardens had been planted. Students were cultivating, weeding, fertilizing, learning. The first harvest had come in—mâche, arugula, mustards, lettuces, kale, bok choy, carrots, turnips, beets, garlic, fava beans, and tomatoes—and now the kids were learning to cook. They produced a lavish banquet for their parents. Ten students came down from the Uni-

In the Edible Schoolyard kitchen

versity of Montana to build a ramada (an open porch of logs), through which climbing plants would be trained to provide shade. Using Japanese joinery instead of nails, the students and a designer built a tool shed from a single redwood tree harvested from a certified-sustainable forest. There were new plantings, of citrus trees, apples, plums, ground cherries, black currants, hazelnuts, figs, raspberries, edible bamboo, kiwifruit, scarlet runner beans, chayote, and—for tea, fragrance, and beauty—hibiscus, jasmine, and passionflower. And they planted one of Alice's favorite things in the world, a mulberry tree.

Mister Rogers' Neighborhood and *The Oprah Winfrey Show* broadcast on location from the Edible Schoolyard. Eleven apple trees were trained to an espalier. Alice persuaded the Berkeley school district to phase out all foods derived from cows given bovine growth hormone and all foods derived from genetically modified crops. And the crops kept rolling in—corn, blackberries, lemon verbena, mint, gourds, tomatoes, onions, leeks, peppers, basil, parsley, broccoli, collard greens. The students were raising, harvesting, cooking, serving, and eating them all. They had come a long way from microwaved hamburgers and soda pop.

· MULBERRY ICE CREAM CONES ·

This is another favorite dish that I like to make myself. Once upon a time, at the restaurant we had been getting these mulberries from a particular farmer, and they were always fantastic eaten raw on the fruit plate. But then one of the cooks made them into ice cream, and it was an awakening for me. I went right down to the pastry department and I said, "I want this every day. Every day." They always hate that, when I say, "This is so good I want this every day on the menu." They do it for about a week and then it's gone, and I don't see it again until the next year. We made mulberry ice cream cones for the twenty-ninth birthday of the restaurant, and Fanny and her friends served them out in front of the restaurant. It was the best thing anybody had ever tasted for two dollars.

We made the cones, too. We used one of those sort of Swedish waffle irons. You make a batter with flour and sugar and butter and a little bit of vanilla, and I think it has a little milk. You put a little bit in the iron, and then you press it closed, and in a minute it puffs up like a little thin waffle. We've got a little cone made out of wood, and you just roll the hot waffle around the cone. I suppose you could make it on a griddle. You have to have it really thin.

For the mulberries, you take the stems out and crush the berries in a blender, and push them through a sieve. If you like a rougher texture, you just use a sieve with bigger holes. You make a custard with egg yolks and half-and-half and sugar and cream. You strain that, and then you chill it. When it's nice and cold, you fold in the berries and put the whole thing into an ice cream freezer, and there you are!

I like to pour a little chocolate in the bottom. It makes a wonderful surprise.

In 1998, an astonishing offer came to Alice, one that could dramatically extend the range of her influence. Hélène David-Weill, director of the Museum of Decorative Arts at the Louvre, asked Alice if she would like to establish a restaurant in that ancient palace. She had refused for twenty-seven years even to consider opening another Chez Panisse, but this was different. The first image that rose into her mind was of a vegetable garden in the Jardins des Tuileries, to grow the fruits and vegetables that the restaurant would serve. A teaching garden. The restaurant would have 330 seats—almost seven times the size of the downstairs dining room at Chez Panisse. "Were there no French chefs for such an undertaking?" asked the *New York Times*. "Mrs. David-Weill said she did not find them. 'Probably there are very good people in France, but they didn't come to us.'"[2]

Probably there are very good people in France? Imagine the *scandale.* The first restaurant in the history of the Louvre not in the hands of a Frenchman? Not even a Frenchwoman? Alice was in raptures. She drew up a mission statement:

> A platform, an exhibit, a classroom, a conservatory, a laboratory, and a garden. It must be, in a phrase, an art installation in the form of a restaurant. . . . Amidst the grandeur of the Louvre, the restaurant must feel human, reflecting the spirit of the farm, the terroir, and the market, and it must express the humanity of the artisans, cooks, and servers who work there.

And then she went to take a look at the space. There was room for ninety diners, not three hundred. The idea of a kitchen garden in the Tuileries was met in official quarters with a sharply raised eyebrow. The only place for a prep kitchen was a gloomy, low-ceilinged basement. In *The New Yorker,* Adam Gopnik wrote:

> After Alice left Paris, *Le Figaro* published an interview with her in which she gently reviewed her concerns about the Rungis market [the main wholesale food market that supplied most restaurants in Paris]. THE MARKETS IN PARIS ARE SHOCKING! was the headline on the piece, whose effect, from a P.R. point of view, was that of a Japanese baseball player who after a trip to Yankee Stadium is quoted in a headline saying, "YOU CALL THAT A BALLPARK?"[3]

"We were intending that it would be truly part of the museum, that it would be like an exhibit in the museum," Alice says. "But the administrative part of the Louvre gave me a contract as if I was opening a fast-food concession. I was so charged up I wanted to go ahead and do it anyway. But I had a lot of people advising me, and they all said, 'Do not sign that paper.'"

Did she regret the loss of that grand opportunity? "Not a bit. It would have been awful. Besides, by then I was into Slow Food, and that was so much more what I wanted to do."

. . .

THE SLOW FOOD MOVEMENT had been following a path that would inevitably cross that of Alice Waters. It was just a matter of time.

On March 22, 1986, a McDonald's had opened on the Piazza di Spagna, in the heart of Rome, within easy littering distance of Bulgari, Valentino, Prada, and the city's most expensive hotel, the Hassler Villa Medici. In the distant Piedmontese town of Bra, a thirty-six-year-old activist named Carlo Petrini was horrified. Soon Carlo and several dozen of his supporters were in Rome, marching up and down in front of that archetype of fast food, carrying bowls of penne and placards proclaiming, in McDonald's native tongue, SLOW FOOD!

Carlo Petrini had founded Italy's first radical radio station. He had established a folk music festival where the musicians not only played onstage but marched into people's living rooms. He abhorred the industrialization and standardization that were creeping into the Italian way of eating. He and his friends opened a restaurant in Bra to express their credo of honest, hand-made, regional food. They called it Boccondivino, "Divine Mouthful."

Bra lies near the vineyards of Barolo. The makers of Barolo at that time were among Europe's most stalwart upholders of viticultural tradition-alism (some of them still are, though others have succumbed to a specious modernism). The wine was made essentially as it had been for genera-tions. It was harsh and unforgiving in its youth, but after ten or twenty years of maturation, it was transformed into a velvety, richly aromatic wine as fine as any in the world. Barolo epitomized the central tenet of Carlo's philosophy, namely, that to those who attune themselves to time and the land, good things, in time, come. The first advocacy organization he formed was the Libera e Benemerita Associazione degli Amici del Barolo, the Free and Deserving Association of the Friends of Barolo.

Among Carlo's supporters was a group of Milanese intellectuals asso-ciated with the magazine *La Gola* ("The Gullet"). Together they and the Associazione Ricreativa Culturale Italiana (ARCI) helped Carlo form a bigger organization, Arcigola—a pun meaning, roughly, "archgluttony."

Arcigola opposed not only the right wing but also the Green Party, marijuana, and vegetarianism.

Arcigola Slow Food, as it renamed itself in 1987, caught on quickly. By 1989, it had a membership of eleven thousand in Italy alone, and chapters were springing up all over Europe. The Arcigolosi, as they styled themselves, published widely, most often in *L'Unità,* the Communist Party daily. Their mission was to convert their starchy, self-abnegating fellow leftists into fellow hedonists—in unconscious emulation of what had happened twenty years before in Berkeley.

Slow Food. In those Anglo-Saxon, seemingly nonsensical words Carlo saw the dawning of his life project. Slow Food International (which had dropped the incomprehensible "Arcigola") wouldn't be just opposition to fast food. It would be about how to live. The hurry and hassles of America had already infected Milan and were working their way south. Pesticides were poisoning Italian waters. Industry was turning Italian workers into automatons. Grandmothers' recipes and techniques were undergoing a mass extinction as the new generations of women left their stoves for offices. Psychotherapy, antidepressants, tranquilizers, and plastic surgery, all growing fast, were no match for the modern anxiety that was afflicting the rapidly, radically changing society of Italy.

The Slow Food movement precisely mirrored Alice's mission, and in Carlo Petrini, she recognized a magnetism, an energy, and a determination equal to her own. Slow Food was growing prodigiously, but it was still a mainly European enterprise, with only a skeleton office in New York, fewer than five hundred American members, and no particular American ambitions. But Alice saw immediately that there was no reason that Slow Food couldn't boom in the United States just as it was doing in Europe. It just needed leadership.

Carlo had come to dinner at Chez Panisse once, in February 1988, and Alice had met him then, but her own focus at that time was strictly local. By 1999, Slow Food was emphasizing biodiversity as well as cultural conservation, and Alice was thinking big about education and biological conservation. She heard Carlo give a talk in San Francisco, recognized the

Carlo Petrini and Alice

prospects for powerful synergy, and said to Cristina, "We've got to get involved with this."

Carlo and Alice hit it off instantly. He didn't speak English, she didn't speak Italian, but—sometimes with the aid of a translator, and sometimes without—they seemed to understand each other perfectly. They agreed that it was time for expansion in the United States. Patrick Martins, an American who had been working for Slow Food in Bra, moved to New York to set up a fully staffed office, one capable of handling the growth that Alice and Carlo hoped for. Alice joined the board of Slow Food USA, and the office at Chez Panisse became its de facto West Coast headquarters.

Carlo visited the Edible Schoolyard and promptly concluded that school gardens ought to be on Slow Food International's agenda. "Alice," says Carlo (through a translator), "is a person who distinguishes among people very quickly, sometimes in an eyeblink. And she is a person who reconciles sweetness and tremendous determination. She has a great capacity for building things, because she knows how to bring people together."

On May 20, 1999, Chez Panisse gave a dinner to honor Carlo Petrini and Slow Food and to inaugurate the Berkeley "convivium," or chapter, which Alice and Cristina had just formed. Jean-Pierre Moullé moved a butcher block into the dining room, along with a tank of live trout. Risking a recurrence of the famous blue-trout disaster of 1973, he killed the fish one by one with a quick blow to the back of the head, and immediately plunged them into boiling court bouillon. The diners cheered.

Apéritif & hors d'oeuvres
NV Prosecco di Valdobbiadene Brut, Adriano Adami
❦

Local Pacific king salmon with lime oil and basil
Santa Barbara warm white asparagus with an herb vinaigrette
1997 Grüner Veltliner Federspiel, Im Weingeberge, Waschau, Nikolaihof
❦

Live rainbow trout au bleu with beurre mousseux
Sierra morel and pea ragout with a taste of grilled squab breast
1997 Green and Red Vineyard Chardonnay, Napa
❦

Braised Crystal Creek goat with roasted garlic, new potatoes,
and Berkeley Gardens salad
1997 Dolcetto d'Alba, Priavino, Roberto Voerzio
❦

Bellwether ricotta cheese and rhubarb
Chino Ranch strawberry sherbet and rose petal granità
1995 Handley Brut Rosé, Anderson Valley

Every one of the ingredients, as well as the wines, reflected the shared creed of Carlo Petrini and Alice Waters: local, just in season, and the work of dedicated artisans.

. . .

RICHARD MAZZERA resigned as general manager of Chez Panisse in March 1998, and joined Stephen Singer and two other partners in opening Bar César. The board of directors of Chez Panisse called for a thorough audit, and discovered that once again, the restaurant was in a financial shambles. Mario Daniele was hired as the new general manager, and immediately began a program of industrious accounting, cost control, and close oversight. After two years of that, the restaurant was, for the first time, making real money—enough, by the year 2000, to donate nearly $150,000 to the Chez Panisse Foundation.

Also in 1998, David Tanis had returned, cooking at the restaurant and café as needed but occupied primarily in helping Alice write *The Chez Panisse Café Cookbook,* which was published in September 1999, shortly after the death of the man whose books had inspired so much of the café's cooking, Richard Olney.

After many tumultuous years as not-chef, not-quite-chef, sous-chef, chef, and co-chef, Jean-Pierre Moullé resigned again on February 1, 2000, and returned with his wife, Denise, to France, once more certain he would never return. Alice asked David Tanis to be co-chef with Christopher Lee.

David's hair was graying now. Behind his big dark-framed glasses and under his shaggy brows, his dark eyes seemed to have a newly sharpened focus. He loved Chez Panisse, and his style of cooking was in perfect accord with it, but he had become psychologically independent of the restaurant now, and he was good enough to cook wherever in the world he wanted. Bob Carrau says,

> It appears to me that Alice finds people to work with who have these interesting personal, and maybe idiosyncratic, ways of working. Like her suppliers, or a lot of the cooks, and the chefs, and the artists, they're usually local, found in her backyard, her life. Then she collaborates with them, and the process infuses them with a certain sense of self and vision and confidence, and then something happens—like their work gets better, better known, and so forth, and so here these

artists have been born, but they're not the same anymore. They're not the naïve individuals they once were. Many times they aren't comfortable collaborating with Alice in the same way anymore. They want more say, more control, more money. So Alice watches them flourish and bloom and ultimately has to watch them move on.

THE YEAR 2000 also brought a change that would be as momentous for Chez Panisse as the arrival of Cristina Salas-Porras had been for Alice: the ascendancy of Gilbert Pilgram to general manager. Cristina had brought order and focus to Alice's life, and had become indispensable to her. Following the recovery that Mario Daniele had wrought, Gilbert wanted to bring further order and profit to Chez Panisse. He, too, quickly became indispensable. What was most important to Alice, she finally felt entirely comfortable leaving Chez Panisse in someone else's hands. Gilbert Pilgram, Alice believed, would allow her to climb the vertiginous heights of her dreams without looking down.

Gilbert is tall, thin, with long, lank, prematurely silver hair and pene-

Gilbert Pilgram and Alice

trating gray-blue eyes. He nearly always wears a fitted Hermès shirt with single French cuffs and a bright, floppy Hermès bow tie. A Mont Blanc pen peeks from the pocket. Gilbert personifies what Chez Panisse has become: secure in his skin, conscious of being at the top, confident in the future.

He grew up in Mexico City, where his family, of German descent, had a chocolate factory. Intended by his family to take it over, he majored in food science at the University of California at Davis. While there, he discovered he was gay, started spending weekends in San Francisco, and decided against a career as a chocolate magnate. After a couple of unsatisfying jobs for big food companies, he went to work at a prestigious law firm, and went on from there to earn an MBA at Golden Gate University. "Meanwhile, I was cooking all the time," he says.

Everything I did was god-awful. When they thought I wasn't looking, my friends would throw the food out the window.

I met Richard [Richard Gilbert, his companion of twenty-three years] at the law firm. We knew a painter who was also a waitress at Chez Panisse, and she suggested that I see if I could get a place as an intern. Which I did. Thirty years old, and working for no money.

I'd have fired myself. Jacques Pépin came to be chef for a little while, while Paul took some time off to work on his book. Pépin took one look at my technique and told me to get lost. I worked at Campton Place in San Francisco, and I went with Judy Rodgers and Catherine Brandel to this wine expo in Europe. All unpaid. Thank God Richard was a lawyer. Then Catherine started cooking at Chez Panisse, and she got me a real job there, doing prep in the café. Six dollars an hour.

Eventually, I made it up to sous-chef, and finally co-chef with Russell Moore, in the café. Russ and I were going to start our own place, but then Mario left and Alice persuaded Russ and me to stay. When she asked me to be general manager, she offered me a share in the restaurant equal to her own.

I felt very lucky. This restaurant is a living thing, you know.

People have been here twenty years. Everybody really cares about what they're doing. From the menu meeting on, the cook has total responsibility for the dish. That's what makes our food so different. At Jean-Georges, you make Jean-Georges's food. Here you are a chef. It is your kitchen, your dish.

It was difficult for me to get across the idea of sustainability. I say we have to take care of ourselves. There's a difference between charitable and sustainable. Slow Food and the Edible Schoolyard are very well, but my concern has to be the people of the restaurant. We've got to be profitable enough to pay a living wage. Alice likes to keep the restaurant as affordable as possible, and so one of the things I need to point out to her every now and then is that we need to generate enough income that we can pay everybody well. It is not sustainable to do twenty benefits a year for the foundation. It is sustainable to do a couple of them a year, but to also do a couple of events for profit—what I jokingly call benefits for Chez Panisse. I think the restaurant has a responsibility to pay above market, because what we ask of people is way above market.

"Gilbert can be very hard to argue with," Alice says.

Another thing that makes us different [says Gilbert] is that you have the sense that people will take care of you. If you get into a bit of personal trouble, the restaurant will step in—observing your privacy of course—to help you. You know you are not simply punching in, punching out, and getting a paycheck. We do a very substantial contribution to the 401(k). It's not unheard of for us to do a contribution of a hundred thousand dollars at the end of the year. You also know that all our watching the bottom line and watching overtime means that at the end of the year, we can have a very generous sharing—to the tune of two hundred fifty, two hundred seventy thousand dollars. We have a system of points to divide the money. So if you're in the dish room and have been doing really good work, you get points for that. How long you've been here earns you certain points. Another is how many hours you've worked. And then there's merit, which is completely discretionary. A dishwasher who has worked here full-time and worked very hard through the year could get another three thousand dollars. In the restaurant business, especially at the low end of the pay scale, that's not small potatoes.

Pat Edwards, Pat Waters, and Richard Mazzera had all tried to bring a modicum of serious management to Chez Panisse, and Mario Daniele had succeeded, but none of them exercised power over Alice, and her unbossability limited how much even Mario could accomplish. When Alice wanted to spend money, or give it away, she did it, and nobody could stop her. Gilbert would not have official authority over Alice either; but he was determined to govern the business of Chez Panisse. "I knew that she was used to having her way about everything," he says, "and if I was going to do what I intended to do as G.M., that was going to have to change. Initially it was very difficult. I was always saying to her, 'Alice, am I running this place or not?'

"Finally we got to the point where I could say, 'Alice, you're driving me crazy, and this is why.'"

The perfect freedom Alice had foreseen for herself in the Gilbert era was turning out not to be so easily gained, simply because she could never quite let go of the restaurant.

The culture of Chez Panisse did not lend itself readily to Gilbert's governance:

At first, I rubbed a lot of people the wrong way, because tightening needed to be done. In the downstairs crew, you'd break for dinner while the seatings changed, and back then you would get to open a bottle of whatever you wanted. But if you were an upstairs cook, you didn't get to sit down and have a bottle of Château Margaux. At the end of the shift, sometimes, suddenly Champagne would start to flow. That came from everybody's pockets. And I got people to understand that at the end of the year, I would rather have three thousand dollars going into my 401(k) and six thousand come to me as a bonus rather than drink that money through the year.

We've also had a problem of misplaced generosity toward customers. The easiest thing for a waiter is to give a glass of Champagne to everyone at the end of a meal. I don't subscribe to that school of thought at all. Alice does. When you do it all the time, I think you devalue the gift. A restaurant can be generous in exceeding its customers' expectations. If someone has ordered two glasses of wine, and you see that they have finished their second glass and they still have a little bit left of their main course, well, let me just top you off a little bit. But if we're giving whole lunches and dinners away all the time—I joke with Alice, saying, "Well, what do you do when someone really has a reason to celebrate? Do you send them home with the staff member of their choice?" You have to husband your generosity, and then you can make the person really feel special.

"Gilbert can drive me crazy," says Alice, "but in a way that's what I hired him to do. He's turned Chez Panisse into a real business."

Gilbert explains:

Our revenue last year was almost seven million dollars. Profit is not as much as you would think—around ten percent. It would have been bigger if we hadn't given a quarter of a million in bonuses. It would have been higher if we hadn't contributed a hundred fifty thousand dollars to the 401(k). For health insurance we pay seventy percent, and the employee pays thirty. Our part of that annually is over a hundred thousand dollars. This is a very good place to work. And it's sustainable.

WITH ANOTHER BLOWOUT fund-raising dinner for the Clintons in March 2000, Alice's last chance was at hand: Less than a year remained in the president's term in office. The menu was spectacular, with three iterations of his favorite course, dessert:

Truffled risotto fritters and vegetable crudités
❦

Dungeness crab salad and Fairview Gardens white asparagus
with watercress mayonnaise
❦

Petaluma duck leg braised with new garlic;
fava beans with rosemary noodles
❦

Tangerine granità
❦

Warm chocolate fondant with pecan ice cream
❦

Candies, candied fruits, and mint tisane

Alice did not buttonhole the president at the dinner itself, but on March 20, 2000, she wrote him a letter more imperative than any she had yet dared:

Dear Mr. President:

Although these are the final days of your presidency, I still believe that Thomas Jefferson's dream of a government informed by the values of a nation of independent farmers can be realized through your example. Therefore I encourage you to show the world your concern for the environment with this simple and beautiful gesture:

Mr. President, plant that garden on the White House grounds! . . . I can think of no more powerful way to ground your legacy than to leave behind you a kitchen garden and the compost pile to nourish it. . . .

With respect and admiration,
Alice Waters

On April 28, 2000, the president wrote back to Alice. Note that by now he was just plain Bill:

Dear Alice:

It was good to see you in California last month. I really enjoyed the evening—your cooking is such a treat.

Thanks for your suggestion about planting a kitchen garden on the White House grounds. Since I took office, Hillary and I have been interested in the idea of growing fresh herbs and vegetables here at the White House. But we decided that an informal kitchen garden would not be in keeping with the formal gardens of the White House and the historic planting guidelines developed in the 1930s. Instead . . . Hillary requested that the National Park Service plant and maintain a vegetable garden on the roof of the Executive Residence. In addition, the East Garden has been planted with garden herbs that our chefs use for our meals, and the National Park Service maintains a compost recycling pile at our greenhouse. . . .

    Sincerely,

    Bill

Two weeks later, on May 12, 2000, Alice fired back:

Dear Mr. President:

    . . . I apologize for being so insistent, but I have the impression that you and Hillary may have made up your minds about a different garden than the one I have been proposing. An informal garden would indeed be out of keeping with the traditional formality of the White House grounds, but . . . as you probably know, L'Enfant's original plan for the capital city was inspired by the layout of Versailles, and at Versailles the royal kitchen garden is itself a national monument: historically accurate, productive, and breathtakingly beautiful throughout the year. . . .

    Respectfully,

    Alice Waters

Bill and Hillary Clinton knew a thing or two about stubbornness, too. Neither replied, and that was the end of the correspondence.

FOR THE THIRTIETH BIRTHDAY of Chez Panisse, Alice was dreaming big. She knew that if she could gather into one occasion the whole history of Chez Panisse and of her other accomplishments, the immensity of her vision would be manifest to all.

I thought we should have probably about five or six hundred people. I was going to use the Escoffier model: For every hundred people, there would be a full kitchen and a head chef. Then one day I was just sort of spouting off to the chancellor of the university [of California at Berkeley], wondering whether there was any place on campus that could handle a number like that, and he said, "Well, you know, you might want to come and look at the main library." I thought, Oh, my God! I'd never expected an offer like that.

Then I was looking at a book about L.A. at the turn of the century, when there were farms in Pasadena. There was this picture of some sort of big reunion in Iowa. There were these big long tables and all these people sitting with their hats on. Outdoors, under the trees. That became my *idée fixe*. This young woman took me around the whole campus, and every location was better and better, and then I saw the campanile [a replica of the one at San Marco in Venice], and the plaza below it. And there we had it.

For a long while I thought our office could run it. I thought we were doing okay until I realized that we were not. We were in deep water. Well, then, thank God for Cristina, and thank God for Carolyn Federman.

Carolyn Federman is slight, pretty, and animated, with long dark hair and a broad smile. Her manner tends toward the amused. "I interviewed with Cristina first," she recalls,

and she had to talk Alice into interviewing me. I had never done anything like this before. I did coordinate this one event when I was just out of college, a three-day music festival, and there were a lot of components, and I had also planned my wedding. So I was familiar with—you know, you do the music, you do the catering, you do the blah blah.

My interview with Alice was funny. She had this binder with sheet protectors, with all these pictures of what she envisioned the birthday would look like, and all these little notes. And when she opened the binder, all the pages fell out, and she was also talking, and she couldn't concentrate on what she was trying to say, so I took the binder from her and said, "Why don't I do this while you talk?"

Right then, I knew that we were going to be a good combination.

Once again, Alice was taking a highly risky chance on someone who had scant qualifications ("I planned my wedding") but who seemed to "get it."

She told me all the different things she wanted to have going on, and I walked out of there thinking, This woman is absolutely nuts.

Alice was trusting everyone to do their thing. Well, she did change the menu the day before the event. We were sitting down, all the chefs, and I was trying to take charge of the meeting, and David Tanis just stopped the conversation. He said, "She's never worked with Alice, has she?"

I kept thinking, These people are crazy, but it turned out everybody really knew their stuff one hundred percent. You could just really trust that when they said they were going to do something, they would do it.

Sunday, August 19, 2001, was a hot day for Berkeley, broiling in the sun though, as always, chilly under the redwoods. There were six hundred guests, paying $500 each, with the proceeds going to the Chez Panisse Foundation. There were sixty cooks in all, and two hundred volunteers waiting tables (in twelve teams, each with its own captain). Fritz Streiff composed the invitation:

As the aromatic smoke of lambs turning slowly on spits wreathes the base of the Campanile, we will welcome you with a sparkling apéritif and a *panisse*. . . . Just down the hill at the Bancroft Library, you will have an opportunity to view an exhibition that in-

Tables set for the thirtieth-anniversary party, 2001

cludes original Chez Panisse art, posters, menus for special occasions, cookbooks, and other memorabilia, and you may join in a silent auction of Chez Panisse menus and other ephemera.

. . . A leisurely lunch will fade imperceptibly into dinner—a feast prepared outdoors by our extended family of chefs and friends and interspersed with toasts and entertainment by some of the wonderful writers, musicians, poets, and personalities who have brought such life to Chez Panisse over the years. We will converse, dance, eat, and drink until sunset.

Dress as if for a grand holiday picnic or a Sunday town square civic celebration. . . .

As we look back and celebrate thirty years of Chez Panisse with this idealized evocation of communitarian and agrarian values, we are also looking forward—to a delicious twenty-first-century revolution in education that will bring about a saner and healthier future for our children. . . .

The menu:

RECEPTION AT THE CAMPANILE
Dario Cecchini's pork specialties from Panzano
Panisses, radishes, and almonds

LUNCH À LA FAMILLE ON THE ESPLANADE
Summer vegetable salads
❦
Provençal fish soup cooked in the fireplace
❦
Spit-roasted barons of Canfield Farm lamb with chanterelles
Spicy lamb and mint sausages
Fresh shell beans
Herb salad
❦
Cheese from Jean d'Alos
Apple and plum jellies
❦
Mulberry ice cream cones
Friandises and tisanes

WINES DONATED BY KERMIT LYNCH, WINE MERCHANT
Prosecco brut Bosco di Gica, Adriano Adami
2000 Bandol rosé, Domaine Tempier
1999 Bourgogne Blanc, Côte Chalonnaise Les Clous, A & P de Villaine
1999 Gigondas, Domaine les Pallières
1999 Muscat de Beaumes-de-Venise, Domaine de Durban

Lunch began with the Prosecco at one o'clock, accompanied by baskets of figs, olives, cherry tomatoes, hot roasted almonds, and salty, hot *panisses* (the indigenous Marseillais chickpea fritters after which the Pagnol character was named). At two thirty, as the Baroque Philharmonic Orchestra blasted out fanfares on valveless period horns, the diners took their seats at the long, white-linened tables arrayed on the lawns. The Gigondas had come from Kermit Lynch's own vineyard, the Bandol rosé from Lulu's.

Dario Cecchini, the famously eccentric butcher from Panzano-in-Chianti, in clown-striped pantaloons and purple cowboy boots, recited Canto V of Dante's *Inferno* in booming Italian, from memory. Alice had asked the choreographer Mark Morris to sing the menu, but he ended up singing "Let's Have Another Cup o' Coffee." San Francisco Symphony conductor Michael Tilson Thomas banged out his just-composed "Marche Triomphale de la Cuisine" on an upright piano:

CHEZ PANISSE! CHEZ PANISSE! CHEZ PANISSE,
Haute cuisine of revolution!
CHEZ PANISSE! CHEZ PANISSE!
We're your veteran foody institution.
We lead off the ev'ning news with our stews and ragouts.
Our attention to detail is deft and manic.
We refine obscure old goop into ecstatic soup.
We won't serve a toothpick if it's not organic!

CHEZ PANISSE! CHEZ PANISSE!
Fighting fast-food assassins' wretched base crud!
CHEZ PANISSE! CHEZ PANISSE!
On our guard to redeem each virgin tastebud!
We won't serve what we suspect's not politic'ly correct.
We're immune from fickle fashion's shoves and pushes.
We won't whisk our meringues for those types who harangue.
It's not likely that we'll beat around the Bushes!

CHEZ PANISSE! CHEZ PANISSE!
Roast, sauté, simmer, sear, and fricassee!
CHEZ PANISSE! CHEZ PANISSE!
Marinate, steam, reduce, and you will see—ah . . .
What do you say after the blood and sweat and tears?
What do you say after these thirty years?
What do you say? What do you say
But a four-star Hip Hip Hooray!

It's more than just a restaurant!

It's a proud credo we can flaunt!

Doing our bit for food each night!

Keeping the torch of taste alight!

Bravo and Bis!

And if you please

We'll never cease!

CHEZ PANISSE!

CHEZ PANISSE!

Fanny and Alice at the thirtieth

Theater and opera director
Peter Sellars and Lulu Peyraud

Pat and Marge Waters, Alice's parents

Alice at the thirtieth

*David Goines and his
friend Tati Argue*

An instrumental quartet serenaded the tables with Pagnolian tunes. An honor guard of Alameda County sanitation men passed in clangorous parade, spinning their garbage cans into the air like majorettes' batons. U.S. senator Barbara Boxer read a tribute to Alice. There were messages of congratulation from Senator Dianne Feinstein and Bill and Hillary Clinton.

Christopher Lee supervised the chefs—Jean-Pierre Moullé, Judy Rodgers, David Tanis, Jonathan Waxman, and Chris's new co-chef as of 2001, Kelsie Kerr. Twenty hindquarters of lamb sizzled gently above ten charcoal grills.

It was a blazing day, but Cristina had thought of a countermove: A nurse in a World War I uniform made her way among the tables distributing sunblock. Alice was everywhere at once, kissing, laughing, receiving congratulations, proud—and dressed in high Alice style: "I was wearing a maroon sort of tunic, and sort of short pants under it. I mean not short pants, capri. There was a little handmade bolero top with colored flowers embroidered on it. And a little kind of, what would you call it? A little cloche, that my friend Jeanne d'Alessio made for me."

The stage set depicted the oak-savanna hills of California somewhat in the style of Grant Wood. Flushing bright pink, Alice took the microphone and paid tribute to four women who had informed her idea of what a great female cook might be: Marion Cunningham, her close friend, longtime assistant to James Beard, and editor of the modern *Fannie Farmer Cookbook*; Edna Lewis, the grande dame of southern cooking; Lulu Peyraud; and Julia Child. (Julia, ill, was unable to be there.) Alice seemed flustered, overwhelmed.

A number of Alice's friends were appalled by her rambling, disjointed speech, in which she gave credit to no one. "What I was was high on Bandol rosé," says Alice by way of reply. "There's a film of me speaking, but you can't understand a word I'm saying."

Davia Nelson, a veteran of radio and film production, sympathizes with Alice's sometimes extreme difficulties in front of crowds:

Alice likes to be a presence, but being on a stage just gives her vertigo, makes her levitate. We always say, "Did you stay in your body that time?" Sometimes I watch her words come out of her mouth like little birds getting hatched. It's so painful to watch her find her words. Just this little neck stretching up to the sky. I always think it's like one of the saints trying to get a vision, only she's just trying to get to the next sentence. I can hear it caught in her throat. When only the simple phrase "thank you" needs to come out, her nerves are jangling and she bumbles her next line, and she'll say, "I'd like to thank mmm . . ."—and it just gets lost.

Alice's dad recalled the unsteady beginnings of Chez Panisse. Fanny, just having turned eighteen, said a few quiet words of admiration. Various others from the far reaches of Alice's vast personal geography raised a good many toasts.

The day passed slowly—languid, joyful, loquacious, and a shade elegiac as the sun sank toward the Bay. As dusk came on, a film crew projected onto the white granite of the campanile a montage, edited by Tom Luddy, of scenes from Marcel Pagnol movies, and the guests, all sated, many exhausted, slowly dispersed.

17.

AN EXTRAORDINARY
DAY IN ITALY

2001–2002

When Yale freshmen and their parents arrive on the campus each September, the president of the university gives a party in the enormous backyard of his enormous house to welcome them. Fanny Singer was one such freshman in September 2001, and her mother, Alice Waters, was with her. Alice and Fanny had just taken a look around Commons, the cavernous dining hall where Yale's thirteen hundred freshmen and a good many graduate students take their meals; just the smell of it—that ineffable fragrance of steam tables and soup—turned Alice's stomach. When Alice made her way through the receiving line to Yale president Richard Levin, she shook his hand and said, "I'd like to help you with the food here at Yale."

"Well," she says, "I was probably the three-thousandth hand he'd shaken that day, and he was just in a zone." She asked him why the food at Yale shouldn't live up to the quality of the scholarship there.

President Levin's wife, Jane Ellen Aries, recognized Alice, and in a moment they discovered that both Fanny and the Levins' kids had attended the Mountain School, a one-semester program of Milton Academy, in Vershire, Vermont, where the students work and live on an organic farm.

Alice started in, rapidly firing off ideas for the food system at Yale, but this was a receiving line, after all, with hundreds of hands for the president of the university still to shake. "Can you come and talk to me about this?" he asked Alice.

"I think he was thinking that I might do a dinner at his house. Anyway I went, and I talked to him." She told him he should revolutionize the way students were fed at Yale. And on she went, about local, organic, seasonal, fresh produce, and growing it right there on campus, and integrating the garden work with the academic curriculum. Yale had some vacant lots, surely? She described the Edible Schoolyard, and Slow Food International's campaign for similar projects in Europe.

"He said we'd have to talk to the vice president in charge of finance.

"Okay, so I did. The vice president said, 'My family had a farm, and all the farmland is being paved over, and I'm interested in doing something to support the farmers in New England.' I didn't even have to propose this myself. There was already a student group called Food from the Earth with about five hundred members working to get better food served. So the timing was right, and it got going very quickly."

The big question was whether the money could be raised—that is, whether Alice could raise it.

Certainly she could, Alice said, having no idea how.

Her plan was to start with a pilot project at one of Yale's twelve residential colleges. A steering committee was appointed, and chose Berkeley College (the name was a coincidence).

The Yale Sustainable Food Project would be a first step toward preserving what remained of Connecticut's centuries-old farming and fishing cultures. It would conserve rural landscapes and wildlife habitat. Would students have to give up their burgers and pizza? Certainly not, Alice declared. "We're going to have grass-fed organic hamburgers and an outdoor pizza oven."

Alice was thinking of what replication of the project could mean for the small farmers and artisans who were the front lines in what she was now calling, in an echo of the sixties and the Free Speech Movement, the Delicious Revolution. She saw school and college programs proliferating rapidly across the country and abroad. Soon after starting work on the Yale project, she said, "At Chez Panisse we buy from about seventy-five farms, and for some of them we're the only customer. Just think when you multiply that out to twelve thousand!"

Carlo Petrini had said that doing food right was going to have to become fashionable, even glamorous, for the revolution to take hold. It was happening now.

By 2002, the Yale project had hired Seen Lippert, a former Chez Panisse cook, to develop its menus. The project manager found a neglected one-acre plot on Yale property, from which students soon were clearing dying hemlock trees and tangled undergrowth. Alice found an executive at Aramark, the giant industrial food distributor, who—miraculously, in view of the company's reputation for frozen industrial food—was willing to find local organic farmers and deliver their produce. The Yale administration was by now enthusiastically in favor of the project.

The Chez Panisse Foundation had recently received an impressive gift out of the blue, from a woman in New York who did not want her name made public. Alice had not met the donor, but she made a point of doing so on her next visit to New York. Alice left that meeting with a promise from the anonymous donor to fund the start-up of the entire Yale project single-handed, with a gift (in addition to her earlier one) of $800,000.

On October 2, 2002, Alice held a dinner at Berkeley College to announce the college's commitment to be serving 100 percent organic food by the following fall. It wasn't long before Yalies from all eleven other colleges were angling to transfer into Berkeley.

· TO FEED THREE HUNDRED YALIES ·

I've always thought that I wanted to do the chicken paillard. At the restaurant we just pound skinless, boneless, organic chicken breasts flat with a mallet, down to about a quarter of an inch thick. I don't know exactly how you would do them on a mass scale, but I think it could be done. Somebody could invent something that would pound those chicken breasts. I think it could be an easy thing in terms of service.

I think it could be done for hundreds of people. *Bang, bang,* two minutes on the grill and then just serve it up—off the grill and onto the plate. Throw some fresh herbs on it, maybe a little lemon juice. They do have a grill at Berkeley now. It would make a great sandwich.

I think they'd be really good with some kind of French bread. I spread a little aïoli, some rocket, what else? Maybe a little tapenade spread—just olive oil and garlic and olives. They could do this on a mass scale just as easily as I do it in my kitchen at home.

Something like long-cooked pork, pork shoulders, would be great for a school. You could serve it with some beautiful winter greens. At the restaurant, we kind of braise the shoulder. We start with a *mirepoix* with herbs and a little wine, and add a little water to the bottom of the pan and long-cook it, covered, at low temperature.

Then we open it and it can get a little brown, but it should be falling off the bone. You don't have to bone it beforehand; it bones itself. You can take off all the meat and either leave it in larger pieces and serve it as a main dish, or break it apart and use it for a sandwich. It makes the greatest sandwich. Sometimes we purée the vegetables, sometimes we just serve it with the vegetables in it and they're all sort of melted. Or you can strain it out and serve just the juice. If it's flavorful enough, you don't have to do anything. And if it isn't, you can reduce it a little—after you've taken the fat off, of course.

Requests for information and for visits were coming in to the Edible Schoolyard virtually every day from start-up school gardens across the United States. Hundreds of visitors to the project came away inspired. After much romancing from Alice, the Berkeley Unified School District set a goal of serving organic food in all its schools. "That's ten thousand students!" Alice says. "We raised a quarter of a million dollars for that. Every school is going to have its own cafeteria and a full-service kitchen. We're going to get the junk-food vending machines out of there." Berkeley's Center for Ecoliteracy produced a comprehensive *Guide for Creating School Gardens as Outdoor Classrooms.* By 2004, there were garden programs in four hundred school districts in twenty-two states.

Alice was in and out of Chez Panisse. When she was there, she remained the merciless taster and critic, the dust-speck inspector, the perennially fussing lighting director, the change-everything-at-the-last-minute menu reviser. "I was very happy with the restaurant," she says, "though I was never satisfied. What I liked most was that when I wasn't there, I could sense that things were going along just as if I had been there. Gilbert was on top of everything. Cristina was my lifeline. If a problem came up, Cristina made sure I knew about it, wherever I was. Of course, there was always pressure on the chefs. That never stops. Still, it's always a pleasure for me to work with such talented cooks."

David Tanis resigned in 2001, and Alice replaced him from within the *famille Panisse,* with the shy, pretty, cerebral Kelsie Kerr. Chris Lee remained as the other co-chef. Also in 2001, *Gourmet* magazine named Chez Panisse the best restaurant in the United States. "And all I ever wanted," Alice said, "was to be like a little Michelin one-star restaurant.[1] I still don't want people to come with such great expectations. But I should be grateful, too. They keep us full all the time. They keep us in the black."

When Alice was not at Chez Panisse, she was focusing with increasing clarity on the events that could have the most significant consequences. "I want to live the change I want to see," she said. "That's what Gandhi said. I try to express that in what I'm doing. When I write a book, I want it to be beautiful. I want it to be straightforward, honest, and authentic.

I want to express the values that are important to my life. I really work at doing that. I can't say that I always do that successfully, but I try."

In April 2002, *Chez Panisse Fruit* was published. The eighth book to carry the Chez Panisse name, it was the most beautiful yet, thanks in great part to Patricia Curtan's superb linoleum-cut prints. As in the vegetable book, each fruit had its own print and its own little essay. The recipes were mostly simple and straightforward, never disguising the fruit.

The particular freshness, candor, and congeniality of tone that characterize all of Alice's books were at their best in *Chez Panisse Fruit*. The naturalness and ease of the narrative voice certainly had its source in Alice's own voice, but it was the product of an elaborate interpersonal back-and-forth that is typical of how Alice arrives at her fully formed ideas. Most often her interpreter has been Fritz Streiff, though it's not uncommon for Alice to consult with Cristina Salas-Porras, Patty Curtan, and other friends who she knows "get it." Round upon round of dialogue and editing may ensue.

Two classic Alice themes emerge in this technique: first, relying on friends, never doing anything alone; and, second, like the cooking at Chez Panisse, producing an effect of apparent simplicity that is underlain by layers of experiment and subtlety. Fritz's touch is to be found in nearly every speech Alice gives, every paragraph she publishes. Though he's always paid for the major work, there are a lot of little chores that are just what Fritz wants to do, because he's a member of the family. He watches the restaurant's menus with a ruthless eye for bad French, misspellings, and off-kilter usage. His jaunty personal style—the white suits, the bow ties, the air of bottomless gloom beneath the cheer—is in itself a Chez Panisse institution.

Alice has always loved Fritz, in the way of an occasionally exasperated mother. Asked in her kitchen at home what she might make him for lunch one chilly winter day, she improvised this little scenario.

Frustration and resolution:
Alice and Fritz Streiff at work

· LUNCH FOR FRITZ ·

I have this beautiful ham, from Heritage Foods, this company that's trying to support all the rare breeds of pigs and cattle and turkeys and ducks around the country. So first I'd run out in the garden. My latest thing for making sandwiches is to pick whatever herbs are in the garden and chop them up fine and mix them sometimes with a little garlic, with a little vinegar and oil, into a sort of savory herb paste. It's interesting to have it change all the time because it's based on whatever is in the garden.

I really believe in toast. It's rare you can have bread that's beautiful, freshly made. So, okay, I'll dampen the bread a little and toast it on the grill. Then spread on the herb paste. Slice the ham, thin, on top of that. I have some great sweet onion marmalade, and I'd put that on top. Leave it open-face.

And I've got these different winter chicories from Bob Cannard for a salad. He has the most beautiful chicories in the world. I'd use little tiny bits of Treviso, and the Castelfranco, which is lime-green with little splashes of maroon. Right now there's something about the cold that really brings out the radicchio's deepest maroon. And the insides of the escarole are so yellow. It makes just a glorious salad.

And that's it, Fritz.

ALICE WATERS has lived in the same house for twenty-three years, and like Chez Panisse it has grown in subtlety and refinement without sacrificing its fundamental modesty. The house is a small, narrow bungalow built in 1908 in the Craftsman style. There is no longer a garage. Behind the house there is the studio she and Stephen built together. Behind the studio is a tiny guest cottage, just big enough for a bed and a little chest. "Sometime, if you have a little too much wine at Chez Panisse," she tells a friend, "come and stay here." The whole backyard is a garden, with raised beds, rows of tiny lettuces year-round, herbs, raspberries, Meyer lemon trees, swarming vines, and a towering hundred-year-old redwood.

Like many houses long lived in and loved, Alice's house has come to express the inner life of its owner. One's first impression on entering is apt to be of thorough old-fashionedness. It is darkish inside, as so many Berkeley houses are, its furnishings neither spare nor busy, its atmosphere deeply quiet. It smells of wood smoke, apples, old rugs. The living room is densely populated with books, pictures, flowers, a grand piano, memorabilia.

"I'm sure I'd have moved on by now, but Fanny will never let me," Alice explains. Fanny's bedroom walls are covered with a dense collage of photographs, clippings, memories.

Alice's bedroom is mauve, tidy, and bright. Adjacent is a lush Turkish bath. "That time I was traveling in Turkey, camping, in the late sixties, we went to a bathhouse. It was underground, with the hot water dripping from overhead, from a thermal spring. I wanted that feeling."

The heart of Alice's house, of course, is the kitchen, a very old-fashioned place indeed, reflective of her commitment to simplicity. Though when not at home, she is surrounded by all the beeping, bossy digital paraphernalia of the twenty-first century, Alice manages to thrive at arm's length from nearly all of it. She does not touch computers. "Well, I did get one, so people could send me photographs," she says, "but I still haven't been able to make it work. I can't even send e-mail. Have to get one of my wonderful assistants to handle correspondence." A friend will program her cell phone's auto-dialer. She does not own a microwave oven or a food processor. The highest-tech device in her kitchen is a little toaster oven, which she painted dark green to match the walls. Her favorite cooking devices—in the spirit of Lulu Peyraud—are the two wood-burning ovens and the open hearth built into her kitchen wall. She likes wire whisks, good knives, terra-cotta casseroles, *non*-nonstick pots and pans (especially the cast-iron ones). "My favorite tool in the world is the mortar and pestle. I love my mortar and pestle."

A big oval table topped with marble sits at the sunny end of the kitchen, surrounded by mismatched wooden chairs. A corner cabinet houses thick pottery plates, also of differing but harmonious styles. A bay

Alice in her kitchen at home

window looks out onto the garden through a tangle of vines. On the shelf below the window is a clutter of antique cookbooks, art books, baskets, bottles. On the walls are paintings—of a brioche, of a bowl of garlic—and photographs, one depicting the original cast of Marcel Pagnol's Marseille trilogy.

The inner kitchen—small, narrow, and ergonomically just right—has a copper sink, a butcher block, shelves crowded with bowls, plates, pots. Flanking the big professional stove is a long worktable, with plenty of room for people to prep and cook together. "I don't think I've ever had people over and made the whole meal myself."

The late R. W. Apple, Jr.—known to his friends as Johnny—was associate editor of the *New York Times* as well as a legendary gourmet and a longtime friend of Alice's. Recalling an incident vividly illustrative of Alice in her kitchen, he once said:

The *Times* asked me to get Alice to cook Thanksgiving dinner in advance, so we could run the story right before Thanksgiving. We went to her house, and the usual cast of characters was there. And then something required anchovies. And out came this gorgeous tin of salted anchovies. Big, round, discus-sized. And she couldn't find a can opener. So here's this turkey on a spit that she is basting with the branch of a rosemary bush, but there was no can opener. Finally she found one, but it was a ten-minute, fifteen-minute search for a can opener in the kitchen of the queen of freshness.

BY THE FALL OF 2002, when Slow Food USA was not quite three years old, it had signed up some seven thousand members and established about a hundred American convivia, as its chapters are called. Slow Food International had seventy-four thousand members in fifty countries. In Italy, Slow Food has been adopted into the regional governments of Emilia-Romagna and Tuscany and is guiding agricultural policies there. (If a similar policy revolution could be effected in American agricultural states, it would turn American farming on its head. For Alice, it would be a dream come true.) Slow Food formed a publishing company, Slow Food Editore, which has produced some sixty books. Slow Food Editore also publishes a quarterly journal, *Slow: The International Herald of Taste and Culture,* in English, French, German, Italian, Japanese, and Spanish. Recognizing that three-quarters of agriculture's genetic diversity and half of its livestock breeds were lost in the twentieth century, Slow Food's "Ark of Taste" program searches the world for endangered varieties of domestic plants and animals, farm products, and traditional dishes, and opens them to wider markets by means of what Carlo Petrini calls "virtuous globalization"—without which many would be doomed to extinction.

It is not commonly known that biodiversity on traditional farms is often higher than that found in national parks, wildlife refuges, and the other reserves that are usually thought of as the "arks" on which rare species are saved. Industrial agriculture, on the other hand, with its vast acreage of monocrops and its exclusion of virtually all other life from the fields, is one of the most powerful destroyers of biological diversity.

Recognizing the immense biological and cultural importance of traditional farming and inviting people into awareness of it through the pleasures of the food those farms produce are the guiding principles of what Alice calls the Delicious Revolution. Traditional conservation is based in considerable part on negative emotions—guilt and shame for the damage we have inflicted on our home planet, anger at those who continue to hurt it. Slow Food's and Alice's way is based on gratitude and joy—celebrating the beauty of the earth, eating its delicious bounty, participating as animals in its ecosystems. That is a revolution in conservation. It is powerful indeed, because it preserves the ways of human life that sustain biodiversity.

The writer Verlyn Klinkenborg lives on a traditional farm in upstate New York, celebrated in his editorial columns in the *New York Times*. Choosing to live as he and his wife do, he writes, "really comes down to living as close to wildness as we can. I realize that now. What makes it easier is that so many wild creatures don't mind living near us."[2]

In October 2002, Slow Food's biennial Salone del Gusto ("Hall of Taste") gave powerful proof of the movement's growing reach. Into a former Fiat factory in Turin—transformed in the 1990s by the architect Renzo Piano into one of the world's grandest public spaces—came 138,000 people to wander among more than six hundred booths and galleries representing eighty countries. There were literally miles of exhibitors—sausage maestros, cheese wizards, pig breeders, tomato conservers, olive orchardists, winemakers, bakers. All were artisans of the old, authentic specialties of local traditions around the world—Anglesey sea salt, herbed Scottish sheep cheese, kangaroo salami, organic Brazilian chocolates, Istrian truffles, Swiss cannabis pastilles, Genovese tuna belly, Wiltshire herb jellies, Tuscan chestnut cookies, goose prosciutto, hundreds of handmade beers, wines, and liqueurs. Most of these wonders were for sale; many of the artisans proffered free samples. There were little three-sided booths in which to sit down with a glass of wine, some cheese, and a piece of bread, few of them familiar beyond their regions of origin.

The Salone also comprised hundreds of tastings, exhibits, seminars, field trips, and superlative meals, foremost among them some sixty-five lunches and dinners at restaurants scattered across the nearby Piedmontese countryside.

On October 27, 2002, Alice and a brigade of cooks from Chez Panisse were to create a dinner at the Ristorante Real Castello di Verduno, near the vineyards of Carlo Petrini's beloved Barolo. Most of the Slow Food feasts were being prepared by the restaurants' own staffs, using familiar local ingredients to make classic local dishes. The Chez Panisse chefs, on the other hand, had seen the Verduno kitchen for the first time only that morning and, except for the bread and vegetables, had not been able to buy their own provisions.

The fish was lousy, and it was Sunday, with every fish market in Italy closed. Alice wanted the squab legs grilled, but there was no grill, or firewood. The pears were hard as bricks. The porcini were full of worms.

But each of those problems, over the course of the day, would be solved. When Alice arrived from Turin, she found her crew at work in the Chez Panisse way, quiet, intent, unhurried. Two chefs from the restaurant were there—Christopher Lee and Russell Moore—along with cook Amy Dencler and several Chez Panisse alumni temporarily lured away from their jobs elsewhere in Europe.

Conferring with Alice, and at six foot two towering over her, Chris Lee was mild-spoken in the manner that betokens restrained authority. After one look at the mass of pre-chopped sea glop meant to be the base for the fish stock, Russ Moore—with years of Chez Panisse experience—had thrown the whole mess out. They had planned to serve small portions of some meaty fish surrounded by an intense seafood broth, but none of the big whole fish they had was fresh enough. Russ said that if he could find some good little Mediterranean reef fish, he could make a *passato*—a thick soup passed through a food mill.

And then there were the Burlottos. These were the owners of the castle—the three sisters Gabriella, Elisa, and Liliana Burlotto, plus Elisa's daughter Alessandra Buglioni di Monale, the chef. The Burlottos were annoyed, and no wonder. They had waited up the night before to welcome the Chez

Panisse brigade, who didn't pull in till two in the morning. The team was late because they had stopped at Elena Rovera's Cascina del Cornale—an all-organic co-op, which was supplying the beautiful vegetables and bread for the Chez Panisse dinner—and Elena had insisted that they stay for dinner; then they'd gotten lost on the way to Verduno. They could have called, but they had not. Alessandra was now in her office with the door closed.

"Cristina?" whispered Alice worriedly. "You've got to talk to her."

With a long intake of breath, Cristina knocked, entered, and closed the door behind her.

Alessandra had curtly informed the Chez Panisse chefs that the only remaining possibility for fish was the supermarket. But Russ was now beaming at a just-arrived box of fat pink Mediterranean lobsters. Where had it come from? "I called a friend who called a friend."

Tall, wide-eyed, with a nearly constant thin, bemused smile and a shock of brown hair standing straight up at the summit, Russ moved with the meditative tranquility of a man who loves what he's doing. (He was until 2006 co-chef of the Chez Panisse Café.) His idea of the fish *passato* underwent a quick transformation: With the shells of those beautiful lobsters, some saffron, and some Pernod, Russ could make a rich, clear, bouillabaisse-scented broth. He would cook it on an open fire of oak and vine cuttings, which one of the cooks had scrounged up in the village, and the smoke would almost imperceptibly rusticate the aroma of the soup—an old *truc* of Lulu Peyraud's.

Leeks, onions, and fennel lay chopped in neat piles, ready for Russ's broth. Squab stock was simmering. In the main hall of the castle, under a high frescoed ceiling, Alessandra Buglioni di Monale and Cristina Salas-Porras, having emerged from the office, exchanged elaborate compliments. Alessandra looked no older than twenty, no heavier than eighty pounds, with the breastless body of a prepubescent boy. She had a fine-boned, elfin face, with prominent dark eyes, black hair, and translucent ivory skin.

The number of guests was supposed to have been limited to fifty-five, but Alice wanted to squeeze in another fifteen, including Carlo Petrini and her friend Mikhail Baryshnikov, whose White Oak Dance project was performing in Turin that week. "Alice wants there to be a particular spirit in the room," Cristina implored, adding, "We're very happy to be in this beautiful place."

"We also are very happy to have you here," replied Alessandra in lilting English, "but this is a problem." She had turned away friends and regulars of her own, she explained. Places were set for fifty-five, and no more.

Alice sniffed a pear and frowned, watched closely by Chris, Russ, and Amy. Amy Dencler, a cook from the downstairs kitchen at Chez Panisse, was tall, broad-shouldered, with wide-set, watchful eyes, short salt-and-pepper hair, and a shy, self-contained manner. The pears were her dish for tonight. They didn't have much of a perfume, and they seemed awfully hard, but Alice wanted pears and these were the best to be found.

Was Alice about to have one of her ideas? "She'll just say, 'Here's how I want a thing to be,'" said Russ, "and it's up to us to figure out how to do it. I try not to say no unless it's truly impossible." But no inspiration came to Alice this time, and Chris's and Russ's shoulders visibly softened.

"Now," proclaimed Alice, slipping into an apron, "I'm going to do the one little thing that I really like to do best, prep the salad"—especially when the greens are as vibrantly alive as these were: three kinds of radicchio, including the delicate Castelfranco variety—pale yellow speckled with pink—and *pane di zucchero* [sugar loaf], a creamy-green, tight-leaved chicory. A stillness came over Alice's features as she worked.

Cristina joined Alice in tearing the greens into casual but careful squares. "No luck?" asked Alice.

"None," said Cristina.

"There seems to be no way to get through to her," murmured Alice, meaning Alessandra. "She won't even look me in the eye."

In one of the dining rooms, Umberto I, king of Italy from 1878 to 1900, glowered down from a print on the wall, staring fiercely out the window at some of the best vineyard land in the world. On the sideboard below Umberto were arrayed eight bottles of the Castello di Verduno's wines, including Barolo, Barbaresco, Dolcetto d'Alba, Barbera d'Alba, and Verduno's own Basadone (which in Italian evokes "Kiss the ladies"), made from an ancient and genetically unique grape native to Verduno known as pelaverga piccolo, which was saved from extinction on that very estate.

These wines were the work of Gabriella Burlotto, Alessandra's aunt, a small, blue-eyed gentlewoman elegantly dressed *à l'anglaise* in tweed and suede. She is the first woman in four generations of winemaking Burlottos. She asked Chris Lee if he'd like to come down to the cellar for a little tasting. The wines were sensational, each one deeply true to its type, the Barolo brooding and earthy, the Barbaresco like velvet, the Dolcetto cherry red and cherry fragrant, the Barbera spicy and pungent, the Basadone pure, juicy, with a flavor like no other.

Chris's report on the wines elicited from Alice a pained wince. "Why aren't we serving *them*?" she groaned. "The wines for tonight are from Tuscany"—which in Italian terms, and according to the Chez Panisse way of thought, was as far away as the moon.

Alice and Chris assembled a trial version of the squab dish, the separated breasts and legs arranged just so on the salad—not architectural, just balanced. They studied the plate together, shifting a leg here, a leaf there. "I thought about julienning the greens," said Alice, "but then I thought, No, the hot squab might wilt them too fast, and anyway I like the colors like this. It's lovely, Christopher, don't you think?" She moved the squabs' ankles an eighth of an inch closer together, then put them back as they were.

An event such as the dinner that night would be a big money loser for Chez Panisse. But Alice had, as usual, bigger aims than profit: "It's important to express the philosophy of the restaurant." And a great Chez Panisse dinner might just inspire a wealthy and/or influential attendee to take up the cause of organic farming, enlightened consumption, healthy oceans, better European agriculture policies.

Meanwhile, Russ had improvised a cook camp on the gravel courtyard in front of the castle, crisscrossing oven racks across stacks of bricks to create a distinctly unsteady-looking grill. "It's going to be dark out here," he murmured, indicating the complete absence of lighting on the castle façade.

Alice appeared, smiling contentedly at the makeshift apparatus. "I'm going to skewer the legs," Russ explained. "It shouldn't be too bad."

"Can you use rosemary skewers?" asked Alice. "I love those."

Soon the stock was boiling away, lobster legs poking out haphazardly. Frustrated, Russ complained, "The pot's too small. So I've got to make the stock extra-strong and then dilute it."

Russ's girlfriend, Allison Hopelain, appeared, bearing two precious gifts: a glass of wine and a penlight.

In the kitchen, Alice began cutting yard-long strips of focaccia for the grill. Soon a test pear came out of the oven, looking dull brown and shriveled. Amy spooned an ivory sauce around a pear half. She, Chris, and Alice all took a taste. Alice pronounced the *crème anglaise* too sweet. She didn't like the almond stuffing, either. "It's too—something," she said, trailing off. Amy nodded as if she understood, and went back to work.

Five thirty. The kitchen door flew open, hard enough to bang against the wall. It was Chef Alessandra, catching nobody's eye, cruising between the tables and ranges, looking at this, looking at that, then cruising out without a word. Alice and Chris shared a quick uneasy look. The numbers issue was still not settled.

A bucket of sparkling-bright squid arrived, closely followed by Alice, grinning with delight. "Shall we fry them?"

The obvious question was where fried squid could possibly fit in tonight's menu, but Russ didn't ask it. He just said, "I'm not sure."

"Well, you know, you've got to do something with it."

Alice has a horror of waste, but she also has faith in her chefs. "I don't do anything, really," she said. "I'm not a chef. I just let them do what they do so well. They are the best, you know." She followed that statement with a soft, proud lifting of the chin. When Alice speaks with love, as she was speaking then, she tends to tip her weight ever so slightly forward, onto the balls of her feet, poising her body as though to rise, a shift from stillness to intention.

"It's nice squid. We'll have it ourselves, after service," said Russ.

Alice half tripped over a bag of potatoes. She held a potato under her nose, held it up in the light, turned it slowly around. Chris moved toward her warily. There were no potatoes on the menu either. "Ahhh," she sighed, inhaling the loamy scent. "Let's split them and boil them and roast them."

"We could grill them," suggested Chris.

"Let's grill them!" exclaimed Alice.

So now Russ's teetering crisscross of oven racks would be producing fish soup, grilled focaccia, grilled squab legs, and grilled potatoes—all in the dark. It didn't seem possible.

"This is my job," he said. "I can do it by feel."

An experimental assembly of the first course was ready—a cardoon salad with anchovies. The cardoons tasted curiously nondescript, though the anchovies, fresh from the Mediterranean that morning and marinated all day in garlic and olive oil, were sublime. Amy fiddled with the dressing: adding lemon juice, and then tasting; adding shallots, and tasting again; adding a little finely chopped anchovy and tasting yet again. She squeezed in more lemon, and tasted.

Then Christopher tasted the dressing. "Some parsley would be good," he said. "And there are beautiful chives in the garden." Alice grabbed a basket and scuttled toward the garden.

Russ, just in from the dark, called, "Alice, plus, while you're out there, we need herbs for the soup. Whatever looks good." She returned, aglow, with a huge bouquet of chives, parsley, lovage, rosemary, and mint spilling out of the basket.

As evening came on, Alice's posture grew slightly S-shaped; she looked softer, soft-boned, and then, as she seemed to catch herself sagging, she squared her shoulders and stood up straight, as if in resolution.

"I'm infusing the oil for the crostini with truffles," Chris reported.

Russ was chopping fennel and the small, flat red onions known as *cipolline,* which he would sauté and then mix with the chopped lobster meat. He lifted a steaming, just poached lobster tail toward Alice. "I thought, Just kind of herby, oily?"

Alice nodded serenely. Another Chez Panisse dish had been invented on the spot from materials at hand. A heap of the lobster mixture would ride a little raft of grilled focaccia floating on each bowl of broth.

Amy started in on the mountain of pears, halving and coring; the skin stayed on. Lindsey Shere materialized in the kitchen, a guest tonight but happily at home in the kitchen as well. She showed Amy how to cut a flat spot on the back of each pear half so it would be stable. Amy seemed to be moving remarkably slowly. Indeed, everybody did. Russ was slowly skewering the pigeon legs. Alice at that moment was off in a corner, slowly cleaning up the waste and trimmings from her salad greens.

It was six forty-five. The potatoes, once boiled, seemed awfully fragile. Russ broke one easily in half. "Maybe a vinaigrette?" he suggested.

"I think we can still grill them," said Chris. "Look." He halved a few more potatoes, then delicately threaded two skewers through each three halves, forming a compact, self-propping square.

At seven o'clock, the Castello dining-room staff, all of them women in white blouses and black skirts, came pouring into the kitchen. A grim chill seemed to grip the room. Suddenly, Cristina burst into song—a version of the song that Michael Tilson Thomas had written for the thirtieth-anniversary party: "Alice in a palace!" she sang.

"Chez Panisse!" chorused the whole *brigade de cuisine* at the top of their lungs.

"It's not just a restaurant, it's a proud credo we can flaunt!"

"Chez Panisse!" boomed the cooks.

After the boisterous song, calm returned. Alice withdrew with Cristina in her wake, and the preparation slowly continued.

Out in the halls of the castle, everything was still. Alice and Cristina descended from upstairs in impeccable dresses and makeup. Alice's coiffure was new, and rather shocking, with sprouts of blond and orange standing up amid her usual light brown.

Baryshnikov, smoking a cigarette, was the first to arrive. Soon the halls were thronged. A consul appeared in the doorway and paused there, his entourage lingering behind him. He waited on the threshold to be welcomed, then gave up and moved inside. A restaurateur from New York was quite sure it was all a fraud and the food was going to be lousy; she considered the reputation of Chez Panisse to be a fiction promulgated through the all-too-easily-gulled food media. Film people arrived, along with Slow Food members and staff, gourmets from half a continent away, a contingent of Alice's friends. It was a jolly and good-looking crowd.

Russell Moore, Alice, and Christopher Lee
at the Castello di Verduno

When the first course, cardoons and anchovies, was served, there were some sniffs of consternation. To many here it seemed awfully plain and unadorned.

In fact, it wasn't great. It was merely very, very good. It was indeed plain and unadorned—a few slices of poached cardoon, a sparkling anchovy, some mild green oil, and that was it. The fish soup, with its rafts of lobster, came next. It made a striking impression—deep and mysterious, powerful and delicate at once: indubitably great.

Out front, Russ was picking up squab legs with his fingers, tossing one here, another there, over the waning coals. He was out of firewood. But the legs were crisp and juicy—cooked to rosy perfection—as were the slightly rarer sautéed breasts with which they were reunited in the kitchen. The sauce of reduced stock was subtle but potent, a subliminal intensification of the meat's basic flavor. The potatoes were a bit dry, but a nice-enough foil for the rich, almost livery pigeon meat. The pears had never softened, but their flavor was intense, the stuffing was a contrastingly sweet sort of almond crunch, and the *crème anglaise* wrapped them in satin smoothness.

With the exception of the New York restaurateur, whose low expectations had apparently been met, the diners appeared quite blissful. The flavors had been pure and clear. The meal had not been heavy in the slightest. People had talked and laughed and made new friends. A few may have been revising their notions of what constitutes great food.

Alice, who had won the seating battle by sheer force of will, made sure that Alessandra shared in the praise. The crowd leaned forward, silent, to catch Alice's soft voice as she told them that all the ingredients tonight had been organic and local, that virtuous farming means better tasting food. "How we eat," she said, "can change the world."

18.

AN ORDINARY AFTERNOON AND EVENING AT CHEZ PANISSE

2003–2006

Jean-Pierre's coming back!" cried Alice in delight, and relief. It was July 2003, and Christopher Lee was leaving, to open his own restaurant in Berkeley. Jean-Pierre Moullé had returned from France once again, though he would be just filling in, as co-chef with Kelsie, until Alice and Gilbert found a replacement for him. But for once, the perfect person did not fall out of the sky into Chez Panisse at just the perfect moment. By the fall, after a couple of months of peaceful relations and superlative food, Alice realized that there was probably no one as creative, as disciplined, as intelligent, and as well versed in the Chez Panisse way as Jean-Pierre Moullé. Alice, Gilbert, and Jean-Pierre all agreed that he should stay.

This was a mellower, more mature Jean-Pierre. His hair was longer and had gone silver, but his body was still lean and compact, and his ready grin still flickered a hint of wickedness. He was getting along with

Jean-Pierre Moullé

Alice very nicely now. To a friend he said, flashing the grin, "It helps that she's here not very often."

Sylvan Brackett succeeded Cristina Salas-Porras as Alice's assistant in 2003, when Cristina resigned for full-time motherhood and part-time consulting. Cristina continued working on individual projects with Alice, and remains inextricably woven into Alice's life.

Sylvan had worked as a Chez Panisse cook and then as Cristina's backup since 2000. He seemed tailor-made for Chez Panisse and Alice: "At Reed College, I did my senior thesis on the emergence of the idea of taste in seventeenth-century France, and how that corresponded with the emergence of a distinct French cuisine. It was a rather cynical idea—that taste is something made up, to distinguish people from different classes."

Sylvan is not a cynic, but he is a close observer. Alice, he says,

Sylvan Brackett

doesn't use the jargon. She refuses to learn the table numbers. She'll say, "You know, the table by the window!" "The booths!"

I would say seventy-five percent of the stuff we do in the office is not affiliated with Chez Panisse. The money from the restaurant is funding the other efforts, and this is a point of contention. Gilbert is not a big fan of the Slow Food movement.

This sounds as if Chez Panisse might sustain itself more easily without Alice's being there at all. Sylvan:

I can't imagine Chez Panisse going on without Alice. But I can see her at ninety-nine, receiving people, looking over menus, and complaining about this or that. Saying she likes this person or doesn't like that person, and, "This waiter needs to cut his hair."

Alice with David Tanis after his return to be downstairs co-chef

In early 2004 Kelsie resigned to work with Alice on her next book and to spend more time with her young daughter. To preserve the co-chef system, Alice and Jean-Pierre created a new version of it: He would be chef—not co-chef, not quasi-chef, not chef-without-the-title, but *chef*—for six months, and then David Tanis would return for six months, and so on. Each would spend his six months off in France. The chef's workweek would be just five nights. On Mondays, when the downstairs restaurant serves its simplest dinner—often the old regulars' favorite—the longtime cook Phillip Dedlow would take the helm.

On Alice's sixtieth birthday, in April 2004, Cristina asked her what she thought she should be able to look back at ten years hence. Alice by then had the world for her stage. In 2003, the *American Masters* series on PBS, which for more than twenty years has been documenting "our most outstanding cultural artists," had broadcast a film by Doug Hamilton, *Alice Waters and Her Delicious Revolution*. Alice was the only chef ever to be chosen as an American Master. Also in 2003, she was elected vice president of Slow Food International, second only to Carlo Petrini. The Edible

Schoolyard and the Yale Sustainable Food Project were widely known, and just as Alice had hoped, similar projects were taking root in both America and Europe. What more could she hope to achieve? Alice gave Cristina's question a lot of thought.

The scope of her interests was global now. Alice's life now would be devoted to changing the world in the biggest ways possible. Her involvement in one new project after another meant that more and more of her time would be spent on airplanes and in places far from Chez Panisse.

All that involvement would also elicit criticism. What Alice's closest friends recognized as persuasiveness, others called manipulation. Susie Buell, a philanthropist and political activist, and one of Alice's true intimates, says,

Alice can't stop. She has to keep finding new things, and it's exhausting. She's very driven by her passions, her concerns, her curiosity, her anxiety about why we're not living better, why we're not taking care of ourselves. So she creates this character, this nonstop creator of everything. And it's true, it's authentic, it does come from within.

She's manipulative in a way, but she has to be. It's not a bad thing. That's the way you get things done. Every great person is manipulative. She does her little baby-talk thing, and she kind of pouts, and she wants things to happen her way. She has to convince people. And she adores men. She's the greatest little flirt. That's all very manipulative.

Some of her best friends won't talk to her sometimes for a while, because they feel that her expectations are too much, that they just can't be there for her the way she needs them to be so that she can have her way, have her thing done. But in the end, when the result comes, I don't think anybody would have done it any differently.

Davia Nelson sees good reason for Alice's increasing concentration on people of influence, but she insists that there is nothing exclusionary about Alice's circle, or circles, of friends:

Alice will worship heroes. They're in "the first circle." David Brower was in it, and Michael Pollan is. Wendell Berry. Carlo Petrini. And a Tibetan van driver and a butcher in Italy. Her first circle isn't about being famous, even though Baryshnikov is in it, and Peter Sellars. The first circle is about, Are you committed, are you passionate, do you want to change the world, are you a force for change?—even if you're a kindergartner. She recognizes that spark of passion in people.

ONE FRIDAY in the fall of 2004, a visitor came to observe an ordinary day at Chez Panisse. At one o'clock in the afternoon, Jean-Pierre went over the evening's reservations with Robert Messick. As usual, the restaurant was going to be full. There was a honeymooning couple, which always warrants special attention, and there would be a group from Slow Food. Glasses of complimentary Champagne were to be offered to the newlyweds and the Slow Food people.

Next Jean-Pierre checked his supplies. In the chilly air of the breezeway outside the kitchen door were stacked garden flats of root vegetables—turnips, carrots, rutabaga, parsley root, salsify, and Jerusalem artichokes, all just in from the Chino Ranch. The Chez Panisse van, having delivered its burden of compost to Bob Cannard's farm that morning, was expected back at the restaurant shortly. Jean-Pierre slid back the massive polished copper door of the walk-in cooler. In the walk-in hung a half dozen back halves of lambs, dark with aging. There was only one bag of fresh coriander seeds left. "These are hard to get," he said, "and it's not so many, but smell—powerful, no?" There were no Meyer lemons where they were supposed to be. He asked the pastry department if they could spare a dozen Meyers, and they could. A cook squeezed past with a hotel pan (a large, shallow, rectangular stainless steel container) filled with parboiled purple cabbage. Jean-Pierre grabbed a piece and munched. "Too salty," he said. Oversalting is the curse of many cooks' overworked, and therefore sometimes benumbed, palates.

Dhondup Karpo arrived with the van. He is Tibetan, one of a number of political refugees whom Chez Panisse has employed through the years;

there are also Afghans, Vietnamese, and Cubans. "Khalil Mujadedy," Alice says, "comes from an extremely prominent family in Afghanistan. The queen of England stayed at his family compound when he was young. But he came here as a dishwasher who hardly spoke English. Now he's become an indispensable part of the restaurant. He can fix anything. He can build anything. He's made copper railings, lamps, beautiful things.

"Dhondup—same thing—indispensable. These people work so hard. People who visit the kitchen don't see them, they're always behind the scenes, but Chez Panisse couldn't function without them."

Three cooks, including Jean-Pierre, hurried into the breezeway to see what the day's bounty would be. "Beautiful chervil," he said. "Beautiful, beautiful, tiny watercress." He took a small bite. *"Pow!"* he exclaimed. Just picked, it had a sharp pepper-and-licorice bite that would fade in half a day or less.

He ordered that the herbs and vegetables be taken immediately into the garde-manger—the room where cold food is prepared. "The café has been grabbing stuff early, because they're here first," said Jean-Pierre. "Look at this." He opened the heavy door of the dark room where house-cured hams, *zamponi* (stuffed pig's trotters), and salami were aging. "They put vegetables in here. That's why we have mold on the hams. I want them to use the wine room, but Jonno"—Jonathan Waters, the wine buyer (no relation to Alice)—"is resisting. Of course I'm resisting his wine list. Too many overextracted reds. Not enough Bordeaux." The grin flashed again—Bordeaux is Jean-Pierre's hometown. "Those giant wines, these zinfandels with sixteen percent alcohol, they overwhelm the kind of food we make. Where is my Savoy cabbage? You see? It's gone."

Michael Peternell, Russell Moore's co-chef in the café, came in to consult with Jean-Pierre about a sauce. Cal, as he is known, is tall, blond, elegantly well-spoken, and formally polite. Like many of his predecessors, he has been an artist, lived in Italy, and found a culinary home at Chez Panisse—while also able to live a real life at home with his wife and children. "I had time off when my son was born," he says. "Recently, I took some time to build my kids a tree house. There aren't many restaurants where something like that is possible. There's so little friction in our kitchen. Sometimes it amazes me how nice these people really are. And how good. All of them. How well the others like what I'm cooking, and the menus I write—that's the real measure, for me, of how I'm doing. And then they always have the opportunity to make changes in the dishes they're doing. So we've all got pride of ownership in what comes out of our kitchen."

AT NOON, leftovers from the day before were set out in a nook off the kitchen. Cooks, waiters, bussers, and office staff descended on them hungrily. These were not just any leftovers. There was a whole chocolate tart that didn't sell the night before. There were glistening slices of roast pork sprinkled with herbs; bowls of sparkling salads and vegetables. Staff lunch at Chez Panisse is one of the best meals to be had in the Bay Area. Unfortunately, everybody always seems to wolf it down in ten minutes. For these devotees of Slow Food, lunch is distinctly non-slow.

At two o'clock, the downstairs kitchen brigade took seats at an unset table in the dining room. In the low fall sunshine and without its golden lamps on, the room looked rather beat-up, the wood trim dinged, the chair legs gouged. Grass, leaves, string, and flower petals littered the floor: Carrie Wright and her assistant were improvising a new display of flowers.

Jean-Pierre took his seat not at the head of the table but modestly off to the side, studying a wrinkled handwritten menu and saying, "We pretty much have everything"—meaning that they could, if they chose, serve the same menu that was printed on the sheets stacked next to the front door and posted at www.chezpanisse.com.

"Okay, apéritif—Prosecco with a little Meyer lemon syrup." (There are always rows of bottles of fruit syrups in the walk-in, all house-made.) "Then we have"—he read from the menu—"warm salad of winter chicories with cèpes, pancetta, and eggs. Fish and shellfish soup with Dungeness crab, Atlantic cod, and fennel. I don't know about the fennel. Bob's chervil is so beautiful." He read again: "Grilled rack, loin, and leg of Cattail Creek lamb with fresh coriander seed sauce and roasted Chino Ranch vegetables.

"Okay. For the soup base we have fish, fish bones, shrimp, clams, mussels. Not too many vegetables, just leeks and fennel. The broth shouldn't be too strong—you want to taste the crab, eh? No aïoli, nothing like that. Maybe a plain crouton. Fennel tops or chervil. Beautiful chervil.

"For the roasted vegetables, we have turnips, carrots, celery root, beautiful cauliflower from Bob—you've seen what we have in the flats."

"I'd like to do the soup," Beth Lells volunteered.

"I'll take the lamb if it's okay," said Ignacio Mattos.

"The salad?" asked Paula Bock.

"Okay, good," said Jean-Pierre. "For the salad, Paula, a warm salad needs more acidity, maybe also mustard, not too much oil. Balance is very important, because when you dress it too much and then heat it, it looks greasy. So start with half the usual olive oil.

"The cèpes you want to sauté first with garlic and parsley, and for them a different vinaigrette. Or maybe roast them with the vegetables, covered, and crisp them at the end."

"I've never done this before," said Paula. "Do you think we could do one batch of the mushrooms for the whole seating?"

"I think maybe we work it out as we go," said Jean-Pierre, diplomatically avoiding direct contradiction. "Maybe small batches will be better. For the soup we have lots of crab—you can use five or six for the broth. And toast with that? I don't know. We decide later.

"The lamb, we make a marinade with dried coriander seeds, fresh cilantro, salt, pepper, thyme, garlic. I'm very excited about this coriander sauce."

Jérôme Waag—son of Alice's old friend Nathalie, and an artist when not cooking at Chez Panisse—said he would do the vegetables. Jérôme tends to look underslept, undershaved, terrible, thoroughly grumpy, till his sunny smile breaks through. "Maybe I do the turnips separately, eh? And roast the rootier things. I think maybe no potatoes. And we use that beautiful watercress to garnish, eh?"

"Some of these dishes," Jean-Pierre said to a visitor, "will evolve over the course of the day. I don't want to give directions too specific. I want the cooks to use their imagination. But it all has to pass my test—of course."

The Chinos' root vegetables were tiny, many no bigger than marbles.

Jérôme peeled them unhurriedly, creating hundreds of little spheres. The most senior cook in the room, Jérôme had taken the most menial task.

Jean-Pierre peeled the tiny salsify roots as patiently as Jérôme did his turnips. "When you're ready with the broth," he called across the kitchen to Beth, "I want to taste it." He started in on the very knobbly parsley roots. "These are a nightmare to peel," he said, working his way through dozens of them. This was scut work, which anywhere else would be done by interns or the lowest-ranking kitchen staff. But that is not the Chez Panisse way.

All afternoon, the downstairs kitchen was a quiet scene of the same operations repeated over and over: picking crab, shelling shrimp (glistening-fresh, harvested by a small-boat fisherman from one of the few remaining sustainable shrimp fisheries, but not local—they had been flown in over-night from Florida), stirring the lamb stock, turning the roasting bones in the oven, endlessly peeling the tiny root vegetables.

Ignacio broke down the lamb meat with quick strokes of his narrow, scalpel-sharp boning knife. He cut out every white trace of connective tissue. He made the marinade and then massaged it into the meat with his hands.

Paula dried small batches of salad greens with an ordinary plastic pull-cord spinner, always gently so that the leaves wouldn't be bruised or creased, laying the greens on soft white towels, dabbing at them till the last drop of water was gone. This was one place where the unseen pres-ence of Alice hovered—over Paula's salad greens—making sure that they would still look as alive in the dining room as when they arrived in the van.

Just after four o'clock, Jérôme and Ignacio shouldered the immense iron rotisserie out of the wood-burning oven and marched it out to the back, yelling people out of their way at every step. Two café cooks outside were digging into two five-gallon tubs of just-made ice cream—one hazelnut, the other pecan—happily taste-testing as they dug.

Jean-Pierre leaned against the wall with pad and pencil, composing the vegetarian menu, which it was quite possible no one would order: fennel soup with crème fraîche; roasted root vegetables; cabbage leaves stuffed with cèpes and other mushrooms; the same dessert, a Meyer lemon soufflé.

"We do have a problem sometimes," Alice says, "when people want something that's not on the menu. The vegetarians are no worse than anybody else. It's just that most of the time, there's not much we can do. We've bought the materials for that night's dinner, and that's it. Sometimes we can get something brought downstairs from the café, or vice versa, but it tends to break the flow."

By five o'clock, the vegetables, lightly coated with oil, each type separate, were roasting on sheets of parchment paper. A small fire was warming the fireplace. Beth debearded mussels while Jean-Pierre picked over the crab yet again, so that not a speck of shell would make it into the dish. Waiters arrived, in civvies, and started polishing glasses, folding napkins, setting the tables.

"Watch out for salt, Paula," Jean-Pierre called. "The pancetta, you know."

Paula, too intent on her work to look up or speak, nodded in silent acknowledgment.

Beth, stepping in to help Paula, peeled hard-boiled eggs, each yolk barely gelled at the center. The pace was picking up, the temperature in the kitchen rising into the mid-seventies, the cooks as they finished their prep work cleaning up quickly. At Chez Panisse there are no runners, no scullions, to pick up anybody's dirty pots; cooks must run them to the dishwashers themselves, and clean the counter themselves.

At five thirty, Jean-Pierre assembled the waiters and walked them through the menu with a detailed explanation of each dish. "In case anybody asks," he said with a hint of dismay, "yes, the cod is on the yellow list." (Both the Monterey Bay Aquarium and the National Audubon Society have been publishing guides to sustainable seafood. The aquarium's green list is "best choices," the yellow list "good alternatives," the red list "avoid." The Audubon list is rather more strict, green meaning "abundant, relatively well-managed species"; yellow, "significant concerns about a species' status, fishing methods, and/or management"; and red, for fish that have "a lot of problems—such as severe depletion, overfishing, or poor management.")

"But you know we have fishermen working in a way that it's okay to take them," said Jean-Pierre, "so I think it's all right. You explain to the customer if they ask."

The sourcing of fish for Chez Panisse has gone through a long evolution. In the early days, Alice would sometimes go down to the docks of a fishing port and buy directly from the fishermen, inspecting each fish personally. Along the way, she met Paul Johnson, who offered to buy fish for the restaurant. He focused on the finest of the fine, selecting individual fish out of larger hauls. Paul later, with Jerry Rosenfield, founded the Monterey Fish Company, which now has a substantial wholesale business as well as a retail shop in Berkeley. The company sells nothing but sustainably harvested fish, and acts as a sort of adjunct conscience for Chez Panisse.

"That Atlantic cod, for instance," said Phillip Dedlow as he watched Beth Lells poaching it for the soup:

The species is on a couple of these red lists, but the conservation groups have to paint with a broad brush. Monterey finds a small fisherman with a small boat who's fishing with a hook and line, harvesting very small amounts. This whole thing is based on a chain of trust. We trust Monterey, which trusts the fisherman to be telling the truth and doing the right thing. What's important is that these are people who know and trust one another.

Take monkfish. Most monkfish is harvested with these horrible drag nets that scrape the ocean floor—absolutely ruinous. But Paul Johnson has found a fisherman who uses what's called a tickler chain, which floats just above the bottom and stirs up the monkfish into the net but doesn't touch that whole ecosystem of the ocean floor. Also the guy rotates where he fishes—takes only a few fish from a given location, and then lets it rest. So we can feel pretty sure that we're doing the right thing with the fish we serve.

It's the same with the beef, which I'm buying now for the whole restaurant. After we learned from Michael Pollan about all the horrors of feed lots and sick cows and all that, Alice decided she didn't want to use any more corn-fed beef, and we've been searching for over a year now for grass-fed beef that tastes good. And it has to be humanely raised and killed. No chemicals on the land. Totally organic. It hasn't been easy to find. A lot of grass-fed just doesn't taste that great, consistently. What we've been buying from Magruder is the best we've found, but the quality seems to me to be also very dependent on *terroir*. As the grass begins to green up, the beef starts to taste better and better, and then toward the end of the summer when the grass is all going brown, there's a steady decline in flavor until the rains start again in the winter. Plus, we've been having to buy whole cows, and there are all these cuts that we don't know what to do with. It's a big learning process.

The old country-pine table that divides the kitchen from the dining room was hastily swabbed clean, and Shelley Mulhall, the hostess and dining-room manager, quickly arranged two still lifes on it, one of very earthy-looking root vegetables and the many-colored chicories, the other of round brown loaves of Acme bread. At five fifty-six Shelley called into the kitchen, "Four minutes!" Jérôme removed his dirty apron, put on a clean one, and returned to chopping his turnip greens.

Paula set up a sample salad for tasting. She heated the greens briefly in a bowl suspended over hot water while warming the mushrooms and pancetta in the *sautoir* and then sprinkling them with parsley chopped so fine it was almost a powder. The greens went on the center of the plate, and Paula set two quarters of eggs on either side. Jean-Pierre leaned over the salad and added an infinitesimal amount of salt and pepper. He didn't like the look of the eggs and suddenly attacked them with his knife, chopping them into uneven chunks that he then distributed over the top. He lifted a big forkful into his mouth, and five other forks plunged in after his. While they chewed, the cooks all watched Jean-Pierre, awaiting his reaction. He said nothing. Jérôme said, "The dressing is perfect, it just needs a little more. I think it should be a little warmer, and you should warm the eggs to room temperature. You can't taste them when they're cold like this." Jérôme was speaking with the authority of years of experience. Jean-Pierre nodded in agreement.

Jean-Pierre tasted each element of the soup separately. "The broth is too clean," he said, and Beth looked mystified. "A little more salt, I think. Don't worry about the broth. It will get better as the evening progresses."

The waiters donned their simple uniforms of white shirts and black pants. Two bottles of Prosecco were uncorked, and a pitcher of pale yellow Meyer lemon syrup set beside each. The main kitchen counter was wiped clean for plating. Jean-Pierre put on new whites, the fancy jacket with *Chez Panisse* embroidered on the chest. Shelley took her place at the podium.

ALICE WATERS was not at Chez Panisse that night. The regulars know by now not to be surprised if Alice isn't around. When she is, she will seem to be everywhere at once—up to her elbows in a sink washing lettuce; sticking a finger in a sauce and ordaining a dash of lime juice; shoving logs into the fire, and adjusting the rotisserie; inspecting the recycling cache behind the restaurant to be sure that the cans are spotless, the garbage odorless; sometimes in her trimly fitted kitchen whites, sometimes in one of her unique, unknowable-period dresses, making the rounds of the dining room, kissing friends on both cheeks, sitting two minutes here, five there, holding both hands of an admirer, pointing out to a busser a dusty inch of molding. When she is at the restaurant, she will taste every dish produced in both the downstairs and the upstairs kitchens, and she will not be hesitant with her criticism. There are 119 people on the staff of Chez Panisse, and not one of them, ever, argues with Alice's palate.

What is remarkable in Alice's absence is the continuing presence of that palate. Chez Panisse embodies a system of aesthetic discrimination of deep subtlety and hidden complexity. Alice's standards, her taste in everything from the quality of the light to the silkiness of the butter, her ethical standards, her sense of the restaurant as a family—all these stay behind when she is gone, as strong as when she is here. A common remark from one cook to another who has just tasted the first one's dish is, "Alice would love that." Besides the physical one, there is a virtual Alice Waters.

1517 Shattuck Avenue, 2006

THE FACE that Chez Panisse presents to the street is both plain and intricately expressive. Climbing or down-spilling vines weave through an arbor and screen fashioned partly of weathered redwood, partly of gray steel bars punctuated with little steel polka dots. A glass-fronted polished copper box displays the day's menus. Above the narrow entranceway is an arc of raw redwood on which the restaurant's name is jauntily, somewhat roughly painted. Behind the screen is a small enclosed terrace with three redwood benches, a potted camellia, and a Japanese maple growing through the brick floor with tiny violets at its base. An unruly wisteria sprawls upward into the second-story eaves. Strawberry plants line the pinkish concrete retaining wall. Squeezing through the sidewalk and towering over it is an enormous, rather bizarre-looking tree, which nearly

The downstairs dining room, looking west

The kitchen at Chez Panisse

Looking east, into the kitchen

everyone, including the waiters, calls a monkey-puzzle (*Araucaria arau-cana,* a native of Chile), but which is in fact a bunya-bunya (same genus, different species—*Araucaria bidwillii,* from Australia). All this artful jumble—the slow accumulation of Alice's refinements since 1971—does not conceal the building's beginnings as a humble, rambling old house.

That autumn evening in 2004, as the first customers approached, a waiter walked quickly across the terrace waving a delicately fragrant burning branch of rosemary—the first of several subtle gestures of welcome devised by Alice.

It was one party's first meal ever at Chez Panisse. Handrails of hammered brass led them up six steps to a landing beneath layered raw wood gables. A heavy redwood door opened into a narrow foyer containing a bench, a small table, a rug, and a primitive space heater along the baseboard. Two narrow windows peeked into the dining room. Double doors led to the second foyer, a warmer place, suffused with the golden light particular to Chez Panisse.

A beaten-brass vase was overflowing with autumnal flowers, vines, and leaves—manifestations of nature's abundance being another of Alice's customary gestures of welcome. A narrow stairway on the left led to the café upstairs. To the right was a redwood podium, behind which Shelley Mulhall waited. Shelley found the party's reservation in her leather-covered book and noted the table location.

"Welcome to Chez Panisse," she said, and gestured toward the dining room.

Downstairs at Chez Panisse—the original dining room—is not an easy restaurant to get into. It is best to call for a reservation precisely a month ahead, preferably first thing in the morning. Robert Messick will answer the phone as he has been doing for the last twenty-two years: "Good morning, Chez Panisse." He reminds each caller that there is no choice on the menu, but that one can phone early in the week to find out what's planned, or look it up on the restaurant's Web site. He also tells the caller that what will actually be served may be what was planned, or may resemble it but differ; occasionally a course will have changed entirely.

Following Shelley into the dining room, the first-time diners slipped

past a green velvet curtain and into an atmosphere both simple and stu-
diously composed—foremost of aromas, floating from the open kitchen, of
olive oil, garlic, wood smoke, pastry, roasting meat, something frying,
something sweet, a mingling of the scents of haute cuisine and an Italian
grandmother's kitchen. As yet unpeopled, the dining room seemed rather
severe, with white plaster walls, redwood trim, copper sconces, a few mirrors, a couple of offhandedly rustic arrangements of particolor chicories
and raw root vegetables. The room was gently lit, neither dark nor bright,
except at the rear, which was open wide to the strong white light of the
kitchen. The tables were set with plain flatware and glasses, plain white
linen, plain white plates. The woodwork was faintly Japanese in style. The
only immodest elements of the room were the spectacular bursts of flowers,
all locally grown, all proclaiming the season and abundance and welcome.

At each place sat a small cream-color paper folder bearing on its front
a delicate linoleum-block print by Patricia Curtan, of a bowl of tangerines.
Inside was the night's menu:

CHEZ PANISSE

An apéritif

❧

Warm salad of winter chicories with cèpes, pancetta, and eggs

❧

Fish and shellfish soup with Dungeness crab, Atlantic cod, and fennel

❧

Grilled rack, loin, and leg of Cattail Creek lamb
with fresh coriander seed sauce and roasted Chino Ranch vegetables

❧

Meyer lemon soufflé

DINNER: SEVENTY-FIVE DOLLARS

TAX: EIGHT AND THREE-QUARTERS PERCENT

SERVICE: SEVENTEEN PERCENT

Over the next half hour, as all of its fifty seats were filled, Chez Panisse was transformed. The modesty of the dining room is the culmination of the thirty-three years of Alice's pursuit of an aesthetic so refined as to elude most conscious perception of the room as a physical space. What gives it life, in her intention, are people and their pleasure. That night there were shy young couples on important dates, gastronomic pilgrims from afar, wealthy tourists with prove-it looks, sweater-clad regulars leaning back in their chairs and laughing, and the Slow Food contingent, Europeans and Americans together. It was a highly heterogeneous crowd whom, if their common experience worked as Alice intended, the evening would conjoin in a brief community of delight.

To each table came a dish of olives, a basket of bread, and a small pot of butter; to each diner a slim glass of Prosecco, barely fizzy, scented with the house-made syrup of Meyer lemon—an apéritif concocted specifically to harmonize with that night's menu.

The wine list is neither short nor long, none of it cheap, though most of it reasonably priced. The waiters all know the wines well, but for each dinner Jonathan Waters, the restaurant's wine buyer, selects two whites and two reds that he considers particularly harmonious with the menu and good value as well.

A foursome of longtime friends of the house strolled into the kitchen to say hello to the cooks and the chef, and to see what was cooking. If a diner asks a question about the food that his waiter can't fully answer, the diner is likely to be invited into the kitchen, to talk to the cook responsible for the dish. The portions are adequate, but if someone especially likes something, and as long as there's enough, it's not a secret that the kitchen will gladly serve seconds.

The salad was a multirhythmic composition of textures, flavors, and temperatures: the fresh cèpes hot from the *sautoir,* slightly chewy, crisp at the edges, lightly garlicked, dressed with a very small amount of rather piquant vinaigrette, and sprinkled with infinitesimal flakes of parsley; the bits of pancetta warm, crisp, pungent, and salty; the leaves of the various crunchy chicories (red ones, yellow ones, Castelfranco freckled with pink, *pain de sucre* hued from pale at its center to bright green at its leaf tips) barely warm and softening slowly in the warmer vinaigrette, a milder one than that used on the mushrooms; and two quarters of boiled egg at room temperature, spotted with drops of bright green olive oil and glittering with crystals of sea salt.

After a pause came the soup. The stock on which it had been built was too complex for any but the finest of palates to tease out all the flavors, but it was not at all strong. Almost as light as water, it served merely to frame and focus the solid ingredients—half bites of pearlescent Dungeness crab, a small, tender square of house-salted cod, a few slices of poached fennel bulb, a sparse drizzle of finely chopped fennel fronds and chervil.

To drink with these, the waiter suggested a light-bodied white wine, perhaps a sauvignon blanc, a Muscadet, a verdejo—something with plenty of acid, he said, to stand up to the vinaigrette, and not too much fruit, in order not to blur the delicacy of the soup.

The three small slices of grilled lamb, each from a different cut, exhibited three palpably different textures, but they were uniformly rosy, slightly oak-smoky, and caramelized at the edges. There was not a strand of gristle, no silverskin, no rims of fat. They had been moistened with perhaps a tablespoon or two of intensely flavored lamb stock that at the last minute had been briefly infused with a bouquet of fresh coriander seeds. Despite its intensity and the exotic perfume of the coriander, the dark yet still transparent stock so discreetly deepened the savor of the meat that it was nearly imperceptible.

The tiny root vegetables accompanying the lamb were a palette of autumnal color—rust-orange carrots, pale green celery root, soft yellow rutabaga, cream-color parsley root, blue-white turnips, ivory salsify, apple-white Jerusalem artichoke, all bound with a little sweet butter.

Jean-Pierre Moullé favors aromatic, moderately extracted European red wines, with more finesse than power, such as classical Bordeaux and Burgundies, but he knows that the American fashion these days seems to be for the dense, thick, high-alcohol ilk of hot-climate zinfandel, syrah, and various reds from the sun-roasted slopes of southernmost France;

the Chez Panisse wine list offers some of each. The Green and Red zinfandel that is the Chez Panisse house red, which the waiter recommended to the first-time diners, nicely balanced power and finesse. It is the house wine for several characteristically Chez Panisse reasons. Its maker, Jay Heminway, has been a friend of Alice's ever since she was his daughter's teacher at the Berkeley Montessori School; the grapes are grown and vinified in entirely sustainable fashion; and the wine is delicious.

The diners' glasses were rarely empty, and never overfilled. The waiters will gladly chat, especially about the food, but if a party is deeply immersed in conversation, the staff becomes all but invisible. Look up, and someone will be there. There are no "zones"—any waiter will respond to any table.

As the food and the wine and the flowers and the staff did their work, there was more laughter, more talk. Strangers began chatting with one another. Old friends were changing seats. The newcomers, encouraged by the old-timers they had seen doing it, went in for a look at the kitchen and were welcomed.

As the meal wound down, so did the cooks and the waiters. Everybody was loosening up. The barriers of custom that separate stranger from stranger, server from served, frequently soften at this point in an evening at Chez Panisse, and sometimes they seem even to disappear.

Attentive observation by the dining-room staff determined when it was time to whip up the diners' soufflés and set them to bake. The soufflés arrived entirely unadorned. There were no cookies, no sauce—just a small individual bright yellow soufflé, sprinkled with powdered sugar, in the fluted white porcelain ramekin in which it had been cooked, sitting on a white paper doily on a plain white plate. When the first-time diners parted the tops with their spoons and the pure essence of lemon transformed into steam poured forth, they had made up their minds about Chez Panisse. At least a few customers may have shrugged, perhaps complained—portions too small! all this money for such plain food?— and they would probably never come back. But some of the people in the dining room that evening at Chez Panisse knew that they had had an experience they had never had in any other restaurant—somehow clearer, somehow clarifying.

OF THE PRECEDING seven weeks Alice had spent only six days at home in Berkeley. During her time away, she flew to North Carolina to raise money for the Edible Schoolyard; visited the Yale project; spoke at a dinner in New York for an organization that establishes community gardens in vacant lots throughout the five boroughs; flew to London, to meet with her new friend the Prince of Wales, an advocate of sustainable farming, whom she had persuaded to address some five thousand farmers, fishermen, artisans, winemakers, nomadic herders, and aquaculturists from all over the world at a convocation known as Terra Madre, an adjunct of Slow Food's biennial Salone del Gusto in Turin. From London Alice flew on to Turin to give a speech to Terra Madre herself, in which she asserted:

> I believe that the destiny of humankind in the twenty-first century will depend most of all on how people choose to nourish themselves. And if we can educate the senses, and break down the wall of ignorance between farmers and eaters, I am convinced—because I have seen it with my own eyes time and again—people will inevitably choose the sustainable way, which is always the most delicious alternative.

After a number of workshops, meetings, seminars, and more speeches, Alice introduced Prince Charles to the assembled multitude. "Slow Food," he began,

> is traditional food. It is also local—and local cuisine is one of the most important ways we identify with the place and region where we live. It is the same with the buildings in our towns, cities, and villages. Well-designed places and buildings that relate to the local-

ity and landscape and that put people before cars enhance a sense of community and rootedness. All these things are connected. We no more want to live in anonymous concrete blocks that are just like anywhere else in the world than we want to eat anonymous junk food which can be bought anywhere.

The prince is by far the biggest farmer in England, with well over a hundred thousand acres of land, on which he has been setting an example for an agrarian revolution perfectly in line with Alice's ideals—another pilot project, on an Olympian scale.

That evening, Alice returned to the village of Verduno—the scene of her triumphant dinner two years before—this time not as a harried chef but as the guest of the prince, at another restaurant owned by the Burlotto sisters, Cà del Re, which happens to mean "Castle of the King." The restaurant is in fact part of a modest *agriturismo,* a working farm that supplements its income by taking in guests. The next day, Alice and the prince visited one of Slow Food's most extraordinary projects, the University of Gastronomic Sciences—not a fledgling start-up but a complete university built from scratch. Housed in two beautiful old building complexes in the Piedmontese countryside, it has an international faculty of scholars trained in every possible field related to food, including soil science, anthropology, agricultural economics, food law and policy, microbiology, food service systems, plant and animal study, the geography of natural resources, the history of the agricultural landscape, cooking, tasting, and even the semiotics of food. Alice and Prince Charles also attended the annual Fat Ox Festival of a nearby village.

From Italy, Alice flew back to New York, to raise funds for the Chez Panisse Foundation, to lecture at the French Culinary Institute, and to meet with Gilbert Pilgram and David Tanis to ensure David's return as cochef. Then it was on to Washington, where Alice was envisioning a temporary Edible Schoolyard as a living exhibit in the Smithsonian Folklife Festival. She saw it as a likely way to reach important members of the government and thereby to influence national school lunch policies.

The next day she was off to Ann Arbor, Michigan, to address a meeting titled "The Future of the Agrarian Adventure," and then, that night, to oversee a fund-raising dinner for the presidential campaign of Senator John Kerry, whose wife, Teresa Heinz Kerry, was rather more enthusiastic about a garden on the White House lawn than the Clintons had been.

And then, at last, she came home to Berkeley, for six days of non-relaxation. Sylvan welcomed Alice to the Chez Panisse office with a bulging portfolio of obligations—dozens of phone calls, e-mails, restaurant decisions, foundation matters, personnel troubles, supplier questions, all clamoring for her immediate attention.

Those six days were a blur, and then Alice found herself on yet another long journey, this time to Nice, for yet another award, a banquet with the great chefs of Europe, a Bordeaux wine tasting, and—"Thank God!" she said—a couple of halcyon days at Bandol, in the sweet, soft, slow-moving world of Lulu Peyraud.

Paris was still to come, with a blowout seventy-fifth birthday party for Johnny Apple. The rest of the week was for herself, to eat, drink, breathe, and just *be in* Paris, where a bowl of soup, so long ago, set in motion the restless dream that became Alice Waters's life.

As the months rushed by, Alice seemed, impossibly, to be accelerating. The Edible Schoolyard became part of a broader campaign called Re-thinking School Lunch. The Edible Schoolyard exhibit in Washington fed pizza—baked by kids—to a number of influential politicians, as Alice filled their brains with statistics. She changed the food service at the American Academy in Rome from steam-table cafeteria style to freshly cooked, seasonal local foods. The Chez Panisse Café turned twenty-five, with another big celebration. She lectured, she appeared on TV, she was photographed for *Vogue*. She started work on two new books. Gilbert Pilgram, exasperated at his inability to rein her in, resigned as general manager of Chez Panisse, and Alice threw him a grand, affectionate going-away party. He moved to Uruguay, but returned after a few months to buy Vince Calcagno's interest in the Zuni Café in San Francisco.

. . .

AND THEN ALICE BEGAN to take stock. The board of directors of Pagnol et Cie and she agreed that she was, for real this time, perilously close to being overwhelmed; the upshot was a six-month sabbatical—which in the event only slightly resembled a sabbatical. What it resembled was her normal life—office, meetings, phone calls, tasting, criticizing tiny but to her all-important details at Chez Panisse, more talks, more travel.

ALICE HAS TRAVELED somewhat more for pleasure than before, and at home she has begun to calm and clarify her life, with regular sessions of acupuncture, massage, yoga, and psychotherapy. She has lost weight, and toned up. Her friends say she has never looked so radiant. She believes that she has slowed down, though that is not always readily apparent to others.

Some of Alice's longtime friends still see the same little Alice they first knew, unchanged over the years. She does work hard to keep up with her old friends. Amid the swirl of her public life, she clings to private loyalties. She also makes new friends readily. Davia Nelson is a relatively new friend, and she sees recent change in Alice:

> She's more patient now, and more curious. More committed. The culture has caught up to where she has been all along, so these are the years when it's do or die for the planet, and she is part of that planetary crusade. So she is compulsively busy, but I think it's because she sees the sand in the hourglass.

Alice talks rarely of the past or her inner life. When asked when something happened, she often cannot remember. Her emotions are nearly always on the surface, open to anyone's scrutiny, and her mind, it seems, is nearly always on the present and the future. She sees the future in small things, highly specific goals, and at the same time on an almost inconceivably grand scale. "I'm completely dedicating this decade to public education," she says.

There are small things like writing a book and whatnot, but my immediate big hope is that we will have rolled out an organic lunch program in all seventeen schools in Berkeley. And that we will have integrated the curriculums of the grammar schools and the middle schools and the high schools with the school lunch program, and that ten thousand kids will be eating lunch as part of the academic day. And that we will be supporting any number of farmers and ranches and dairies that are within a couple of hours of the school district. And that we will have documented everything that has gone on. And that the children will have actually changed their eating habits, and that we will have stemmed the tide of obesity in Berkeley. That we will have our first graduates out, and that it will be so compelling and so delicious that the state of California will be contemplating a statewide program, and that they will be ready to take over the funding of the Berkeley program.

For Slow Food, my hope is that in ten years it will be a really

Alice and her Edible Schoolyard exhibit in Washington, D.C.

vibrant force for change in every country in this world. Slow Food for me is a huge commitment to seeing things in a global perspective. We can't talk about just the United States. We have to talk in this global way. A global vision.

The change in the scale of Alice's activities has been so great that the quantitative difference may be said to constitute a qualitative one. Yet she remains anchored to the old and the familiar: devoted to the same old restaurant and café on Shattuck Avenue, sometimes as chaotic behind the scenes as ever, nearly always nevertheless conveying an air of serene hospitality and serving a couple of hundred people every day some of the most delicious food they've ever tasted; devoted to Fanny, who has graduated from Yale and is studying art history at the University of Cambridge; devoted to her aging, ailing mom and dad, her sisters, her friends old and new; devoted to her garden, her mortar and pestle, the pleasures of talk and the table.

ACKNOWLEDGMENTS

My wife, Elizabeth, read this book in all its incarnations, including early ones that were pretty rugged going. She is my best critic, and she has been a patient, sympathetic, and loving partner throughout.

Alice Waters cooperated well beyond the scope of any possible obligation, and I will always be thankful for her generosity and sweet spirit.

Alice's friends and colleagues were also generous with their time and insight, especially Charles and Lindsey Shere, Fritz Streiff, Eleanor Bertino, Cristina Salas-Porras, David Goines, Barbara Carlitz, and the tireless, ever congenial Sylvan Brackett. The members of the staff of Chez Panisse were gracious and welcoming, even when I was endlessly underfoot in the kitchen. The chefs in particular—Christopher Lee, Kelsie Kerr, Russell Moore, Cal Peternell, Mary Canales, Alan Tangren, David Tanis, and Jean-Pierre Moullé—epitomized the Chez Panisse culture of intelligence and openheartedness.

R. W. (Johnny) Apple, Jr., who wrote this book's foreword, died on October 4, 2006. He was a dear friend to hundreds, and an inspiration to hundreds. He was both to me, and I will be forever grateful to him.

Colleen Bazdarich gave untold hours of time as my intern. I wish I could repay my debt to her in money, but it would never be enough. She and Wendy Jovero also put in many hours transcribing recordings of my interviews.

Susan Snyder guided me with care and caring through the labyrinthine mysteries of the Bancroft Library of the University of California at Berkeley.

I also owe gratitude to the various photographers whose work appears in these pages, some of whom are uncredited because I was unable to identify them.

I had two especially clarifying work-sabbaticals. The first consisted of two weeks at the incomparably tranquil Mesa Refuge at Point Reyes Station, California; to its creator and patron, Peter Barnes, my hearty thanks. The second mind-clearing interlude was a beautiful winter month at the home of my dear friend Miles Chapin in New York. Sarah Black, an irreplaceable friend as well as one of the clearest-thinking people I've ever known, guided me toward a plainspoken voice in what until then had been a welter of contending styles.

Also in New York, Chip McGrath provided wise, cogent counsel at a time when I seemed unable to get a feel for the narrative as a whole. My first-ever and still-beloved editor, Bobbie Bristol, gave the manuscript a characteristically meticulous going-over. My agent, David McCormick, has been much more than an extraordinary business representative; his editing and editorial advice, though severe enough at times to be painful, prevented what threatened to be an embarrassing case of literary obesity.

At the Penguin Press, Liza Darnton, Alexandra Lane, Lindsay Whalen, and the boss, my esteemed editor Ann Godoff, have helped me in a thousand ways.

My father, Charles T. McNamee, Jr., ninety-three fierce years old, never let up encouraging me: "When are you going to finish that damn book, Tommy? Don't you want to get paid? Lord have mercy!"

NOTES

CHAPTER 2. SOUP, 1944–1965
1. Alice Waters, *The Chez Panisse Menu Cookbook* (New York: Random House, 1982).

CHAPTER 3. VERY SIXTIES, 1965–1966
1. See http://en.wikipedia.org/wiki/Sustainability: Wikipedia defines *sustainability* somewhat more elaborately, as "a systemic concept, relating to the continuity of economic, social, institutional and environmental aspects of human society, as well as the non-human environment. It is intended to be a means of configuring civilization and human activity so that society, its members and its economies are able to meet their needs and express their greatest potential in the present, while preserving biodiversity and natural ecosystems, and planning and acting for the ability to maintain these ideals in a very long term. Sustainability affects every level of organization, from the local neighborhood to the entire planet."

CHAPTER 5. VERY BERKELEY, 1971–1973
1. Alice Waters, "The Farm-Restaurant Connection," *The Journal of Gastronomy* 5, no. 2 (Summer/Autumn 1989).

CHAPTER 6. JEREMIAH, 1973–1975
1. Most people think of television as a much later invention, but the date here is correct.

2. The French here is incorrect, but it is what was printed on the menu. Correct usage would be *plat de fromages*.
3. See http://comenius.guymoquet.tripod.com/es1/cuisinier/corps.htm. Translation by the author.
4. Anthony Blake and Quentin Crewe, *Great Chefs of France* (New York: Harry N. Abrams, 1978).
5. This dictum is widely quoted in French gastronomic literature, but I have been unable to find the original source. Translation by the author.
6. Interview by Naomi Wise and Carol Field, *City* (San Francisco), April 16–29, 1975.
7. Jeremiah Tower, *California Dish: What I Saw (and Cooked) at the American Culinary Revolution* (New York: Free Press, 2003).
8. Kim Severson, *San Francisco Chronicle*, August 3, 2003.

CHAPTER 7. LAST BIRTHDAY? 1976
1. *New West*, May 9, 1977.

CHAPTER 8. ENNUI AND INSPIRATION, 1977–1978
1. Alice Waters and the cooks of Chez Panisse, in collaboration with David Tanis and Fritz Streiff, *Chez Panisse Café Cookbook* (New York: HarperCollins, 1999).

CHAPTER 9. CREATION AND DESTRUCTION, 1979–1982
1. Ella Elvin, *New York Daily News*, May 2, 1979.
2. Lois Dwan, *Los Angeles Times*, November 4, 1979.
3. Colman Andrews, *New West*, June 1979.
4. Mark Blackburn, *New York Times*, July 18, 1979.
5. Arthur Bloomfield, *San Francisco Focus*, March 1981.
6. Craig Claiborne, *New York Times*, June 3, 1981.

CHAPTER 10. REBAPTISM BY FIRE, 1982
1. Jeannette Ferrary, *San Francisco Chronicle*, August 1, 1982.
2. Paul Bertolli, with Alice Waters, *Chez Panisse Cooking* (New York: Random House, 1988).

CHAPTER 12. ALICE TAKES FLIGHT, 1985–1986
1. Charles Michener, with Linda R. Prout, *Newsweek*, November 29, 1982.
2. Barbara Kafka, *Vogue*, November 1982.
3. Jason Epstein, *House & Garden*, February 1983.
4. Stan Sesser, *San Francisco Chronicle*, November 25, 1983.
5. Marian Burros, *New York Times*, September 26, 1984.
6. Jeffrey Alan Fiskin, *California*, February 1985.
7. David Sundelson, *Nation*, September 25, 1982.
8. Robert K. Merton, "The Matthew Effect in Science," *Science*, January 5, 1969.
9. Blake Green, *San Francisco Chronicle*, August 14, 1984.

Chapter 13. Death and Life, 1986–1987
1. Alice Waters, Chez Panisse sustainability statement, draft, 2000.
2. Charles Shere and the Chez Panisse Board of Directors, "Our Commitment to Sustainability," in *Chez Panisse Purveyors,* privately published, 2001. See http://www.chezpanisse.com/pgcommit.html.
3. Alice Waters, "The Farm-Restaurant Connection."
4. Mark Santora, *New York Times,* January 12, 2006.
5. Stan Sesser, *San Francisco Chronicle,* June 9, 1987.

Chapter 15. Star Power, 1991–1994
1. See http://www.etymonline.com/index.php?search=foodie&searchmode=none.
2. Michael Bauer, *San Francisco Chronicle,* March 17, 1993.
3. GraceAnn Walden, *San Francisco Chronicle,* August 13, 1993.
4. *Chicago Tribune,* August 13, 1993.
5. Monterey Bay Aquarium Seafood Watch: http://www.mbayaq.org/cr/cr_seafoodwatch/sfw_restaurants.asp.
6. See http://www.compass-group.com.
7. Rebecca Williams, Carol Ness, Carissa Remitz, and Deb Wandell, *San Francisco Chronicle,* February 15, 2006.

Chapter 16. Into the Great World, 1995–2001
1. Marian Burros, *New York Times,* August 14, 1996.
2. Marian Burros, *New York Times,* June 10, 1998.
3. Adam Gopnik, *New Yorker,* October 26, 1998.

Chapter 17. An Extraordinary Day in Italy, 2001–2002
1. In October 2006, in its "red guide" for the San Francisco Bay Area, Michelin awarded Chez Panisse just that—one star.
2. Verlyn Klinkenborg, *New York Times,* April 30, 2006.

INTERVIEWS

In addition to these formal interviews, nearly all of them recorded, there have been many follow-up phone calls and e-mails.

Anderson, Bruce: September 23, 2005
Andrews, Colman: December 15, 2003
Apple, R. W., Jr.: December 31, 2003
Aratow, Paul: April 14, 2004; October 21, 2004
Asher, Gerald: November 10, 2004
Bauer, Michael: August 26, 2004
Bertino, Eleanor: April 10, 2003; May 10, 2004; May 17, 2004; October 27, 2004;
    July 29, 2005
Bertolli, Paul: September 30, 2003
Bishop, Willy: October 30, 2003; November 24, 2003
Brackett, Sylvan: March 3, 2004
Budrick, Jerry: October 29, 2004; November 17, 2004
Buell, Susie Tompkins: December 18, 2003; October 6, 2005
Cannard, Bob: December 19, 2003
Carlitz, Barbara: May 12, 2003; October 21, 2004; September 1, 2005
Carrau, Bob: October 10, 2003; January 19, 2004
Clarke, Sally: May 13, 2005
Constable, Ene: January 12, 2004
Cooper, Penny, and Rena Rosenwasser: November 22, 2004

Crumley, Steve: September 17, 2003
Cunningham, Marion: April 21, 2003
Curtan, Patricia: December 18, 2003
Danner, Mark: January 26, 2004
Dedlow, Phillip: October 18, 2005
Dencler, Amy: September 4, 2003
Donnell Lily, Nancy: April 20, 2004
Edwards, Pat: February 28, 2005
Epstein, Jason: December 10, 2003
Federman, Carolyn: September 26, 2005
Finigan, Robert: October 28, 2003
Flanders, Sara: July 26, 2004
Glenn, Carrie Wright: November 11, 2004
Goines, David: September 24, 2003; August 9, 2004
Goines, David, and Richard Seibert, September 6, 2005
Guerrero, Marsha: February 6, 2004
Gussow, Joan: December 10, 2003
Hamilton, Doug: December 30, 2003
Harrison, Jim: November 4, 2004
Heminway, Jay: June 22, 2004
Isaak, Anne: December 9, 2003
Jones, Sharon: May 8, 2003
Kerr, Kelsie: November 7, 2002
Knickerbocker, Peggy: December 19, 2003
Kraus, Sibella: March 25, 2005; September 26, 2005
Kummer, Corby: January 27, 2004
Labro, Claude and Martine: July 18, 2003
Lee, Christopher: February 13, 2003; September 4, 2003
Luddy, Tom: June 5, 2003
Lynch, Kermit: May 8, 2003
Marcus, Greil: June 22, 2004
Martins, Patrick: December 8, 2003
Maser, Jim and Laura: September 24, 2003
Messick, Robert: September 29, 2003
Meyer, Danny: December 9, 2003
Moore, Russell: November 7, 2002; July 30, 2003
Moullé, Jean-Pierre: October 8, 2003; March 7, 2005
Murphy, Sue: January 2, 2004
Nelson, Davia: May 3, 2004
Neyers, Barbara: July 5, 2006
Opton, Gene: November 11, 2004
Peternell, Michael: June 5, 2003
Petrini, Carlo: October 12, 2005
Peyraud, Lulu: July 17, 2003
Pilgram, Gilbert: September 4, 2003; September 26, 2005

Pisor, Ellen Waters: June 30, 2005

Reichl, Ruth: December 12, 2003

Rodgers, Judy: November 24, 2003; April 2, 2004

Salas-Porras, Cristina: September 12, 2002; November 7, 2002; February 11, 2003; March 3, 2004; October 10, 2005

Sandefer, Lee Ann: May 7, 2004

Savinar, Tim: May 5, 2003

Scheer, Robert: November 4, 2003

Seibert, Richard: November 10, 2003

Shere, Charles and Lindsey: July 15, 2002; April 2, 2003; October 17, 2003; November 29, 2003; March 6, 2004

Singer, Fanny: December 30, 2003

Singer, Mark: December 8, 2003

Singer, Stephen: June 3, 2003

Streiff, Fritz: June 23, 2003

Sullivan, Steve: October 31, 2003

Tangren, Alan: April 24, 2004

Tanis, David: July 24, 2003

Tower, Jeremiah: May 17, 2003; February 4, 2004

Trillin, Calvin: December 15, 2003

Waag, Nathalie: April 19, 2004

Waters, Alice: August 13, 2001; October 27, 2002; November 20, 2002; February 2, 2003; February 5, 2003; March 11, 2003; March 13, 2003; March 24, 2003; April 3, 2003; April 11, 2003; July 1, 2003; October 3, 2003; October 9, 2003; November 25, 2003; December 4, 2003; January 12, 2004; January 13, 2004; January 21, 2004; February 27, 2004; May 19, 2004; July 15, 2004; July 29, 2004; August 5, 2004; November 10, 2004; January 5, 2005; September 22, 2005; October 13, 2005; January 3, 2006; May 9, 2006; July 3, 2006; July 5, 2006; July 9, 2006

Waters, Jonathan: October 3, 2003

Waters, Pat and Marge: April 21, 2003

Waxman, Jonathan: February 2, 2005

Wise, Victoria (née Kroyer): October 20, 2003; June 11, 2004

BIBLIOGRAPHY

A number of the following works are not cited in the text, but all contributed to my understanding of Alice Waters and Chez Panisse.

Alexander, Christopher, Sara Ishikawa, and Murray Silverstein. *A Pattern Language.* New York: Oxford University Press, 1977.

Arnold, Ann. *The Adventurous Chef: Alexis Soyer.* New York: Farrar, Straus & Giroux, 2002.

Beard, James. *Delights and Prejudices: A Memoir with Recipes.* New York: Macmillan, 1964.

Berger, Frances de Talavera, and John Park Custis. *Sumptuous Dining in Gaslight San Francisco, 1875–1915.* Garden City, N.Y.: Doubleday, 1985.

Bertolli, Paul, with Alice Waters. *Chez Panisse Cooking.* New York: Random House, 1988.

Blake, Anthony, and Quentin Crewe. *Great Chefs of France.* New York: Harry N. Abrams, 1978.

Bocuse, Paul. *Paul Bocuse's French Cooking.* New York: Random House, 1977.

Brillat-Savarin, Jean Anthelme. *The Physiology of Taste.* Translated and annotated by M. F. K. Fisher. San Francisco: North Point Press, 1986.

Britchky, Seymour. *The Lutèce Cookbook.* New York: Alfred A. Knopf, 1995.

Caen, Herb. *Herb Caen's New Guide to San Francisco and the Bay Area.* Garden City, N.Y.: Doubleday, 1957.

Chabon, Michael. "Berkeley." *Gourmet,* March 2002. Reproduced at http://www.michaelchabon.com/berkeley.html.

Chapel, Alain. *La Cuisine: C'est Beaucoup Plus que des Recettes.* Paris: Éditions Robert Laffont, 1980.

Claiborne, Craig. *The New York Times Guide to Dining Out in New York.* New York: Atheneum, 1970.

Claiborne, Craig, Pierre Franey, and the editors of Time-Life Books. *Classic French Cooking.* New York: Time-Life Books, 1970.

Cooper, Artemis. *Writing at the Kitchen Table: The Authorized Biography of Elizabeth David.* New York: Ecco Press, 1999.

Curnonsky. *Traditional French Cooking.* New York: Doubleday, 1989.

———. *Traditional Recipes of the Provinces of France.* Translated and edited by Edwin Lavin. Garden City, N.Y.: Doubleday, 1961.

Daria, Irene. *Lutèce: A Day in the Life of America's Greatest Restaurant.* New York: Random House, 1993.

David, Elizabeth. *French Provincial Cooking.* London: Michael Joseph, 1960.

Davidson, Sara. *Spare Change: Three Women of the Sixties.* Garden City, N.Y.: Doubleday, 1977.

De Groot, Roy Andries. *The Auberge of the Flowering Hearth.* Hopewell, N.J.: Ecco Press, 1973.

Echikson, William. *Burgundy Stars: A Year in the Life of a Great French Restaurant.* Boston: Little, Brown, 1995.

Fernández-Armesto, Felipe. *Near a Thousand Tables: A History of Food.* New York: Free Press, 2002.

Fitch, Noël Riley. *Appetite for Life: The Biography of Julia Child.* New York: Doubleday, 1997.

Forbes magazine. *Forbes Magazine's Restaurant Guide.* Vol. 1. New York: Forbes, 1971.

Foster, Lee, ed. *The New York Times Encyclopedic Almanac 1971.* New York: The New York Times Book and Educational Division, 1969, 1970.

Frommer, Arthur B. *Frommer's Dollar-wise Guide to California.* New York: Simon & Schuster, 1966.

Girardet, Frédy, with Catherine Michel. *The Cuisine of Frédy Girardet*. Translated and annotated by Michael and Judith Hill. New York: William Morrow, 1985.

Goines, David Lance. *The Free Speech Movement: Coming of Age in the 1960s*. Berkeley, Calif.: Ten Speed Press, 1993.

Gourmet magazine. *Gourmet's France*. New York: Gourmet Books, 1978.

Hess, John L., and Karen Hess. *The Taste of America*. Urbana and Chicago: University of Illinois Press, 1972–2000.

Imhoff, Daniel. *Farming with the Wild: Enhancing Biodiversity on Farms and Ranches*. San Francisco: Sierra Club Books, 2003.

Jutkovitz, Serena. *SJ's Winners: An Exceptional Approach to Round-the-World Wining and Dining in the San Francisco Bay Area*. San Francisco: Russian Hill House Books, 1982.

Kimbrell, Andrew, ed. *Fatal Harvest: The Tragedy of Industrial Agriculture*. Washington, D.C.: Island Press/Foundation for Deep Ecology, 2002.

Kuh, Patric. *The Last Days of Haute Cuisine: America's Culinary Revolution*. New York: Viking, 2001.

Levenstein, Harvey. *Revolution at the Table*. Berkeley: University of California Press, 2003.

Lovegren, Sylvia. *Fashionable Food: Seven Decades of Food Fads*. New York: Macmillan, 1995.

Lynch, Kermit. *Adventures on the Wine Route: A Wine Buyer's Tour of France*. New York: North Point Press, 1988.

Merton, Robert K. "The Matthew Effect in Science." *Science,* January 5, 1969, 56–63.

Montagné, Prosper. *Larousse Gastronomique: The Encyclopedia of Food, Wine, and Cookery*. New York: Crown Publishers, 1961.

Nabhan, Gary Paul. *Coming Home to Eat: The Pleasures and Politics of Local Foods*. New York: W. W. Norton, 2002.

Olney, Richard. *The French Menu Cookbook*. Boston: David R. Godine, 1970; rev. ed., 1985.

———. *Simple French Food*. New York: Macmillan, 1974.

Olsen, Alfa-Betty, and Marshall Efron. *Omnivores*. New York: Viking, 1976, 1979.

Pagnol, Marcel. *Marius Fanny César*. Paris: Le Club du Meilleur Livre, 1956.

Patrick, Ted, and Silas Spitzer. *Great Restaurants of America*. New York: Bramhall House, 1960.

Pellaprat, H.-P., et al. *The Art of French Cooking*. Translated by Joseph Faulkner. New York: Golden Press, 1962.

Pellegrini, Angelo. *The Unprejudiced Palate: Classic Thoughts on Food and the Good Life*. San Francisco: North Point Press, 1984.

Petrini, Carlo, ed., with Ben Watson and Slow Food Editore. *Slow Food: Collected Thoughts on Taste, Tradition, and the Honest Pleasures of Food*. White River Junction, Vt.: Chelsea Green Publishing Co., 2001.

Pico, Leonce, ed. *Restaurants of San Francisco*. Fort Lauderdale, Fla.: Gourmet International, 1963.

Planck, Nina. *Real Food: What to Eat and Why*. New York: Bloomsbury, 2006.

Rabaudy, Nicolas de. *La Cuisine de Chez Allard*. Paris: Éditions Jean-Claude Lattès, 1982.

Reardon, Joan. *M. F. K. Fisher, Julia Child, and Alice Waters: Celebrating the Pleasures of the Table*. New York: Harmony Books, 1994.

———. *Poet of the Appetites: The Lives and Loves of M. F. K. Fisher*. New York: North Point Press, 2004.

Robbins, John. *The Food Revolution: How Your Diet Can Help Save Your Life and the World*. Berkeley, Calif.: Conari Press, 2001.

Root, Waverly, and Richard de Rochemont. *Eating in America*. New York: William Morrow, 1976, 1995.

Rorabaugh, W. J. *Berkeley at War: The 1960s*. New York: Oxford University Press, 1989.

Ruhlman, Michael. *The Soul of a Chef: The Journey Toward Perfection*. New York: Viking, 2000.

Schlosser, Eric. *Fast Food Nation: The Dark Side of the All-American Meal*. New York: Houghton Mifflin, 2001.

Shere, Lindsey Remolif. *Chez Panisse Desserts*. New York: Random House, 1985.

Slow Food Editore. *Terra Madre: 1200 World Food Communities*. Bra, Italy: Slow Food Editore Srl, 2004.

Sokolov, Raymond. *Why We Eat What We Eat: How Columbus Changed the Way the World Eats*. New York: Touchstone, 1991.

Stein, Jean, and George Plimpton. *Edie: An American Biography*. New York: Alfred A. Knopf, 1982.

Theophano, Janet. *Eat My Words: Reading Women's Lives Through the Cookbooks They Wrote*. New York: Palgrave Macmillan, 2003.

Todhunter, Andrew. *A Meal Observed*. New York: Alfred A. Knopf, 2004.

Toklas, Alice B. *The Alice B. Toklas Cookbook.* New York: Harper & Brothers, 1954.

Tower, Jeremiah. *California Dish: What I Saw (and Cooked) at the American Culinary Revolution.* New York: Free Press, 2003.

———. *Jeremiah Tower's New American Classics.* New York: Harper & Row, 1986.

Troisgros, Jean and Pierre. *The Nouvelle Cuisine of Jean and Pierre Troisgros.* London: Macmillan, 1980.

Visser, Margaret. *Much Depends on Dinner.* New York: Grove Press, 1986.

———. *The Rituals of Dinner.* New York: Grove Weidenfeld, 1991.

Waters, Alice. *Chez Panisse Fruit.* New York: HarperCollins, 2002.

———. *The Chez Panisse Menu Cookbook.* New York: Random House, 1982.

———. "The Farm-Restaurant Connection." *The Journal of Gastronomy* 5, no. 2 (Summer/Autumn 1989): 113–22.

———. Foreword to *Lulu's Provençal Table: The Exuberant Food and Wine from Domaine Tempier Vineyard,* by Richard Olney. New York: HarperCollins, 1994.

———. Foreword to *My Father's Glory and My Mother's Castle,* by Marcel Pagnol. New York: North Point Press, 1986.

———. Foreword to *Slow Food: The Case for Taste,* by Carlo Petrini. New York: Columbia University Press, 2001.

———. "Tea and Cheese in Turkey." In *The Kindness of Strangers,* edited by Don George. Melbourne: Lonely Planet Publications, 2003.

Waters, Alice, with Bob Carrau and Patricia Curtan. *Fanny at Chez Panisse.* New York: HarperCollins, 1992.

Waters, Alice, and the cooks of Chez Panisse. *Chez Panisse Vegetables.* New York: HarperCollins, 1996.

Waters, Alice, and the cooks of Chez Panisse, in collaboration with David Tanis and Fritz Streiff. *The Chez Panisse Café Cookbook.* New York: HarperCollins, 1999.

Waters, Alice, Patricia Curtan, and Martine Labro. *Chez Panisse Pasta, Pizza, & Calzone.* New York: Random House, 1984.

Wechsberg, Joseph. *Blue Trout and Black Truffles: The Peregrinations of an Epicure.* New York: Alfred A. Knopf, 1966.

Wuerthner, George, and Mollie Matteson, eds. *Welfare Ranching: The Subsidized Destruction of the American West.* Washington, D.C.: Island Press/Foundation for Deep Ecology, 2002.

INDEX

Page numbers in *italics* refer to illustrations.

ILLUSTRATION CREDITS